12.99
IN4 N
(Wil)

Feminist Social Psychology

0335153305

Feminist Social Psychology:

Developing Theory and Practice

edited by

SUE WILKINSON

OPEN UNIVERSITY PRESS

Milton Keynes   ·   *Philadelphia*

Open University Press.
Open University Educational Enterprises Limited
12 Cofferidge Close, Stony Stratford,
Milton Keynes MK11 1BY, England
and
242 Cherry Street,
Philadelphia, PA 19106, U.S.A.

First published 1986
Copyright© 1986
The editor and contributors

British Library Cataloguing in Publication Data

Feminist social psychology: developing theory
  and practice.
  1. Social psychology
  I. Wilkinson, Susan
  302   HM251
  ISBN 0-335-15329-1
  ISBN 0-335-15330-5   P6K

Library of Congress Cataloging in Publication Data

Feminist social psychology.
  Bibliography: p.
  Includes indexes.
  1. Social psychology — Addresses, essays, lectures.
2. Social psychology — Great Britain — Addresses, essays,
lectures.   3. Feminism — Addresses, essays, lectures.
4. Feminism — Great Britain — Addresses, essays, lectures.
5. Sex role — Addresses, essays, lectures.
  I. Wilkinson, Sue.
  HM251.F376   1985   302   85-29739
  ISBN 0-335-15329-1
  ISBN 0-335-15330-5 (pbk.)

Editorial and Production Services by
Fisher Duncan Ltd, Chiswick, London W4 4PH
Phototypeset by Dobbie Typesetting Service, Plymouth, Devon.
Printed in Great Britain by St Edmundsbury Press, Bury St Edmunds, Suffolk

To my parents

Contents

vii

Section 2: Practice

Notes on Contributors

HAZEL BECKETT was a postgraduate student at the University of Bath between 1981 and 1984. Her research project was entitled *The Development of Expectations of Self and the Future in Adolescence*. She now works for the Economic and Social Research Council in the secretariat to the Education and Human Development Committee.

SUSAN CONDOR studied undergraduate psychology at University College, Cardiff and, after a period working with adolescent boys in care, returned to academic life and gained a Ph.D from Bristol University. She has since conducted research at the University of Kent and University College, Cardiff, and is currently teaching intergroup relations, the psychology of women and women's studies at Loughborough University. Her main areas of research interest include the analysis of behaviour and communication between women in groups, and the extension of social psychological models of intergroup relations and social representations to incorporate the experience of women.

CHRISTINE GRIFFIN is a lecturer in social psychology at the University of Birmingham. She has been involved in youth service provision for girls and young women since 1979, when she also began a study of young women and the transition to un/employment at the Centre for Contemporary Cultural Studies, Birmingham University. This is reported in her book *Typical Girls? Young Women From School to the Job Market* (Routledge, 1985). Since then she has also worked on a study of youth unemployment and racism in the Leicester job market at the Centre for Mass Communication Research, Leicester University.

CATHERINE ITZIN is currently conducting research on ageing for Newham Health Authority and the University of Essex. She is also a Ph.D student at the University of Kent, an active counsellor, and the author of several books—the most recent of which is *How to Choose a School: A Parents' Guide to Selecting the Best Secondary School for their Child* (Methuen, 1985).

CELIA KITZINGER completed her doctoral thesis *The Construction of Lesbian Identities* at the University of Reading and is currently employed as a research fellow [*sic*] in the School of Education, Leicester University. She has recently completed a study on concepts of human rights and has also done research on attitudes to the trial and acquittal of Clive Ponting and on the subjective experience of unemployment. Her main academic interests are social constructionism and the development of Q methodology within that framework.

JUDI MARSHALL took a psychology degree at Manchester University and then went into market research in industry. A set of happy coincidences led her to the Management Sciences department at UMIST, where she was a teaching assistant and did research on job stress amongst managers and their spouses for a Ph.D. She also began writing (with Cary Cooper)—mainly about stress. Since 1978 she has been a lecturer in organizational behaviour in the School of Management, University of Bath, and she completed a major cycle of research with the publication of *Women Managers: Travellers in a Male World* (Wiley, 1984). Her current interests are women in management, organizational cultures and change, and the development of qualitative research methods.

PAULA NICOLSON is a senior lecturer in psychology in the Department of Sociology at North East London Polytechnic. She is currently completing her Ph.D on depression following childbirth, and has previously done research on midwives' attitudes to working in hospitals, and also on therapeutic communities. She has published on these topics and is also co-author of a textbook on applied psychology for social workers.

JANET SAYERS trained as a clinical psychologist at the Tavistock Clinic and now teaches social psychology, social work and women's studies at the University of Kent. Her most recent book is *Sexual Contradictions: Psychology, Psychoanalysis and Feminism* (Tavistock, 1986).

VALERIE WALKERDINE lectures at London University Institute of Education, where she is also the director of a research unit on Girls and Mathematics. Her recent publications include, as co-author with Henriques *et al.*, *Changing the Subject: Psychology, Social Regulation and Subjectivity* (Methuen, 1984).

MARGARET WETHERELL is a lecturer in social psychology at the University of St. Andrews. Her main research interests lie in the field of group influence and representations of majority/minority relations. She is currently working on a study of racist thought among the white majority in New Zealand. She is co-author with Jonathan Potter and Peter Stringer of *Social Texts and Context: Literature and Social Psychology* (Routledge, 1984).

SUE WILKINSON is a lecturer in psychology at Liverpool Institute of Higher Education (where she teaches social psychology and psychopathology), and an honorary research fellow [*sic*] in the Department of Psychology at Liverpool University (where she is currently conducting research on a number of aspects of life stress, particularly in the elderly). Her main academic interests are in the exploration of self and identity (particularly within the context of social relationships); theories and methods in social psychology; and social factors in psychopathology. She has done some extra-mural teaching in women's studies and hopes shortly to begin some work on women's experiences of self.

Acknowledgements

I would like to thank, first of all, the contributors to this volume: both for their sustained efforts over a relatively short time period, and for their responsiveness to my requests for amendments to their contributions. Their enthusiasm for the project has made the job of editing comparatively painless. I have also derived considerable support from the realization that a 'community' of feminist social psychologists is beginning to develop and would like to thank all those who are contributing to this through their research and organizational efforts.

Thanks are due to the people who have assisted in the production of the book — both practically and psychologically. In particular: John Skelton of Open University Press for his enthusiasm for the idea from the outset; two anonymous reviewers for valuable suggestions regarding the format and content of the book; Dr J. Burke, Rector of Liverpool Institute of Higher Education, for supporting the project; the office staff of St. Katharine's College, LIHE, for retyping sections of the manuscript; and John Wilkinson for word-processing assistance, several hundred cups of coffee, and — well, he knows the rest.

The editor and publishers would also like to thank the following for permission to reproduce previously published material in this volume: Longman, for material from Matthews *et al.* (1978) *Early Mathematical Experiences* (Figures 1 and 2, Chapter 4); Royal Medico-Psychological Association, *British Journal of Psychiatry* (Table 1, Chapter 8).

Sue Wilkinson

Introduction

Sue Wilkinson

This volume seeks to reflect increasing interest in feminist research in social psychology, which is now a rapidly growing area of research activity. The direct precursors of the book were two symposia on feminist research in social psychology, which I convened at the British Psychological Society's Social Psychology Section annual conferences in 1983 and 1984. Each symposium was followed by an extended discussion period in which there was considerable debate about the nature of feminist research: for example, how such research may be characterized and what its implications are for the practising social psychologist. The interest and debate generated by these symposia prompted me to pursue some of the issues raised in them, by means of this book.

The first aim of the book is simply to collect together a body of the social psychological research that seems to me to be feminist in orientation, emphasis or intention. Ten people, all currently active in conducting research of this type, were invited to contribute chapters (three of the ten having been contributors to the original symposia). The choice was difficult because the book is very much a 'first step' in a lively and developing field, and I would not claim that it is necessarily representative of all the types of feminist research that are currently being conducted; it certainly does not represent much more than a small sample of all the topic areas where feminist researchers are currently active. I have limited it to British work both for reasons of space and because it seems likely that there may be some national differences in definitions and foci of feminist research (I will return to this later); but I have tried to represent both relatively 'established' and relatively 'new' researchers. I have limited it to social psychology because that is the area I know best—but I use the term in its broadest sense to cover the social processes operating within a wide range of social institutions, such as the family, the school, the workplace, the medical profession and the media. Thus some of the topic areas covered may appear to cut across the more traditional divisions of social, developmental, occupational and clinical psychology.

The second aim of the book is to contribute to the debate about the characterization and practice of feminist research—and in this sense the book

1

is an exploration of what such research is or could become. In briefing the contributors I was concerned not to impose any set definitions upon them, but, rather, to encourage them to indicate in their contributions the ways in which they regard their work as feminist. In this way I hoped that some common themes might be established, while diversity was still encouraged to flourish; I also approached my review of other people's views of feminist research (Chapter 1) in this way.

Still mindful of appearing prescriptive, or of squeezing diverse research into restrictively narrow definitions, I do not intend an extensive review of such themes here. In several ways, the most important word in the title of the book is 'developing': the field of feminist research is young and changing rapidly. However, I am conscious of the fact that editors are expected to define the scope of their material and, by way of orientation to the contents of the book, will suggest two particular 'themes' that appear central to the contributions and, thus, particularly characteristic of feminist research.

First, feminist research is based on an exploration of women's own knowledge and experience, in a disciplined, scholarly and rigorous way. A female perspective is to be regarded as central to the research, not as an additional or comparative viewpoint. Two extensions of this argument are common, and well represented in this volume (although not in all chapters). First, many feminist researchers argue that because knowledge is socially constructed, and thus dependent on a given social, cultural and historical context, the exploration of women's knowledge must be grounded in the specific contexts in which such knowledge is generated; the existence of multiple—and often inconsistent or contradictory—perspectives is also acknowledged (see e.g. Walkerdine, Chapter 4—although her position goes further; Wetherell, Chapter 5; Condor, Chapter 6; Itzin, Chapter 7; Kitzinger, Chapter 9). Second, many feminist researchers include, as central, an analysis of the role of power in determining the form and representation of social knowledge, either in relation to women's position in society (see e.g. Walkerdine, Chapter 4; Condor, Chapter 6; Itzin, Chapter 7; Nicolson, Chapter 8), or in considering the role of the researcher in her/his research (see, e.g. Kitzinger, Chapter 9; Griffin, Chapter 10; Marshall, Chapter 11).

The examination of the researcher's role is also a part of the second main theme of feminist research that I would like to identify here. This is the view that feminist research is not simply the extension of traditional research in non-sexist ways, and/or including topics of relevance to women; rather, it entails a critical evaluation of the research process, in terms of its adequacy in tapping women's experience. Thus, in feminist research, considerable reconceptualization (of ideology, theory and method) is likely to be necessary—and some of the research will not look like traditional science, nor be capable of evaluation by traditional criteria. (The question of possible criteria for the evaluation of feminist research is referred to in Chapter 1, and considered in more detail in relation to qualitative methods by Judi Marshall in Chapter 11.) Theories and methods will be 'borrowed' from a range of disciplines (see Wetherell, Chapter 5, for an example), criticized (e.g. Sayers, Chapter 2; Condor, Chapter 6; Nicolson, Chapter 8), and developed (e.g. Beckett, Chapter 3; Kitzinger, Chapter 9).

In Chapter 1, I discuss some of the terminological distinctions that others have made within the field, distinguishing between 'non-sexist', 'feminist' and 'women's studies' research. In particular, it will become clear that feminist research is both distinct from (and much more than) non-sexist research, and that a feminist psychology is more focussed in a disciplinary way than multidisciplinary women's studies. Here, however, I would like to add a further differentiation: that of 'feminist psychology' from 'the psychology of sex roles' (which, I would argue, may or may not be feminist).

The psychology of sex roles (currently a more active field in the USA than the UK, although British work is expanding) seems to focus more on content than approach: a good example of it is the volume edited by Frieze *et al.* (1978). The term refers to a body of research which covers a broad spectrum: beginning (generally) with differences between the sexes (in personality, abilities, social roles, motivation/ achievement, psychological disorder, and so on), and seeking to explain the origin and maintenance of these in terms of sex role socialization and sex role stereotyping. Alternatively, such research may begin with observations of social practices and seek to determine their differential organization for, or differential effects on, the two sexes. Central to the area are attempts both to measure gender identity (e.g. Bem, 1974) and to delineate the social processes that influence it.

A feminist critique of much of this work is fast developing, however, and, interestingly, parts of this are also critical of earlier feminist analyses. For example, Stanley and Wise (1983, Chapter 4) criticize socialization theory and the concept of gender role; while Eichler (1980, Chapter 3) and Thomas (1985) discuss conceptual and methodological problems in the measurement of gender identity. This critique is extended in this volume by Wetherell (Chapter 5) and Condor (Chapter 6). Wetherell criticizes instruments such as Bem's Sex Role Inventory for reinforcing one set of assumptions about femininity and masculinity, without recognizing either that these are socially and culturally specific, or that individuals may be flexible in their use of different versions of sex role identity in different social contexts. Condor argues that some feminists have pointed out the debilitating influence of sex role traditionalism, without considering how women actually perceive and experience such sex roles—which may be in a favourable way. Similarly, but more generally, other contributors point to the complexity of and contradictions in women's accounts (e.g. Sayers, Chapter 2; Nicolson, Chapter 8).

The organization of the volume is as follows. It begins with a review chapter, in which I consider both how feminist research has been characterized in the existing literature, and how some of the suggested formulations bear a striking similarity to certain types of so-called 'new' social psychology (i.e. ethogenic and related research). The remainder of the book is divided into two sections: 'Theory' and 'Practice'. Since, as I point out in my review in Chapter 1, one of the feminist arguments is the interdependency of theory, method and research topic, this distinction is necesssarily somewhat arbitrary. Nevertheless, the chapters in the Theory section are weighted more towards the use and development of particular theories in feminist research, while the chapters in the Practice section tend to focus on specific empirical research projects, and/or the use of particular research methods within these projects.

Within the Theory section, the contributions represent not only a wide range of theories but a variety of positions regarding the usage of these theories. The first three chapters take existing theories (psychoanalysis, cognitive developmental theory, post-structuralism) and either use them critically and in feminist ways, or develop them substantially to encompass female knowledge and experience. The remaining two chapters begin with a critique of existing social psychological theory (on gender identity and sex role beliefs, respectively), and go on to suggest substantial feminist reconceptualizations. Within the Practice section, the first two chapters describe feminist research projects in areas where (predominantly) male practitioners perpetuate particularly deleterious images and assumptions about women's role and status (the media and the medical profession, respectively). The remaining three chapters focus more specifically on methodological issues, moving from a discussion of particular methods (Q, qualitative cultural analysis) to a consideration of how to use qualitative methods rigorously.

The first chapter in the Theory section, by Janet Sayers, is a critical examination of the value of psychoanalytic theory for feminist research in the area of sexual identity. Sayers considers both the value of Freud's account of infant development and the defences in enabling women to achieve individual psychological change, and its limitation in failing to acknowledge the need for collective social change. The second chapter, by Hazel Beckett, focusses on the role of cognitive developmental theory in studying identity development in adolescence. Beckett presents both a critique of cognitive developmental theory as inadequately representing the thinking of adolescent girls, and a development of the theory from a feminist perspective, based on the work of Gilligan in the USA (e.g. 1982) and on her own empirical data.

Valerie Walkerdine's chapter explores the ways in which post-structuralism may be of value in examining the assumptions and expectations that surround women and girls in their 'everyday' roles as mothers, teachers and children. In deconstructing the multiple positionings of women and children in our society, Walkerdine demonstrates the contradictions inherent in women's position in relation to child care, and in girls' school performance and developing sexuality. Margaret Wetherell continues the deconstruction theme, but her chapter takes as its starting point the social psychological study of gender. Wetherell is critical of current approaches to the definition and measurement of femininity and masculinity, which 'fix' gender identity into normative categories, presumed invariant across social and historical context. She argues that social psychology could learn from a similar debate within the discipline of literary criticism, and proposes the concept of a 'linguistic repertoire' as a way forward. Accepting this model would entail not only an acknowledgement that femininity and masculinity are shifting states, but also that they are produced through language rather than being discoverable 'realities'.

The final chapter in the Theory section, by Susan Condor, looks at another aspect of the sex role system: women's sex role related beliefs. Condor argues that feminism's greatest potential impact in this area (stressing the need for a critical re-examination of existing theories and methods in terms of women's actual experience) is yet to be realized. Like Wetherell, she is critical of existing sex role attitude scales, as linguistic forms that often adopt male values. Starting from an intergroup relations perspective, she reinterprets 'traditional' women's expressed attitudes towards existing sex roles as demonstrating 'ingroup favouritism', rather than 'group self-hatred'. Finally, in a reflexive self-criticism of her own work, she presents a caveat to feminist social psychologists regarding 'objectification' of their 'subjects': other women.

Catherine Itzin's chapter bridges the Theory and Practice sections and also takes up the social construction theme again. Its focus is a review of the ways in which sexism is linked with ageism in the representation of women in the media. Itzin surveys newspapers, television, birthday cards and, particularly, magazines to demonstrate the power and pervasiveness of the stereotypes. She also considers how the stereotypes function, both in reflecting women's oppression and assisting in its construction; and how the messages of patriarchy are reinforced by the interests of capitalism.

Next, Paula Nicolson's chapter documents her attempt to develop a feminist approach to depression following childbirth. Nicolson criticizes traditional research in the field on ideological grounds: its attempt to define and account for women's behaviour, while refusing to recognize either its variety and complexity or its dependence on power relations in society. She places the 'results' of a standardized measure of 'post natal depression' side by side with women's own accounts of early motherhood—and finds very little correspondence. The chapter looks at ways in which the incorporation of personal accounts constitutes a feminist methodology—and at what else is needed. Celia Kitzinger's research on lesbianism is also based on women's own accounts and also addresses the question of a feminist methodology. Kitzinger advocates the use of a specific technique—Q methodology—for processing these accounts. Her analysis details five emergent 'versions' of lesbianism, and emphasizes the importance of the particular social context and ideological purpose in the construction of any one account. She concludes by considering how Q methodology could be developed within a feminist framework.

In the penultimate chapter, Christine Griffin discusses qualitative methods (and, in particular, qualitative cultural analysis) rather more broadly, within the context of her study of the transition to un/employment for young women in Birmingham. Griffin also reflects on her own role in the research; the political nature of research; and the necessity for feminist social psychology to take a central place in teaching and research. The discussion of qualitative methods broadens still further in the final chapter, when Judi Marshall, drawing on her own experience in conducting a study of women managers, discusses how the researcher might attempt to use such methods rigorously, and what criteria might be used to evaluate her/his success in this. Marshall also takes the reflexive examination of her own role in the research further than do the other contributors, relating it to her developing feminism.

Finally, I would like to end by emphasizing (as, indeed, do a number of contributors to this volume) that a feminist perspective is important not just for feminist researchers, but for *all* research in social psychology—and indeed in social science more generally. A feminist perspective may be regarded as having far reaching implications regarding changes in research practice. Not only does it strengthen and develop the now well established critique of positivist science, it provides a deeper and more extensive questioning both of the form and function of research, and of specific theories and research techniques. Out of this questioning comes both an active development of traditional ways of doing research and a committed exploration of alternative modes of investigation.

Feminist research activity may be evaluated by a range of criteria, but central to these is the ability of its theories and methods to illuminate women's experience. However, and again as noted by other contributors, the implication of making women's experience central is not, for most feminists, to focus exclusively on women. It is, rather, to utilize the female perspective to foster the development of a more genuinely *human* psychology; to deepen our understanding of the *whole* of human experience—both female and male.

REFERENCES

Bem, S. (1974). The measurement of psychological androgyny. *Journal of Consulting and Clinical Psychology* **42**, 155–62.

Eichler, M. (1980). *The Double Standard*. London, Croom Helm.

Frieze, I. H., Parsons, J. E., Johnson, P. B., Ruble, D. N. and Zellman, G. L. (1978). *Women and Sex Roles: A Social Psychological Perspective*. New York, Norton.

Gilligan, C. (1982). *In a Different Voice: Psychological Theory and Women's Development*. Cambridge, Mass., Harvard University Press.

Stanley, L. and Wise, S. (1983). *Breaking Out: Feminist Consciousness and Feminist Research*. London, Routledge & Kegan Paul.

Thomas, A. (1985). The meaning of gender in women's self-conceptions. Paper presented at the British Psychological Society Social Psychology Section annual conference, Clare College, Cambridge, September.

Chapter 1

Sighting Possibilities:[1] Diversity and Commonality in Feminist Research[2]

Sue Wilkinson

The main objective of this chapter is to survey a fairly large body of literature in psychology, sociology and women's studies (Reinharz *et al.*, 1983), to determine how 'feminist research' has been characterized, particularly from the viewpoint of a social psychologist interested in conducting such research. The body of literature reviewed here is restricted to formulations of feminist research, rather than actual research projects, as the following chapters provide detailed examples of these. I do not intend in this review to prescribe in any sense what feminist research ought to be, but rather to indicate what it could be, by presenting a diversity of suggestions and commenting on commonalities. In this way I hope I may engage both feminists and non-feminists, perhaps indicating to the former a range of ways in which they might consider the research enterprise, and perhaps demonstrating to the latter both the importance of feminism and how this importance may be reflected in research practice. As Westkott, a feminist researcher, writes:

> To imagine a different world requires first of all the ability to perceive the world differently and to open ourselves to formerly denied possibilities. (1983, p. 216)

A second objective of the chapter is to point up the extensive parallels between the feminist critique of mainstream social science, together with some of its suggested alternatives, and the 'crisis' debates in social psychology in the 1970s, together with the advocacy of the so-called 'new' social psychology, i.e. ethogenic and related research.

The structure of the chapter is as follows. I will begin by considering some terminological distinctions; move on to the feminist critique of traditional research and its suggested alternatives; and then examine some of the issues and implications associated with feminist research, including the similarity between some of its suggestions and those of the 'new' social psychology.

TERMINOLOGY

First, I would like to distinguish between 'non-sexist', 'feminist' and 'women's studies' research. The term 'non-sexist' has generally been taken to mean avoiding sexist practices (such as the assumption that all the researched are male and that women's experiences of the world are just like men's), but in so far as this implies that there is 'some absolute standard of objectivity by which . . . research (can) be evaluated', which nowadays few social scientists would accept, the more positive and precise term 'feminist' has been more widely used (Morgan, 1981, p. 86). A large part of this chapter, and indeed this volume, will, of course, be concerned with a further elaboration of feminist research, but a useful starting definition is that offered by Klein:

> Feminism for me implies assuming a perspective in which women's experiences, ideas and needs . . . are valid in their own right. (1983, p. 89)

Of course, many feminists would go further and invest feminist research with an ideological commitment to supporting the aims of the Women's Liberation Movement and/or working for political change (e.g. Erlich, reported in Stanley and Wise, 1983a, pp. 24–26).

The terms 'feminist research' and 'women's studies' are sometimes used interchangeably; however, they may also be differentiated in two distinct ways. 'Women's studies' is generally used as an all-embracing term to cover both academic research utilizing a wide range of different approaches to the study of women, and the establishment of multidisciplinary courses on the social and cultural context of being a woman. The term 'feminist', in its first sense (and the sense in which it will be used in this volume), is reserved for more focussed research of a particular kind, which starts from the perspective of Klein (see above) and tries to work through its implications in the research process; as such, of course, it may be subsumed by 'women's studies' research. In its second sense, 'feminist' is equated with taking conscious political action to change women's position in society, i.e. the term is used to refer to the activist side, in contrast to the institutional sense of 'women's studies' (Callaway, 1981, p. 459).

There is a major debate—clearly, but not impartially, summarized by Bowles and Klein (1983, pp. 1–14)—over whether women's studies should stand alone as an autonomous discipline or whether feminist scholarship should be integrated into, and, it is hoped, effect change in, existing disciplines, so that eventually women's studies as a separate entity becomes obsolete. Advocates of the former view claim that the present structure of disciplines cannot accommodate feminist claims and that the changes required are too extensive and radical to be achievable in the forseeable future; while those who support the latter position hold a cumulative view of change from within, and argue that separate women's studies will always remain a special interest 'ghetto' outside traditional academia, not to be taken seriously. The problem of being taken seriously is a very real one for feminists, and one to which I will return.

THE FEMINIST CRITIQUE

To be for women is to be simultaneously critical of androcentric theories that reflect sexist society, and of methods that constrain empirical research of significance to women. (Gould, 1980, p. 461)

Content, Ideology and Theory

Some feminist criticisms of mainstream social scientific research are directed at its content: in particular, the extent to which women are either ignored or 'invisible'. As Millman and Kanter note, often it is assumed that there is a 'single society with respect to men and women, in which generalisations can be made about all participants' (1975, p. xiii), yet 'not only do men and women view a common world from different perspectives, they view different worlds as well' (Bernard, 1973, p. 782). There has been a call for more research to fill in gaps in our knowledge of women (e.g. Daniels, 1975) and some of the advocates of autonomous women's studies stress its 'corrective emphasis', i.e. adding women into existing research areas where they have been overlooked or left out (e.g. Tobias, 1978). So far, the principal concern appears to be with removing sexist bias from social science, with no challenge to its fundamental assumptions or ways of conducting research (Bernard, 1973).

More sophisticated critiques include a consideration of the 'ideological apparatus' of society: thus Smith (1978) writes of the ways in which women have been systematically excluded from men's culture, and of the way in which the framework of issues in her discipline, sociology, reflects its development within a male universe (Smith, 1974). Others take the argument further and argue that when women have been considered within the traditional approach to knowledge, their experience has been distorted and misinterpreted, because they have been considered in relation to a masculine norm (see, in this volume, for example, Beckett, Chapter 3; Griffin, Chapter 10) or in terms of man-made stereotypes. For example, Eichler (1980, Chapter 3) argues against the use of masculinity-femininity scales as a 'scientific reinforcement' of sex role stereotypes; others who have conducted this kind of analysis include Weisstein (1970); Parlee (1979); and Vaughter (1976); (see also Wetherell, Chapter 15, this volume). Even some contemporary feminist theory, such as that on socialization and gender role, is criticized by other feminists as too firmly based on 'models which embod(y) the values and power divisions of sexist society' (Stanley and Wise, 1983a, p. 96); (see also Condor, Chapter 6, this volume). Furthermore, research in which women are not related to a male norm is systematically devalued, as Bernard notes:

> A great deal of research focuses on men with no reference at all to women; but when research is focused on women, it is almost always with reference to men. If comparisons are not made with men, the research is viewed as incomplete. Research on women in their own right, without reference to a male standard, is not viewed as worthy of male attention. (1973, p. 787)

Methodology

The feminist methodological critique tends to be stated separately. It questions some of the values implicit in mainstream social science research and expresses dissatisfaction with its methodological characteristics both *per se* and because they are inadequate to tap many aspects of women's experience.

First, traditional social science is taken to task for failing to specify the assumptions on which it is based (Sherif, 1979): for example, the priority given to rationality and objectivity, and the necessity for replicability and generalizability. In addition, attention is paid to the demonstration that traditional research is very far from value-free; in particular, it is argued that male values are enshrined in research practice — in some of the ways indicated below. (In this volume, Griffin (Chapter 10), in particular, reinforces this argument.)

Several feminist writers have extended Bakan's (1966) distinction between 'agentic' and 'communal' tendencies of human existence (identified as principally masculine and feminine respectively) to the characterization of modes of research (Carlson, 1972; Fox Keller, 1978; Reinharz, 1983, pp. 167–170). This distinction is also explored elsewhere in this volume (see, in particular, Wetherell, Chapter 5; also Condor and Marshall, Chapters 6 and 11). 'Agentic' research, which involves 'separating, ordering and quantifying, manipulating, controlling' is contrasted with 'communal' kinds of scientific enquiry, involving 'naturalistic observation, sensitivity to intrinsic structure and qualitative patterning of phenomena, and greater personal participation of the investigator' (Carlson, 1972, p. 20). Traditional modes of enquiry, it is argued, are based primarily on agentic features. Several of the authors in the volume edited by Millman and Kanter criticize the agentic approach for 'fail(ing) to capture the more important features of the social world' (1975, p. x), while Bernard goes beyond the simple agentic-communal dichotomy to identify a 'machismo factor' in research: the male who 'can play with simulated reality like an Olympian God' (1973, p. 785). In common with Reinharz (1983, p. 170), she also emphasizes the greater prestige afforded the agentic approach over the communal one. (Of course, dichotomies like this are always too simple: Morgan notes that 'qualitative methodology and ethnography after all has its own brand of machismo with its image of the male sociologist bringing back news from the fringes of society, the lower depths . . .' (1981, pp. 86–87).

A second strand of the feminist methodological critique is concerned with the traditional characteristics of mainstream research *per se*. For example, Parlee criticizes the laboratory experiment in the following way:

> Concepts, environments, social interactions, are all simplified by methods which lift them out of their contexts, stripping them of the very complexity that characterises the real world. (1979, p. 131)

This is backed up by other writers who point out the ahistorical, acultural nature of such research (e.g. Mies, 1983, pp. 117–139; also several contributors to this volume). Smith argues that sociologists have only been able to regard their knowledge of society as 'extra-social' because of the operation of specific practices that 'disguise' the social nature of the relationship between knower and known (i.e. anonimity, impersonality, objectivity) (1977, p. 16; see also 1974; 1979).

There has also been criticism of the norm of objectivity; and, in particular, the assumption that the researcher can stand back from those s/he studies, and regard them simply as 'objects' in the physical world. The basic feminist argument points out that this both denies the basic humanness of research 'subjects' and refuses to recognize that researchers are also human; consequently they might not only affect their 'subjects', but also themselves be changed in the process of the research (Stanley and Wise, 1983a, pp. 109–110). Furthermore, such a stance contains the implication that the behaviour of the researcher cannot be explained within the same framework as those s/he studies, i.e. it is non-reflexive (Stanley and Wise, 1983a, p. 73).

THE FEMINIST ALTERNATIVE

> The languages and theories we have to work with still lack the very concepts by which the reality of women's lives can be named, described and understood. Our work needs to generate words, concepts, that refer to, that spring from, that are firmly and richly grounded in the actual experiencing of women. And this demands methods of enquiry that open up our seeing and thinking, our conceptual frameworks, to new perceptions that actually derive from women's experience. (du Bois, 1983, p. 110)

From Content to Purpose

Feminists have argued that there should be a shift in focus from the content of research (research *on* women) to a consideration of its purpose (research *for* women): thus there has been a call 'to develop us' rather than 'to tell them' (Bowles and Klein, 1983, p. 10). Klein has defined research for women as:

. . . research that tries to take women's needs, interests and experience into
account and aims at being instrumental in improving women's lives in one
way or another. (1983, p. 90)

While the emphasis on social change is shared by many feminists, some are
involved in establishing the condition of women's lives as a basis from which
change can take place (e.g. Miller, 1978), while others are directly involved in
action research projects (e.g. Mies, 1983). There is also a debate about the extent
to which the purpose of feminist research should be congruent with the purposes
of the Women's Liberation Movement. Stanley and Wise (1983a, pp. 23-27) and
Kelly (1978, pp. 255-256) reject this suggestion, though for very different reasons,
while Mies (1983, pp. 117-122) argues that it is impossible (although, she implies,
desirable) because of a fundamental contradiction between social scientific theory
and methodology, and the political aims of the Women's Movement. In particular,
she argues that the methodological principles of traditional research are
incompatible with feminism: the shift in ideology must therefore be accompanied
by a shift in research practice.

Theory and Methodology

Although feminists have repeatedly called both for more theory (e.g. Wallston,
1981, p. 606) and better theory (e.g. Stanley and Wise, 1983a, Chapter 2), detailed
accounts of what feminist theory would look like have been far less forthcoming.
Instead, feminists have generally tended to focus on what theory should be based
on (arguing for the inseparability of theory and experience: e.g. Stanley and Wise,
1983a, pp. 45-51); and on how it should be generated (arguing for the
inseparability of theory and method: e.g. Klein, 1983, p. 89). In general, the
argument calls for a broader definition of theory than is generally accepted (Bowles
and Klein, 1983, p. 15) and emphasizes the relativity and arbitrariness of all
truths (Spender, 1983, pp. 27-31). An examination of suggestions regarding the
content of feminist theory seems to suggest two broad lines of emphasis; these
are also, to some extent, reflected in the examples of feminist research contained
in this volume.

The first emphasis is on the social construction of meaning. For example,
Westkott writes that feminism affirms:

. . . the idea of a human being as fully and freely creating herself [sic] and
the world in which she [sic] lives, a process which involves negotiating that
creation through dialogue with others. (1979, pp. 426-427)

This emphasis may be seen in this volume (e.g. Wetherell, Chapter 5; Kitzinger,
Chapter 9). The second emphasis is on the situation of women in society (and
is more obviously linked with the call for social change); within this broad category

of work some researchers are concerned with 'the analysis of subordination of all women' (e.g. Evans, 1982, p. 67; Itzin, Chapter 7, this volume); while others are more concerned to focus on the varying experiences of individual women (e.g. Stanley and Wise, 1983a, p. 172; Nicolson, Chapter 8, this volume). Some seek to combine both strands: thus Gould argues for 'a gynopositive theory of society capable of accounting for both microinteractional meaning and social structure' (1980, p. 462); such research is represented in this volume by Condor (Chapter 6) and Griffin (Chapter 10, for example).

In virtually all the accounts of feminist research I reviewed, (and indeed in all the examples of such research in this volume), there is a broad consensus regarding both the necessity of giving priority to female experience and of developing theory which is firmly situated in this experience. For example:

> We believe that feminist social science must begin with the recognition that 'the personal', lived experience, underlies all behaviours and actions. We need to find out what it is that, as women and feminists, we know. We need to re-claim, name and re-name our experience. (Stanley and Wise, 1983b, p. 205)

> To address women's lives and experience in their own terms, to create theory grounded in the actual experience and language of women, is the central agenda for feminist social science and scholarship. (du Bois, 1983, p. 108)

(In passing, it is interesting to note that while there has been a widespread feminist concern with transcending the confines of 'man-made' language (e.g. Spender, 1980), relatively few attempts have been made to do so: Daly's (1978) *Gyn/Ecology* is one of the few serious or sustained ones.)

One corollary of the focus on experience is the suggestion of new criteria for the evaluation of feminist theory. Thus, Jayaratne argues that 'we can judge feminist theories according to their ability to improve the lives of women' (1983, p. 142), while Parlee argues that in addition to 'the usual scholarly principles of reliability, consistency, logical inference and the like . . .', 'one hallmark of feminist research . . . seems to be the investigator's continual testing of the plausibility of the work against her own experience' (1979, p. 130). This issue is further explored by Judi Marshall (Chapter 11, this volume).

This, in turn, suggests three interrelated theoretical/methodological strands of feminist research. First, there is its reflexive and self-reflective quality, for, as Callaway notes, an emphasis on the centrality of female experience directly implies its corollary: 'ourselves as our own sources' (1981, p. 470; see also Kitzinger, Chapter 9, this volume). Similarly, du Bois has emphasized the way in which the knower is part of the matrix of what is known (1983, p. 111; see also Griffin, Chapter 10, this volume); and Reinharz has required the researcher to ask her/himself how s/he has grown or changed in the process of research (1983, p. 183), as does Marshall (Chapter 11, this volume).

Second, the relationship between the researcher and researched will evidently be very different from that of the traditional 'experimenter' and 'subject'. In feminist research, at the very least, both are to be regarded as having the same status: as participants or collaborators in the same enterprise (e.g. Reinharz, 1983, pp. 180–181). Westkott goes further to emphasize the intersubjectivity of meaning of 'subject' and 'object': taking the form of a dialogue between them from which knowledge may emerge (1979, p. 426). This kind of relationship of necessity leads to a consideration of the moral and political implications of research (see Nicolson, Chapter 8 and Griffin, Chapter 10, this volume); thus some feminists have also stressed the obligation to try to maintain honesty (Klein, 1983, p. 95); the non-hierarchical organization of research teams (Reinharz, 1983, p. 180); and the continual awareness of the policy implications of the research (Wallston, 1981, pp. 609–610).

Third, as Callaway notes:

> Women's research makes explicit the risk of subjective involvement in the bid to gain new theoretical understanding. (1981, p. 470)

This may be regarded as a 'conscious subjectivity (not to be confused with uncritical acceptance of a person's statements), which replaces the "value-free objectivity" of traditional research' (Klein, 1983, p. 94). There has been a concern not to overdo the 'subjective' element of the critique: Evans, for example, argues the need for theory 'to avoid some of the worst excesses of subjectivism and individual interpretation' (1982, p. 67).

Beyond the emphasis on the subjective, the methodological prescriptions made by feminists are quite varied. Perhaps surprisingly, relatively few feminists have argued that there is, or should be, a distinctive feminist methodology. One notable exception is Reinharz (1983), who argues for the adoption of 'experiential analysis', which is based on a 'communal' approach (see earlier). Other feminists simply describe a particular method that they have found useful: e.g. Griffin's description of qualititative cultural analysis (1985; see also Chapter 10, this volume). Where one method is preferred, it generally has subjective, experiential and qualitative elements. Those who argue for a range of methods (e.g. Stanley and Wise, 1983a, p. 136; Jayaratne, 1983, p. 158) do so from a variety of standpoints (and with varying degrees of limitation on what is regarded as acceptable). For example, Klein considers that women's studies is a 'young discipline' and needs to experiment with a range of approaches: she argues for the flexibility required to adapt methods to the needs of each individual research situation, but also for the scrutiny of methods to ensure that they are congruent with feminist principles (1983, pp. 91–100).

Very few feminists eschew 'agentic' methods; some even argue specifically for their use: for example, Kelly, in arguing for complete catholicism of methods, nevertheless characterizes rationality and objectivity as 'the fullest development of our intellectual capabilities' (1978, p. 229), and feels that we disown them at our peril. She argues the dangers of polarizing 'masculine' and 'feminine' approaches—a view also taken by Carlson (1972, p. 21) and Wallston (1981, p. 605), who suggest the integration of 'agentic' and 'communal' methods, rather than the replacement of the former by the latter. (Marshall, Chapter 11, this volume, also shares this view.) In fact, a number of feminists argue for the dissolution of traditional dichotomies: e.g. Westkott (1983, p. 214); Spender (1978a, p. 1), although only du Bois (1983, pp. 111–112) backs this up with a theoretical argument. Wallston (1981, p. 602) joins Bowles (1983, p. 42) in emphasizing methods simply as tools to answer questions, and enjoining the avoidance of 'methodolatry'; du Bois (1983, p. 109) also follows this line.

Still fewer feminists have presented complete 'programmes' for doing feminist research. Where these do exist, they vary greatly in amount of detail, emphasis and degree of prescriptiveness. Thus, for example, Mies presents seven methodological guidelines for feminist research, which she regards as 'an invitation for methodological experiment and innovation': they are political/ideological in tone rather than practical or prescriptive (1983, pp. 122–128). Reinharz presents six 'interacting components' of 'experiential analysis' (1983, pp. 174–183). These are quite detailed and prescriptive, offering a complete alternative model and method for research, which forms the culmination of a personal 'intellectual journey' (Reinharz, 1979). In contrast, Stanley and Wise (1983a) present a much more diffuse account of their view of feminist research. At no one point is a distinct programme outlined, but it is possible to derive a clear view of their proposals from the book as a whole; their emphasis is on the overall ideology and purpose of the research (although its implications for methodology are spelled out), and they do not include any detailed prescriptions.

ISSUES AND IMPLICATIONS

Taking Feminism Seriously: Its Epistemological Implications

One issue that has preoccupied feminist researchers is the question of being taken seriously by traditional academia; and for good reason.

The first facet of the problem is that of admission to the academic establishment. Smith's (1978) paper on the exclusion of women from male culture includes a discussion of academia, while Spender (1981) has focussed on the way one important segment of the latter operates: the role of academic publishers as 'gatekeepers'. An anecdote may serve to reinforce her point. Wallston reports Bart's attempts to substitute 'vaginocentric' for 'phallocentric' terminology (referring to data as dry/wet rather than hard/soft), but notes that she was forced to drop the revised wording in the final published version (1981, p. 605). The second facet of the problem is that of being taken seriously. As Gould notes of her discipline:

> . . . the political essence of feminist sociology does not neatly conform to
> constructed notions of what constitutes 'serious academic work' . . .;
> Non-feminist sociologists do not perceive feminism as an alternative theoretical
> and methodological approach. They more comfortably perceive it as a purely
> political issue . . . (1980, pp. 466–467)

Some feminists appear to regard the answer to this problem as being an attempt to enter the male-dominated academic world on its own terms. Thus, for example, McRobbie argues that feminist research should display the 'qualities typically linked with official [sic] research: rigour, scholarliness, precision and lucidity' (1982, p. 54), while Wallston's solution is to produce work that will be published, even when this conflicts with her feminist principles (1981, p. 599). Others, particularly those who argue for an autonomous women's studies, feel there should be no compromise: e.g. Mies declares: 'New wine should not be poured into old bottles' (1983, p. 120).

Those feminists who emphasize the political purpose of feminist research naturally regard its major scope and implications as being the impetus for social and political change; others, however, prefer to stress the importance of feminism in its own right, and focus on its epistemological implications. However, Westkott notes that the epistemological issues have rarely been explicitly stated in the preoccupation with method (1979, p. 425).

Following this line, first it is argued that not only does feminism challenge the basic assumptions of positivistic science (Weinreich, 1977), it suggests real alternatives to it (e.g. Bowles and Klein, 1983; Stanley and Wise, 1983a), as part of the process of 'redefining knowledge, knowledge gathering and making' (Spender, 1978a, p. 1). Second, in the broader women's studies sense, it challenges the arrangement of knowledge into academic disciplines, cutting across disciplinary boundaries, and offering the possibility of reintegrating them within a single framework (Spender, 1978b, p. 259). It has been argued that autonomous women's studies could even become a 'paradigm' in the Kuhnian (Kuhn, 1970) sense—in this, Coyner (1983, p. 69) finds Mulkay's (1975) adaptations of Kuhn useful; while Reinharz (1983, p. 164) incorporates the social psychological extensions of Davis (1971). Third, and most critical to this line of argument, feminism offers the possibility of a shift in the centre from which knowledge is generated: to look at human experience from the point of view of women (Callaway, 1981, p. 460). The proposal is that:

> . . . women's experiences constitute a different view of reality, an entirely
> different 'ontology' or way of going about making sense of the world. (Stanley
> and Wise, 1983a, p. 117)

As Callaway points out, it is crucial to appreciate that this does not mean focussing exclusively on women, but that:

. . . by looking at human experience from the point of view of women, we can understand male experience and the whole of cultural history with greater depth. (1981, p. 460)

Several contributors to this volume also make this point (see e.g. Beckett, Chapter 3).

Who Can Do Feminist Research?

A second issue raised by the feminist alternative to mainstream social science is the question of who its practitioners are to be. Of course, feminists differ in their answer to this question, just as they differ in their definitions of feminist research. Thus for Kelly, who sees feminist research simply as 'research that is undertaken for feminist reasons' (1978, p. 226), presumably the answer would be 'anyone can'. This view is relatively rare; more common is the answer suggested by Bernard: that only those individuals (male and female) whose 'consciousness has been raised' in relation to feminism can do feminist research—because only they are capable of moving outside the androcentric definition of society (1973, p. 787). Most far reaching are the suggestions made by Stanley and Wise. They argue that only women can do feminist research, because only women are in possession of 'feminist consciousness', i.e. 'a particular kind of interpretation of the experience of being a woman as this is presently constructed in sexist society' (1983a, p. 18). Further, because it is not possible to faithfully represent the reality experienced by other people, Stanley and Wise also propose that researchers should only present themselves and their own experiences, in analytic accounts of research situations and the people in them. They argue that while this cannot be 'representative', it at least has a chance of being honestly representative of the researcher herself; and while it may appear limited, it does offer the opportunity to explore a range of forms of female experience in everyday life (Stanley and Wise, 1983a, pp. 167–173).

The 'New' Social Psychology Revisited?

The third general issue I would like to raise in this section is that of potential similarities between some of the features of feminist research that have been discussed, and those of other types of research. One characteristic that is evident among feminist writers is that often they do not appear to be aware either of their intellectual antecedents or of parallel lines of thought in the traditional academic disciplines. There are some exceptions: sociologists appear, perhaps, to be rather better informed than many of their psychologist counterparts. Westkott, for example, makes reference to both Marxist and interpretive traditions in sociology (1979, pp. 425–427), while Stanley and Wise express an awareness of the influences of interactionism and ethnomethodology on their feminist work (1983a, pp. 137–149). However, it is still relatively rare to find a comment such as Stanley and Wise's:

> The view we have put forward has been at the heart of contemporary debates within the philosophy of the social sciences for many years now, but feminism appears more or less oblivious to this. (1983a, p. 136)

They go on to suggest that the dissociation of feminism from its intellectual heritage is deliberate, indicating the possible ideological reasons for this. (This recalls Holland's comments on Personal Construct Theory some time ago (1970, pp. 111–132).) In a similar vein, Reinharz, writing about feminist methodology, notes:

> . . . these methods already partially exist, but they have been so undervalued that they constantly need to be rediscovered . . . As each 'rediscovery' or contribution is made, it appears new and gets its own name. (1983, p. 173)

Many readers of this chapter will feel that several elements of the feminist critique and its suggested alternatives sound rather familiar: echoing the 'crisis' debates in social psychology in the 1970s (e.g. Strickland et al., 1976) and the advocacy of the so-called 'new' social psychology: ethogenics and related research (Harré and Secord, 1972; Shotter, 1975), together with renewed interest in other person-centred psychologies, particularly Personal Construct Theory (Kelly, 1955): e.g. Stringer and Bannister, 1979. My final objective here is to make explicit some of the direct parallels between the feminist approach and this body of work.

The first similarities to be noted are those at a metatheoretical level. Feminism's emphasis on 'possibilities' (Westkott, 1979, pp. 427–430; 1983, pp. 213–217; Callaway, 1981, p. 457) may also be seen to be shared by Personal Construct theorists. The notion of what is possible is central to the philosophical basis of Construct Theory, 'constructive alternativism':

> But human anticipation—the stuff that life is made of—unfolds its full meaning only when one is keenly appreciative of what might actually happen instead, and when he [sic] comes to forecast the events of his [sic] future in the rich context of all else that may be possible. (Kelly, 1969a, p. 7)

(For a more detailed examination of the concept of possibility in Personal Construct Theory, see Wilkinson, 1981.)

Personal Construct Theory's model of people operating essentially as scientists attempting to predict and control their world (Kelly, 1955, pp. 4–5) also finds direct reflection in the basis of feminism's call for theory to be grounded in personal experience:

> All people derive 'theory' or 'second order constructs' from their experience
> or first order constructs . . . It isn't only social scientists who produce general
> accounts of reality in this way, in spite of what we are frequently told . . .
> Everyone constructs explanations of what they experience in their everyday
> lives. (Stanley and Wise, 1983a, p. 160)

Thirdly, feminists' suggestions that an autonomous women's studies could become a 'new paradigm' in the Kuhnian (1970) sense echoes claims made by Harré and Secord (1972, pp. 19-25) for the 'new' social psychology.

Some of the theoretical emphases of feminist research (in so far as these are apparent) can also be seen in the 'new' social psychology. Thus, the suggestions of Westkott (1979, pp. 426-427) and Stanley and Wise (1983a, p. 117) are very similar to those of Harré and Secord (1972, Chapters 1 and 12) and Harré (1979, Chapter 11) regarding human agency, while these feminist writers' suggestions that self and social world are constructed and negotiated through dialogue with others particularly recalls emphases in the work of Shotter (1975). The need that many feminists emphasize to focus on individual experience (e.g. Stanley and Wise, 1983a, p. 172; Nicolson, Chapter 8, this volume) is, of course, a central tenet of Personal Construct Theory (Kelly, 1955, pp. 8-12; 1969b). In addition, the 'sensitivity to intrinsic structure and qualitative patterning of phenomena studied', which is suggested by Carlson (1972, p. 20) as part of the 'communal' mode of enquiry, recalls both Harré and Secord's suggestions for modelling the behavioural sciences on the method of the advanced sciences (1972, pp. 5-6, 68-77) and Kelly's description of the underlying rationale of the repertory grid (1955, pp. 267-318; 1969c).

The feminist critique of androcentric social science in many respects directly parallels the 'new' social psychology's objections to positivism. For example, the feminist argument that mainstream social science is far from value-free (e.g. Bernard, 1983; Reinharz, 1983; Griffin, Chapter 10, this volume) recalls Sedgwick's (1974) demonstration of the ideological biases in psychology, while the feminist attempt to specify hidden assumptions of the traditional framework (e.g. Reinharz, 1983, pp. 167-170), was undertaken within the 'new' social psychology by Harré and Secord (1972, pp. 29-37). The claim that traditional research neglects historical and cultural perspectives (e.g. Mies, 1983, pp. 117-139; and several contributors to this volume) was made in the 1970s by Gergen (1976) and Triandis (1976). The methodological critique is equally familiar, in its focus both on the details of laboratory experimentation (e.g. Parlee, 1979, pp. 131)—this was undertaken in the 'new' social psychology by Harré and Secord (1972, pp. 27-37)—and in the call for attention to the social context of research, in relation to its purpose (e.g. Klein, 1983, pp. 90-93; Wetherell, Chapter 5, Kitzinger, Chapter 9, this volume); this was argued in the 1970s by, for example, Israel and Tajfel (1972).

In terms of the methodological alternatives suggested by feminists, we see an emphasis on such features as the revaluation of subjective experience (e.g. Klein,

1983, p. 94; Stanley and Wise, 1983b, p. 205; du Bois, 1983, p. 108; Condor, Chapter 6, Nicolson, Chapter 6, this volume). The ethogenic equivalent is Harré and Secord's (1972, Chapter 6) 'open souls doctrine', which entails taking people's accounts of their own experience seriously, while in Construct Theory there is Kelly's so-called 'first principle': if you want to know why a person did what they did, ask them, they just might tell you. There is also commonality in the call for more extensive usage of methods which do justice to this experience, particularly qualitative methods: the arguments of Reinharz (1983) and Griffin (Chapter 10, this volume), for example, being very similar to those of Harré and Secord (1972, Chapters 7 and 14), Harré (1979, Chapter 7), and Kelly (1955, Chapter 7). There is, too, a common emphasis on the importance of the study of language use in social life: the feminist argument (e.g. Westkott, 1983, p. 216; Wetherell, Chapter 5, this volume) being echoed by the priority given to this by Harré (1976). The argument on the need for reflexivity in feminist theory (e.g. Stanley and Wise, 1983a, p. 73) is seen in Personal Construct Theory (e.g. Bannister and Fransella, 1971, pp. 188-189; Marshall, Chapter 11, this volume), although Kelly himself did not emphasize it; similarly the redefined relationship between researcher and researched (exemplified in feminist writing by du Bois, 1983, p. 111; Klein, 1983, p. 95; Reinharz, 1983, pp. 180-183; Griffin, Chapter 10, this volume) is also seen in Personal Construct Theory: e.g. Kelly (1969d). The latter concern is also prevalent in the 'new' social psychology: Mixon (1974), for example, writes of the researcher's moral obligations to those s/he studies, while Elden (1981) focuses on the complete rethinking of the status of the participants in the research, including an increased awareness of the ways in which the researcher is influenced by her/his participation.

The necessity of this type of research being based on a limited number of people, pointed out by the feminists Stanley and Wise (1983a, pp. 171-173), was noted as a consequence of ethogenic research by Harré and Secord (1972, pp. 133-134), and, of course, Personal Construct Theory has generally been regarded as idiographic in nature (e.g. Bannister and Fransella, 1971, pp. 58-60), although it is interesting to note that Kelly himself did not see it essentially as such (1955, p. 113). Finally, Stanley's and Wise's apparently radical suggestions regarding the limitation of social scientific enquiry to accounts of the researcher's own experience (1983a, pp. 167-168) are not new: Stringer has hinted that a social psychology based on the psychologist 'operating her/himself in relation' is the epistemological consequence of taking Personal Construct Theory seriously (1979, pp. 110-111), in so far as for Kelly it is only possible to examine social relations through being-in-relation oneself (Sociality Corollary, 1955, pp. 95-102).

The extensiveness of these similarities between feminist research and the 'new' social psychology should not, of course, be taken to indicate anything like a complete correspondence between the two. The feminist focus on a specifically female ontology (e.g. Stanley and Wise, 1983a, p. 117) is, of course, new—and, as has been argued, of considerable epistemological importance—and there are other important differences. Feminists should perhaps be discouraged from identifying too closely with ethogenics or Personal Construct Theory if this would preclude a critical consideration of the value of these theories for women, or retard the development of distinctively woman-based theory. There is probably little danger of this: Smith, (1977, p. 19), for example, has argued that Harré and Secord's (1972) model of human action does not apply to the experience of a typical woman, who finds that her daily life is largely determined and ordered externally to her; thus she does not have the power to act or exercise control over her position. It should be noted, however, that it is not possible to tell from this brief statement the extent to which her critique rests on an incomplete reading of Harré and Secord, whose concept of 'power' is related to a 'field of possibilities', within which an analysis of the 'enabling conditions' for the exercise of power is central (1972, Chapter 12).

Therefore, it may be argued that, in general, feminist researchers could profit from a greater awareness both of their intellectual antecedents and of parallel lines of thought which have developed in social psychology (and, indeed, in other disciplines — although this is beyond the scope of this chapter). The demonstration that their dissatisfactions with traditional social science are comprehensively shared and that their alternatives are not, in fact, 'new', considerably strengthens the feminist case, and may help to overcome some of the problems of being taken seriously.

NOTES TO CHAPTER 1

1. This phrase is 'borrowed' from Callaway (1981, p. 457).

2. An early version of this chapter was presented in the symposium *Feminist Research in Social Psychology: Extending the Perspective*, British Psychological Society Social Psychology Section annual conference, University of Oxford, 14-16 September 1984.

REFERENCES

Bakan, P. (1966). *The Duality of Existence*. Chicago, Rand McNally.

Bannister, D. and Fransella, F. (1980). *Inquiring Man: The Theory of Personal Constructs* (2nd ed.). Harmondsworth, Penguin.

Bernard, J. (1973). My four revolutions: an autobiographical history of the ASA. *American Journal of Sociology* **78**(4), 773-791.

Bowles, G. (1983). Is women's studies an academic discipline? In: G. Bowles and R. D. Klein (eds), op. cit.

Bowles, G. and Klein, R. D. (eds) (1983). *Theories of Women's Studies*. London, Routledge.

Callaway, H. (1981). Women's perspectives: research as re-vision. In: P. Reason and J. Rowan (eds), *Human Inquiry: A Sourcebook of New Paradigm Research*. London, Wiley.

Carlson, R. (1972). Understanding women: implications for personality theory and research. *Journal of Social Issues* **28**(2), 17-32.

Coyner, S. (1983). Women's studies as an academic discipline: why and how to do it? In: G. Bowles and R. D. Klein (eds), op. cit.

Daly, M. (1980). *Gyn/Ecology: The Metaethics of Radical Feminism*. London, The Women's Press.

Daniels, A. (1975). Feminist perspectives in sociological research. In: M. Millman and R. M. Kanter (eds), op. cit.

Davis, M. (1971). That's interesting! Toward a phenomenology of sociology and a sociology of phenomenology. *Philosophy of the Social Sciences* 1, 309-344.

du Bois, B. (1983). Passionate scholarship: notes on values, knowing and method in feminist social science. In: G. Bowles and R. D. Klein (eds), op. cit.

Eichler, M. (1980). *The Double Standard*. London, Croom Helm.

Elden, M. (1981). Sharing the research work: participative research and its role demands. In: P. Reason and J. Rown (eds), *Human Inquiry: A Sourcebook of New Paradigm Research*. London, Wiley.

Evans, M. (1982). In praise of theory: the case for women's studies. *Feminist Review* (Spring), 61-74.

Fox Keller, E. (1978). Gender and science. *Psychoanalysis and Contemporary Thought* 1, 409-433.

Gergen, K. J. (1976). Social psychology as history. In: L. H. Strickland, F. E. Aboud and K. J. Gergen (eds), op. cit.

Griffin, C. (1985). Qualitative methods and cultural analysis: young women and the transition from school to un/employment. In: R. Burgess (ed.), *Field Methods in the Study of Education*. London, Falmer Press.

Gould, M. (1980). The new sociology. *Signs: Journal of Women in Culture and Society* 5(3), 459-467.

Harré, R. (ed.) (1976). *Life Sentences: Aspects of the Social Role of Language*. London, Wiley.

Harré, R. (1979). *Social Being*. Oxford, Blackwell.

Harré, R. and Secord, P. F. (1972). *The Explanation of Social Behaviour*. Oxford, Blackwell.

Holland, R. (1970). George Kelly: Constructive innocent and reluctant existentialist. In: D. Bannister (ed.), *Perspectives in Personal Construct Theory*. London, Academic Press.

Israel, J. and Tajfel, H. (1972). *The Context of Social Psychology: A Critical Assessment*. London, Academic Press.

Jayaratne, T. E. (1983). The value of quantitative methodology for feminist research. In: G. Bowles and R. D. Klein (eds), op. cit.

Kelly, A. (1978). Feminism and research. *Women's Studies International Quarterly* 1, 225-232.

Kelly, G. A. (1955). *The Psychology of Personal Constructs*, Vol. 1. New York, Norton.

Kelly, G. A. (1969a). Ontological acceleration. In: B. Maher (ed.), op. cit.

Kelly, G. A. (1969b). Man's construction of his alternatives. In: B. Maher (ed.), op. cit.

Kelly, G. A. (1969c). A mathematical approach to psychology. In: B. Maher (ed.), op. cit.

Kelly, G. A. (1969d). Humanistic methodology in psychological research. In: B. Maher (ed.), op. cit.

Klein, R. D. (1983). How to do what we want to do: thoughts about feminist methodology. In: G. Bowles and R. D. Klein (eds), op. cit.

Kuhn, T. (1970). *The Structure of Scientific Revolutions*, (2nd ed.). Chicago, University of Chicago Press.

McRobbie, A. (1982). The politics of feminist research: between talk, text and action. *Feminist Review* 12, 46-57.

Maher, B. (ed.) (1969). *Clinical Psychology and Personality: The Selected Papers of George Kelly*. New York, Wiley.

Mies, M. (1983). Towards a methodology for feminist research. In: G. Bowles and R. D. Klein (eds), op. cit.

Miller, J. B. (1978). *Toward a New Psychology of Women*. Harmondsworth, Penguin.

Millman, M. and Kanter, R. M. (eds) (1975). *Another Voice: Feminist Perspectives on Social Life and Social Science*. New York, Anchor Books.

Morgan, D. (1981). Men, masculinity and the process of sociological enquiry. In: H. Roberts (ed.), *Doing Feminist Research*. London, Routledge.

Mixon, D. (1974). If you won't deceive, what can you do? In: N. Armistead (ed.), *Reconstructing Social Psychology*. Harmondsworth, Penguin.

Mulkay, M. J. (1975). Three models of scientific development. *Sociological Review* **23**, 509-526.

Parlee, M. B. (1979). Psychology and women. *Signs: Journal of Women in Culture and Society* **5**(1), 121-133.

Reinharz, S. (1979). *On Becoming a Social Scientist: From Survey Research and Pariticpant Observation to Experiential Analysis*. San Francisco, Jossey-Bass.

Reinharz, S. (1983). Experiential analysis: a contribution to feminist research. In: G. Bowles and R. D. Klein (eds), op. cit.

Reinharz, S., Bombyk, M. and Wright, J. (1983). Methodological issues in feminist research: a bibliography of literature in women's studies, sociology and psychology. *Women's Studies International Forum* **6**(4), 437-454.

Sedgwick, P. (1974). Ideology in modern psychology. In: N. Armistead (ed.), *Reconstructing Social Psychology*. Harmondsworth, Penguin.

Sherif, C. (1979). Bias in psychology. In: J. A. Sherman and E. T. Beck (eds), *The Prism of Sex: Essays in the Sociology of Knowledge*. Madison, Wisconsin, University of Wisconsin Press.

Shorter Oxford English Dictionary (3rd ed.) (1973). Oxford, Oxford University Press.

Shotter, J. (1975). *Images of Man in Psychological Research*. London, Methuen.

Smith, D. E. (1974). Women's perspective as a radical critique of sociology. *Sociological Inquiry* **44**(1), 7-13.

Smith, D. E. (1977). Some implications of a sociology for women. In: N. Glazer and H. Y. Waehrer (eds), *Woman in a Man-Made World*. Chicago, Rand McNally.

Smith, D. E. (1978). A peculiar eclipsing: women's exclusion from men's culture. *Women's Studies International Quarterly* **1**(4), 281-295.

Smith, D. E. (1979). A sociology for women. In: J. A. Sherman and E. T. Beck (eds), *The Prism of Sex: Essays in the Sociology of Knowledge*. Madison, Wisconsin, University of Wisconsin Press.

Spender, D. (1978a). Editorial. *Women's Studies International Quarterly* **1**(1), 1-2.

Spender, D. (1978b). Women's studies: notes on the organisation of women's studies. *Women's Studies International Quarterly* **1**(3), 255-275.

Spender, D. (1980). *Man-Made Language*. London, Routledge.

Spender, D. (1981). The gatekeepers: a feminist critique of academic publishing. In: H. Roberts (ed.), *Doing Feminist Research*. London, Routledge.

Spender, D. (1983). Theorising about theorising. In: G. Bowles and R. D. Klein (eds), op. cit.

Stanley, L. and Wise, S. (1983a). *Breaking Out: Feminist Consciousness and Feminist Research*. London, Routledge.

Stanley, L. and Wise, S. (1983b). 'Back into the personal' or: our attempt to construct 'feminist research'. In: G. Bowles and R. D. Klein (eds), op. cit.

Strickland, L. H., Aboud, F. E. and Gergen, K. J. (eds) (1976). *Social Psychology in Transition*. New York, Plenum.

Stringer, P. (1979). Individuals, roles and persons. In: P. Stringer and D. Bannister (eds), op. cit.

Stringer, P. and Bannister, D. (eds) (1979). *Constructs of Sociality and Individuality*. London, Academic Press.

Tobias, S. (1978). Women's studies: its origins, its organisation and its prospects. *Women's Studies International Quarterly* **1**, 85-97.

Triandis, H. C. (1976). Social psychology and cultural analysis. In: L. H. Strickland, F. E. Aboud and K. J. Gergen (eds), op. cit.

Vaughter, R. M. (1976). Psychology: review essay. *Signs: Journal of Women in Culture and Society* **2**(1), 120-146.

Wallston, B. S. (1981). What are the questions in psychology of women? A feminist approach to research. *Psychology of Women Quarterly* **5**(4), 597-617.

Weinreich, H. (1977). What future for the female subject? Some implications of the Women's Movement for psychological research. *Human Relations* **30**(6), 535-543.

Weisstein, N. (1970). Psychology constructs the female. In: V. Gornick and E. K. Moran (eds), *Woman in Sexist Society*. New York, Basic Books.

Westkott, M. (1979). Feminist criticism of the social sciences. *Harvard Educational Review* **49**(4), 422-430.

Westkott, M. (1983). Women's studies as a strategy for change: between criticism and vision. In: G. Bowles and R. D. Klein (eds), op. cit.

Wilkinson, S. J. (1981). Constructs, counterfactuals and fictions: elaborating the concept of 'possibility' in science. In: H. Bonarius, R. Holland and S. Rosenberg (eds), *Personal Construct Psychology: Recent Advances in Theory and Practice*. London, Macmillan.

Chapter 2

Sexual Identity and Difference: Psychoanalytic Perspectives[1,2]

Janet Sayers

> When I have promised my patients help or improvement . . . I have often
> been faced by this objection: 'Why, you tell me yourself that my illness is
> probably connected with my circumstances and the events of my life. You
> cannot alter these in any way. How do you propose to help me, then?' And
> I have been able to make this reply: 'No doubt fate would find it easier than
> I do to relieve you of your illness. But you will be able to convince yourself
> that much will be gained if we succeed in transforming your hysterical misery
> into common unhappiness. With a mental life that has been restored to health
> you will be better armed against that unhappiness. (Freud, 1895, pp. 392-393)

With the re-emergence of feminism in the late 1960s, those working in psychology
became alerted to its neglect of sexual inequality and difference, to the fact that,
as one psychologist put it, 'even among female investigators sex differences were
ignored in the majority of papers' (Lloyd, 1976, p. 7). Attention accordingly turned
to the work of those who had studied differences between women and men in their
psychology—to the work say of Matina Horner (1969) indicating that women
might not be driven by the same achievement motives as men. Perhaps, Horner
suggested, women fear success—a remarkable suggestion coming as it did from
someone particularly noted for her success: she was after all the youngest ever
President of Radcliffe! Such exceptions aside, women are generally less successful
than men. Some have explained this as due to girls and women attributing what
successes they do achieve to chance rather than ability (see e.g. Deaux *et al.*, 1975).
Others have explained women's lesser achievements, especially in maths- and
science-related occupations, to their not being sufficiently encouraged in the
relevant subjects at school (see e.g. Sherman, 1978), and to their supposedly
processing visuo-spatial information differently in the brain (see e.g. Goleman,
1978). Still others have claimed that women differ from men in their styles of
moral reasoning—that they are not motivated as men are by individualistic
aspirations and concerns (see e.g. Gilligan, 1977; Chodorow, 1978). Differences

25

between the sexes in their vulnerability to mental distress have also attracted attention — women's greater vulnerability, for example, to depression (see e.g. Beck and Greenberg, 1974), and to eating disorders (see e.g. Orbach, 1978).

Following a decade in which research into sex differences became something of a rage in psychology, psychologists are now beginning to question whether these differences are in fact quite as marked as this research seemed to indicate. There is now a spate of reports showing that women no more fear success than men (see e.g. Paludi *et al.*, 1984); that they no more attribute their successes to external factors than do men (see e.g. Frieze *et al.*, 1982); that the similarities between the sexes are more marked than the differences in their styles of moral reasoning (see e.g. Broughton 1983; Walker, 1984); and that, just as women are rendered vulnerable to depression by not having a job (see e.g. Brown and Harris, 1978), so too are men (see e.g. Oatley, 1984). Some feminists in psychology are now calling for an end to sex differences research. Sandra Bem, noted for her contribution to such research in the 1970s, now argues that the feminist moral of this research, specifically of her work on androgyny, is that psychologists and others should stop dichotomizing behaviour by sex (Bem, 1981), and should seek to overcome their preoccupation with gender difference (Bem, 1983) — hardly an easy task given the multifarious ways in which, whether we like it or not, social relations continue to be structured by sex.

A common problem with this latter approach that once again emphasizes the similarities between women and men in their psychology, and with the earlier approach that emphasizes their differences, is that in point of fact women share the *same* psychology as men and yet also have a *different* psychology from them. This, I would argue, is because their social experience teaches them both to expect the same freedom of action as men, and at the same time teaches them of the limitations on women's freedom of action.

Freud's work is interesting in this context because, virtually alone among psychologists, and albeit only in very preliminary fashion, he drew attention to the way this contradiction shapes women's psychology. My main concern in this chapter will be to outline this aspect of Freud's work and its clinical implications for enabling women to become more fully conscious of, and hence better able effectively to deal with, the contradictions of their social lot. In this its clinical goal, I shall argue, psychoanalytic theory and practice is fully consonant with feminism and its advocacy of consciousness raising. But feminism does not stop here. It goes beyond the task psychoanalysis sets itself. Psychoanalysis regards its job as done once it has rendered its patients conscious of, and able to act on, the conflicts and contradictions in their feelings and experience. Feminism recognizes such individual psychological change not to be enough. It recognizes that the conflicts in women's lives arising from their being treated as both equal and unequal to men can only be permanently removed given social as well as individual change, given the achievement of a society in which women are accorded the same freedom of action as men, in which women's needs are met equally with those of men.

SEXUAL CONTRADICTION IN INFANCY

I shall begin with Freud's account of infant development, of the way the social experiences of infancy bring into being, in girls as in boys, the same psychological desires, the same active as well as passive aims. I shall then go on to describe how he saw this similarity of aims as being affected by the infant's later recognition of sexual difference, of women's passive subordination to men.

On the basis of his work with adult neurotics, sexological accounts of the perversions, and anecdotal observations of children's behaviour, Freud concluded that from the earliest hours of infancy we derive sexual as well as physical pleasure from social interaction with others. Such is the sexual pleasure produced in the baby by being physically looked after by others, says Freud, that it seeks to re-create this pleasure by repeating those aspects of its past social interaction that seemed to give rise to this pleasure. In the first instance, he writes, the baby seeks to repeat these interactions in the passive form in which it originally experiences them, in the form of being the passive object of the care and attention of others. However, it also quickly seeks to repeat these pleasures in active form by seeking to take on the agency of the other, of the mother, say, as it experienced her care in looking after it.

Girl and boy babies, claims Freud, seek to recapture the sexual pleasure they derive from being fed: passively by continuing to be suckled even when sated, actively by seeking to feed others. Likewise, toddlers seek to conjure up the pleasures produced in them by having their toilet attended to and watched over: passively and exhibitionistically by getting their playmates as well as their parents to watch while they urinate; actively and voyeuristically by contriving to watch others at their toilet. Similarly, writes Freud, children seek to intensify the genital pleasures they obtain from being cleaned and clothed. Passively, this can take the form of getting the mother to repeat the actions she makes in dressing them, actions by which they experience themselves to be the passive object of the mother's seduction. Freud records, for instance, a mother telling him how, when she was trying a pair of knickers on her three year old daughter, she had inadvertently brushed against the inner surface of her daughter's thigh, whereupon the child 'shut her legs together on her mother's hand, saying: "Oh, Mummy, do leave your hand there. It feels so lovely"' (Freud, 1909, p. 183). Such incidents can also elicit active aims in the child, says Freud, the aim of repeating these incidents being to capture the sexual pleasure supposedly enjoyed by the mother in actively seducing it, as the child experiences her care. Freud suggests that childhood masturbation expresses just this aim, that children seek to seduce members of their family when they masturbate in front of them. Punished or disapproved of on this account, says Freud, girls and boys seek to repeat this experience: passively and masochistically by imagining or actually getting others to punish and even beat them; actively and sadistically by imagining or actually punishing and tormenting others.

Disapproval of childhood masturbation also has another and crucial effect, according to Freud. For, he says, this disapproval causes the child to recognize what it has until then only suspected, namely that girls do not have a penis. Up until then, writes Freud, the girl like the boy seems to believe that she has a penis which is 'still quite small. But when she gets bigger it'll grow all right' (Freud, 1908, p. 194). Punished, explicitly or implicitly, for masturbating, however, the child recognizes that girls in fact do not have a penis. It construes this fact, in the light of its parents' disapproval of its masturbation, as the effect of girls having been punished with castration for masturbating.

Up until this point, implies Freud, girls consciously believe themselves to have a penis. With their recognition, via the castration complex, that they do not have a penis, comes acknowledgement that the earlier belief of having a penis is in contradiction with reality. This belief is accordingly repressed into the unconscious. It is not, however, thereby done away with. The girl's belief that she has a penis persists, says Freud. This is evident from the analysis of women's dreams and neurotic symptoms. It is also evident in psychosis when women sometimes openly express the belief that they are men—such is the dominance in psychosis of waking as of sleeping life by the hallucinatory, 'primary', and unrealistic processes of unconscious thought.

Normally, however, woman's belief that she is a man (that she has a penis) is unavailable to consciousness. When this belief is repressed, as it generally is, what happens to the traits socially associated with maleness, with being a man? Today these traits apparently include those of being 'aggressive', 'independent', 'not at all emotional', 'objective', 'dominant', 'active', 'competitive', 'logical', 'worldly', 'self-confident', 'ambitious', and 'never conceited about appearance' (Broverman et al., 1970). Of course, the traits socially associated with masculinity vary cross-culturally and historically, as do the traits socially associated with femininity. Freud neglected this variation. He tended to treat masculinity as simply synonymous with activity, femininity with passivity—an equation that succinctly expresses the social fact of men's social dominance but which does not do justice to the fact (recognized by Freud) that men can also be subordinate and passive, women dominant and active. Not only did Freud say little on this score, he also gave little indication of how children come to know of the social equation of activity with masculinity, passivity with femininity. He simply suggested that they first acquire this knowledge through observing their parents' sexual and social intercourse with each other.

Once girls know that activity is socially associated with masculinity, what then happens to the active aims brought into being in them, as in boys, by the social interactions of their infancy—aims that continue to be elicited in them, as in boys and men, by the fact that their social experience teaches them that they have every right to realize themselves as active agents of their own destiny? What happens to this active aspiration in girls and women when they recognize the social limitations and obstacles to their realizing their individual freedom in the way that men can; or when they realize that they are more often treated as passive objects of the agency of others rather than as active agents of their own destiny? Once they recognize that they are not men, that they do not have a penis, girls, as I have said, repress into the unconscious the belief that they are male, since this belief is in contradiction with biological reality. There is, however, no reason on this biological score why they should also repress into the unconscious their active aims, even though these aims are socially equated with masculinity, with being male. Indeed, women are clearly often conscious of, and consciously act on, these aims in themselves. And, of course, these aims constitute the psychological impetus of their individual achievements, and of their collective struggle say as feminists to change society so that women might more fully realize their active aims in the ways open to men.

All too often, however, women succumb to the contradictions resulting from their social subordination. Instead of acting on their so-called 'masculine' aims, they disown them—repressing them, as occurs in neurosis; turning them against themselves, as occurs in depression; or mislocating them in others, as occurs in paranoia. Women's regular disowning of their active aims goes some way toward explaining why, although these aims make women similar to men in their psychology, this is overlooked when attention is paid instead to the differences between women and men in their psychology. Many, however, will be unfamiliar with Freud's account of the defences that I am arguing contribute to this neglect, namely those of repression, introjection, and depression. I shall therefore use the rest of this chapter to outline this aspect of his theory. In the process I shall indicate some of the methods developed by Freud and his followers for undoing these defences such that people might thereby better realize all their aims, active as well as passive, masculine as well as feminine.

> But when that which is perfect is come, then that which is in part shall be done away. When I was a child, I spake as a child: but when I became a man, I put away childish things. For now we see through a glass darkly; but then shall I know even as also I am known. (St Paul, *Corinthians* I, ch. xiii)

REPRESSION AND NEUROSIS

Recognizing themselves to be female, girls all too often repress and, as it were, only 'see through a glass darkly' their 'phallic activity', their active aims, and their 'sexuality in general as well as a good part of . . . [their] masculinity in other fields' (Freud, 1931, p. 376). To the extent that girls and women narcissistically cathect themselves as feminine following their recognition of sexual difference and its social elaboration, and to the extent that they accordingly experience gratification of their erstwhile, conscious, masculine aims as in contradiction with their narcissism or egoism, these aims may be repressed into the unconscious. They can then only be expressed in unrealistic, neurotic form—such is the opposition of the ego to their actual gratification.

This outcome may be illustrated by reference to Freud's account of his treatment of a young woman by the name of Ida Bauer, referred to by Freud as Dora. Dora suffered from a variety of neurotic symptoms: hysterical fainting fits, a nervous cough, a 'tickling in her throat', and anorexia. Anorexia, and other eating disorders in women, are now often explained as arising from women's attempt, so often thwarted in our sexually unequal society, to exercise control over their lives (see e.g. Lawrence, 1984; Maisner and Pulling, 1985). Freud also explained such disorders as the effect of control, specifically of sexual control or repression. He suggested that Dora's oral symptoms represented, in hallucinatory and displaced form, the fulfilment of her repressed, active, sexual and genital aims and desires. Such 'hysterical' symptoms are widespread among women and Freud claimed them to be directly traceable to the social suppression of their sexuality.

Freud sought to treat these symptoms by having his patients freely associate to them. He thereby hoped to uncover and make conscious the unconscious, repressed aims he believed both to be expressed in and to sustain the symptoms of neurosis. Neurotic symptoms, he observed, are sustained by the 'primary gain', by the hallucinatory or illusory gratification they afford the sexual aims they express. Furthermore, people also derive 'secondary gain' from their neurotic symptoms. In so far as others look after them on account of their neurosis, people obtain real gratification of their physical needs by being ill. Women, wrote Freud, are particularly likely to learn of this means of securing the care and attention of others (see Freud, 1905, p. 77), solicitude of which they are otherwise often deprived. Freud came back to this point in his *Introductory Lectures on Psychoanalysis*:

> A woman who is roughly treated and ruthlessly exploited by her husband will fairly regularly find a way out in neurosis, if her constitution makes it possible, if she is too cowardly or too moral to console herself secretly with another man, if she is not strong enough to separate from her husband in the face of every external deterrent, if she has no prospect of supporting herself or obtaining a better husband and if in addition she is still attached to this brutal husband by her sexual feelings. Her illness now becomes a weapon in her battle with her dominating husband—a weapon which she can use for her defence and misuse for her revenge. To complain of her illness is allowable, though to lament her marriage was probably not. She finds a helper in her doctor, she forces her usually inconsiderate husband to look after her, to spend money on her, to allow her at times to be away from home and so free from her married oppression. (Freud, 1916–17, p. 430)

Freud adjured doctors not to collude in this way with the secondary gains women and men derive from their symptoms. If people are to be permanently cured of neurosis, he argued, their neurotic symptoms must be treated not by hospitalization, but in the context that brought these symptoms into being in the first place. In addition, he came to realize that this also means that the unconscious aims that sustain neurotic symptoms must be analysed in the here and now in therapy, as they become evident in the 'transference' relation patients unconsciously seek to establish with their therapists. Otherwise, this relation becomes an obstacle rather than a vehicle of cure.

. Later, Freud came to appreciate that successful treatment of the neuroses depends not only on making conscious the patient's transference to the therapist, nor solely on analysing the primary and secondary gains patients obtain from their symptoms. He realized that it also depends on analysing the resistance of the ego to cure. Neurotic symptoms, he pointed out, cause us pain as well as pleasure. We cling to them as much for the suffering as for the gratification they afford us. The suffering that people derive from their symptoms is the source, wrote Freud, of what he referred to as the 'negative therapeutic reaction'. This resistance to cure, he suggested, is the work of the ego, specifically of the super ego. He hypothesized that this agency of the ego originates in the castration complex. Equating gratification of its genital aims toward members of its family with castration, the ego represses these aims—now characterized by Freud as basically the work of the id. The ego seeks to prevent these aims from being expressed because of the dangers of castration it associates with their expression. It does this by identifying with the parents' prohibition, actual or only suspected, of the child's sexual aims towards them. This identification constitutes the basis of the super ego. It is this that gives rise to the negative therapeutic reaction, to patients' clinging to their symptoms in punishment of the repressed active and passive aims these symptoms express. If the patient is to gain actual as opposed to merely neurotic gratification of the aims that their symptoms express, then the resistance of the ego, or super ego, to these aims being consciously expressed, must needs be undone. That is, the ego itself now becomes the object of analysis.

Up until this point the analyst relies on forming a 'therapeutic alliance' with the healthy part of the patient's ego to bring about his or her cure. With the analysis of the negative therapeutic reaction this alliance breaks down: the ego itself constitutes the principal obstacle to treatment. In men, writes Freud, this resistance stems ultimately from the unconscious belief, retained from childhood, that to submit to another man (as they construe being cured by the analyst) is tantamount to being castrated, as, in their infancy, they then interpreted their mother's submission to the father. In the case of women, implies Freud, the resistance of the ego to cure often arises from the unconscious belief that only by being men, that only by having a penis, can they be cured. Only thus, they believe, can they hope to realize, actually rather than neurotically, the active aims and desires they share with men.

Freud stated that, with this resistance of the ego to therapy, psychoanalysis comes up against the insuperable biological obstacle of sexual difference. In fact, however, men's biological sex is not an insuperable obstacle to men realizing their passive aims. Nor is femaleness an insuperable obstacle to women realizing their active aims. The obstacles to such realization are social not biological. They include the continuing discrimination exercised against women both at work and in the home — whereby, while men are allowed and even encouraged to be active agents of their own destiny, such individualism is frowned on in women as selfish callousness. Women are instead expected unselfishly to subordinate their needs as individuals to those of others.

Although this, and women's social subordination generally, constitutes a major obstacle to women realizing their active aims as individuals, Freud never made these social matters an object of his therapeutic work. I shall return to this point in my conclusion. First, however, I shall outline two other mechanisms described by Freud whereby women (and men) disown their unwanted aims and aspirations; their active aims, say.

INTROJECTION AND DEPRESSION

One such mechanisms is that whereby these aims are turned against the self, as occurs in depression. A tragic example comes from Freud's history of the Wolf Man. It concerns the Wolf Man's sister of whom Freud tells the following tale:

> As a child she was boyish and unmanageable, but she then entered upon a brilliant intellectual development and distinguished herself by her acute and realistic powers of mind; she inclined in her studies to the natural sciences, but also produced imaginative writings of which her father had a high opinion. She was mentally far superior to her numerous early admirers, and used to make jokes at their expense. In her early twenties, however, she began to be depressed, complained that she was not good-looking enough, and withdrew from all society. She was sent to travel in the company of an acquaintance, an elderly lady, and after her return told a number of most improbable stories of how she had been ill-treated by her companion, but remained with her affections obviously fixed upon her alleged tormentor. While she was on a second journey, soon afterwards, she poisoned herself and died far away from home. (Freud, 1918, pp. 249–250)

Freud explained depression, such as took its toll on the life of the Wolf Man's sister, as constituted by the turning against the self of one's unwanted aims, by the 'introjection', in her case, of her previously outwardly expressed intelligence and biting wit.

Introjection of these aims is particularly likely to occur in women given the social association of these aims with masculinity, whereby women are not encouraged, as are men actively, and openly to express these aspects of their personality. And this also holds true of women's feelings of anger and frustration at their social lot. Such is their social subordination that women regularly feel helpless about and discouraged from openly expressing and acting on these feelings. It is therefore little surprise that women tend more often than men to respond to the untoward events of their lives with inward rather than outward aggression and rage, that they are much more likely than men to suffer from depression. (For evidence on this last point see e.g. Hirschfeld and Cross, 1982.)

Depression, Freud implied, is triggered by the unconscious experience of the disappointments of one's life as though they involved loss of those believed to be responsible for these disappointments. Instead of acting on the anger such hardships provoke, people respond in depression as though the people they love and blame for their problems were internal to the self. According to Freud it is the castigation of these 'internal objects' that constitutes the stuff of depression. 'The depressed woman,' he writes,

> who loudly pities her husband for being tied to such an incapable wife as herself is really accusing her husband of being incapable, in whatever sense she may mean this. There is no need to be greatly surprised that a few genuine self-reproaches are scattered among those that have been transposed back. . . . they derive from the pros and cons of the conflict of love that has led to the loss of love. . . . far from evincing towards those around them the attitude of humility and submissiveness that would alone befit such worthless people . . . they make the greatest nuisance of themselves, and always seem as though they felt slighted and had been treated with great injustice. All this is possible only because the reactions expressed in their behaviour still proceed from a mental constellation of revolt, which has then, by a certain process, passed over into the crushed state of melancholia. (Freud, 1917, p. 257)

Such shadow-boxing hardly serves to deal effectively with the external frustrations that give rise to it. This depends on women (and men) acting constructively on the anger they feel about their social lot, on their not turning this anger destructively against themselves. It depends on undoing the defence of introjection to the extent that it is this that impedes women's (and men's) capacity to use their anger to change the external social conditions that elicit it so that their needs—physical, psychological, and sexual—might adequately be met.

Freud himself was pessimistic as to whether this goal could be achieved through psychoanalysis. He implied that in severe depression the ego is so divided between narcissistic cathexis of itself and identification with its disappointing loved objects that it is incapable of forming the therapeutic alliance he held to be necessary to successful analysis. His followers—notably Karl Abraham, Melanie Klein, and object relations theorists like Donald Winnicott—were not so pessimistic.

On the basis of her pioneering analytic work with children and her clinical work with adults, Klein suggested that depression is sustained by unconscious anxiety, lest in acting on the anger and hatred one feels about one's social lot, one might thereby harm and hence lose those one loves and on whom one depends. And, of course, this anxiety is likely to be particularly acute for women in so far as they depend economically as well as emotionally on those they love.

Kleinian treatment of depression involves making conscious the unconscious anxiety about object loss, already referred to by Freud in his account of depression, as this anxiety manifests itself in the transference. This can be illustrated by reference to the Kleinian analyst Hanna Segal's account of a therapy session with a woman who, because of her financial difficulties, had asked Segal to waive her analytic fees:

> . . . the patient opened the session by complaining that my waiting-room was very cold. She also thought, for the first time, that it looked very drab and dreary, and she deplored the lack of curtains in the room. Following these associations, she reported a dream. She said that the dream was very simple — she had just dreamt of a sea of icebergs . . . She said that on waking her first thought was that she was afraid she might soon be in the grip of depression again. . . . She then associated with the icebergs a poem about ancient and deserted ships, looking like swans asleep. They also reminded her of the white and wavy hair of an old friend of hers, Mrs. A., who used to be kind to her, from whom she had had help and whom she had neglected, which caused her a great deal of guilt and sorrow. (Segal, 1973, p. 71)

On the basis of these associations, Segal interpreted to the patient her anxiety lest, by putting her money worries on to Segal, she had thereby used up and lost Segal's capacity to help her:

> I interpreted that the cold waiting-room was the same as the cold icebergs in her dream; that she must feel that her demands to pay reduced fees or no fees at all had completely exhausted and impoverished me — the waiting-room being drab and dreary and without curtains — that she had in fact killed me, so that I had become like a cold iceberg, filling her with guilt and persecution. (Segal, 1973, p. 71)

Those working at the London Women's Therapy Centre describe this aspect of therapy thus: 'At the point of being able to take in the therapist's caring, the woman may become caught up in worrying and fantasizing about the needs of the therapist. . . . She may feel she needs to take care of the therapist in order to keep her there' (Eichenbaum and Orbach, 1985, pp. 93–94). Adopting an object relations development of Klein's approach to treatment, they argue that this aspect of the transference stems from women's experience, as daughters, of being called upon by their mothers to attend to the mother's needs rather than to their own; that mothers thereby prepare their daughters for women's lot of subordinating their needs to those of others.

By thus interpreting and working through (as in mourning) the analysand's anxieties lest they lose the therapist as a helping person, by openly expressing the frustrations and demands to which their social experience gives rise, Kleinians and object relations therapists hope to enable their clients to be able to recognize that it is safe to express and act on these demands not only in therapy but in social life generally. They thereby seek to reassure their clients that it is safe to express and act on the frustration they feel about their social lot rather than giving in to it as occurs in depression.

PROJECTION AND PARANOIA

Women's (and men's) capacity to act on their feelings so as to change and improve their social situation can be impeded not only by their turning these feelings against themselves. It can also be obstructed by their failing to recognize these feelings as their own, instead only recognizing them in projected form as manifested by others.

This can occur in agoraphobia. The analyst Alexandra Symonds describes cases of women who gave up their previous autonomy and independence on marrying, looking to marriage as a place where their ertswhile unfulfilled dependency needs might bc met. Unable to express the anger and frustration caused by the resulting conflict in them between their dependent and independent strivings, lest they thereby put their marriage at risk, these women only seemed able to recognize such feelings of conflict and irritation as they were expressed by others — by their husbands, say. It was this — their 'externalization' or 'projection' into the outside world of their disowned feelings of anger, autonomy, and control — that, according to Symonds, constituted the source of the paranoia underlying their agoraphobia. One woman, for instance, said she could no longer drive because 'she feared that the car would do something that she did not want it to do' (Symonds, 1973, p. 301).

In agoraphobia women parody the helplessness supposed to typify their sex. Their agoraphobia, however, hardly serves to challenge the social subordination of women that gives rise to this characterization of femininity. The same can be said of all women in so far as, unable to own to the anger and bitterness they feel about their social lot, they instead only own to these feelings as they are expressed by men in their aggression and even violence toward women. As Kleinian analyst Jane Temperley points out, by dwelling on men's aggression, women may buy themselves the illusion of innocence (Temperley, 1984). But they do so at the cost of divesting themselves of feelings they might otherwise use to confront and deal with men's aggression towards, and dominance over them.

It is, of course, little wonder that women more easily recognize aggression in men than in themselves given that, by virtue of men's social dominance, aggression is more readily accorded to men. The psychologist Dora Ullian implies that it is precisely this dominance and women's subordination to it, that causes women to be particularly liable to disown their feelings of aggression, fearing lest they be destroyed by these feelings in themselves, so 'fragile and defenceless' do they experience themselves to be (Ullian, 1984). Kleinians seek to make conscious this anxiety for the self that they hold underlies women's (and men's) projection of their hostile feelings. They do this by interpreting this anxiety as it is expressed in the transference.

An example comes from Klein's account of her analysis of a woman who dreamt that:

> . . . she had to deal with a wicked girl child who was determined to murder somebody. The patient tried to influence or control the child and extort a confession from her which would have been to the child's benefit; but she was unsuccessful. I [Klein] also entered into the dream and the patient felt that I might help her in dealing with the child. Then the patient strung up the child on a tree in order to frighten her and also prevent her from doing harm. When the patient was about to pull the rope and kill the child, she woke. (Klein, 1946, p. 20)

Klein interpreted the dream to the patient as expressing unconscious anxiety lest, by expressing her feelings of anger and frustration, the patient destroy or annihilate part of her personality, represented in the dream by the child. The dream, said Klein, also expressed the patient's hope that Klein might protect her from destroying herself in expressing these feelings.

By thus interpreting in the transference the unconscious anxieties women (and men) feel for themselves about expressing the anger and frustrations to which their social relations give rise, Kleinians hope to enable them to own to, and hence to act constructively on, these feelings so as to change and improve their social lot, rather than being simply the passive victims of it and of the negative feelings it provokes in them.

CONCLUSION: FEMINISM AND PSYCHOANALYSIS

Psychoanalysis, I have been arguing, seeks to enable its patients to see more clearly, and to become more fully conscious of, the contradictions in them between their feelings of love and hate, passivity and activity, femininity and masculinity — feelings produced in them by the social interactions of everyday life. Analysts believe that their patients will thereby be enabled actually to realize their aims and desires rather than gratifying them in the merely illusory and magical fashion afforded by the symptoms of neurosis, depression, and paranoia. By contrast, feminism recognizes that if women's needs are to be met alike with those they share with men, they must not only be individually conscious of those needs, but must also collectively struggle to overcome the social obstacles currently standing in the way of those needs being fulfilled. Feminists have accordingly sought to achieve equal opportunities with men in education and employment, and they have campaigned and continue to campaign to maintain and extend the welfare state so that it more fully meets women's as well as men's needs. This has included initiatives by women's groups in pressing for, and in providing health services designed to attend more adequately to women's physical and psychological well-being — initiatives like the Boston Women's Health Collective and the London Women's Therapy Centre.

In so far as women's current social subordination is the cause of their disowning their so-called 'masculine' aims, such that these aims are then expressed in neurotic, depressive, or paranoid form, it is little wonder that psychoanalysis seldom succeeds in permanently relieving women of these symptoms. Freud recognized such symptoms to be caused by the social 'circumstances and the events' of his patients lives (see the opening quotation to this chapter). But he failed to make these circumstances and events — including the social subordination of women — an object of his therapeutic work. Indeed, he adjured his patients not to seek to make any major changes in their social circumstances while they were in therapy with him.

Psychoanalysis might well be effective in divesting women of the illusion that their needs are already met. But if these needs are to be actually and fully met, it is necessary to go beyond this. For these needs will only be met once the social changes for which feminism is struggling are achieved. Individual psychological change is not enough. Social change is also required if women's 'hysterical misery' is to be converted not only into 'common unhappiness', but into the happiness women need, want and desire.

NOTES TO CHAPTER 2

1. This chapter is based on my book *Sexual Contradictions*, which covers in greater detail, and with fuller references to Freudian and post-Freudian psychoanalytic theory, the issues dealt with here.

2. My thanks to Sue Wilkinson for getting feminist social psychology off the ground, for me at least, at the 1983 BPS Annual Social Psychology conference, and for her comments and suggestions on an earlier draft of this chapter.

REFERENCES

Beck, A. T. and Greenberg, R. L. (1974). Cognitive therapy with depressed women. In: V. Franks and V. Burtle (eds), *Women in Therapy*. New York, Brunner/Mazel.

Bem, S. (1981). Gender schema theory: a cognitive account of sex typing. *Psychological Review* 88, 354–364.

Bem, S. (1983). Gender schema theory and its implications for child development: raising gender-aschematic children in a gender-schematic society. *Signs* 8, 598–616.

Broughton, J. (1983). Women's rationality and men's virtues: a critique of gender dualism in Gilligan's theory of moral development. *Social Research* 50, 597–642.

Broverman, I. K., Broverman, D. M., Clarkson, F. E., Rosenkrantz, P. S. and Vogel, S. R. (1970). Sex-role stereotypes and clinical judgments of mental health. *Journal of Consulting and Clinical Psychology* 34, 1–7.

Brown, G. and Harris, T. (1978). *The Social Origins of Depression*. London, Tavistock.

Chodorow, N. (1978). *The Reproduction of Mothering*. Berkeley, University of California Press.

Deaux, K., White, L. J. and Farris, E. (1975). Skill or luck: field and lab studies of male and female preferences. *Journal of Personality and Social Psychology* 32, 629–636.

Eichenbaum, L. and Orbach, S. (1985). *Understanding Women.* Harmondsworth, Penguin.

Freud, S. (1895). With Breuer, J. *Studies on Hysteria. Penguin Freud Library (P.F.L.),* **1**.

Freud, S. (1905). Fragment of an analysis of a case of hysteria. *P.F.L.* **8**.

Freud, S. (1908). On the sexual theories of children. *P.F.L.* **7**.

Freud, S. (1909). Analysis of a phobia in a five-year-old boy. *P.F.L.* **8**.

Freud, S. (1916-17). *Introductory Lectures on Psychoanalysis. P.F.L.* **1**.

Freud, S. (1917). Mourning and melancholia. *P.F.L.* **11**.

Freud, S. (1918). From the history of an infantile neurosis. *P.F.L.* **9**.

Freud, S. (1931). Female sexuality. *P.F.L.* **7**.

Frieze, I. H., Whiteley, B. E., Hanusa, B. H. and McHugh, M. C. (1982). Assessing the theoretical models for sex differences in causal attributions for success and failure. *Sex Roles* **8**, 333-343.

Gilligan, C. (1977). In a different voice: women's conceptions of self and of morality. *Harvard Educational Review* **47**, 481-517.

Goleman, D. (1978). Special abilities of the sexes: do they begin in the brain? *Psychology Today* **12**, 48-59, 120.

Hirschfeld, M. A. and Cross, C. K. (1982). Epidemiology of affective disorders. *Archives of General Psychiatry* **39** (Jan.), 35-46.

Horner, M. (1969). Fail: bright women. *Psychology Today* **3**, 36, 38, 62.

Klein, M. (1946). Notes on some schizoid mechanisms. *The Writings of Melanie Klein,* Vol. 3. London, Hogarth.

Lawrence, M. (1984). *The Anorexic Experience.* London, The Women's Press.

Lloyd, B. (1976). Social responsibility and research on sex differences. In: B. Lloyd and J. Archer (eds), *Exploring Sex Differences.* London, Academic Press.

Maisner, P. and Pulling, J. (1985). *Feasting and Fasting.* London, Fontana.

Oatley, K. (1984). Depression: crisis without alternatives. *New Scientist* **1413**, 29-31.

Orbach, S. (1978). *Fat is a Feminist Issue.* New York, Paddington Press.

Paludi, M. A. (1984). Psychometric properties and underlying assumptions in four objective measures of fear of success. *Sex Roles* **10**, 765-781.

Sayers, J. (1986). *Sexual Contradictions: Psychology, Psychoanalysis, and Feminism.* London, Tavistock.

Segal, H. (1973). *Introduction to the Work of Melanie Klein.* London, Hogarth.

Sherman, J. (1977). Effects of biological factors on sex-related differences in mathematics achievement. In: L. H. Fox, E. Fennema and J. Sherman (eds), *Women and Mathematics: Research Perspectives for Change.* Washington, National Institute for Education.

Symonds, A. (1973). Phobias after marriage: women's declaration of dependence. In: J. B. Miller (ed.), *Psychoanalysis and Women.* Harmondsworth, Penguin.

Temperley, J. (1984). Our own worst enemies: unconscious factors in female disadvantage. *Free Associations* (pilot issue), 23-28.

Ullian, D. (1984). 'Why girls are good': a constructivist view. *Sex Roles* **11**, 241-256.

Walker, L. J. (1984). Sex differences in the development of moral reasoning: a critical review. *Child Development* **55**, 677-691.

Chapter 3

Cognitive Developmental Theory in the Study of Adolescent Identity Development[1]

Hazel Beckett

IDENTITY DEVELOPMENT AND ADOLESCENCE: AN INTRODUCTION

Within this chapter I aim both to challenge current assessments of female identity development and to begin to describe how a new perspective can and should be applied to developmental assessment. I shall use the work of Carol Gilligan (1977) and empirical data of my own to argue the need to expand and strengthen developmental understanding, in order to build a greater explanatory basis for studying the thinking of both sexes, and to work towards a substantive psychological reappraisal of the social domain of identity development. I shall argue that, on the one hand, a cognitive developmental model of identity development could usefully enhance our understanding of adolescence, but also, on the other, that the existing parameters of cognitive development theory are inadequate to yield an analysis of sufficient richness to accurately reflect the thinking of both sexes. This is principally because they are not grounded in the real life experience of both males and females. This chapter will indicate the ways in which a feminist perspective demands and informs a revisionist remapping of the social and cognitive domain, in exploring some features of adolescent identity development, and focussing in particular on the core themes of sex role identity and future aspirations.

There are extensive literature sets on both adolescence and sex roles. However, as Cockram and Beloff (1978) remark, none of the theoretical approaches to adolescence have specifically addressed the psychological development of girls, and, in addition, until relatively recently, the subject of sex role identity has been almost neglected in psychological work on adolescence. Both omissions should be carefully considered. Self-concepts of masculinity and femininity have received much less attention than sex role stereotypes (Rosenkrantz *et al.*, 1968) and masculine and feminine sex role attributes (Bem, 1974; Spence and Helmreich, 1978; — see Wetherell, Chapter 5, this volume, for a critique of this work). There has been less research attention despite, I would argue, the key role of sex role self-concepts in identity development; and despite the critical nature of the relationship of sex role identity to the critical choices we demand of individuals in adolescence when future aspirations and assessments are translated into some form of work decision-making and future planning. Indeed, Kohlberg (1966; 1969) and Loevinger (1966; 1976) have related sex role self-concept and cognitive development; and Pollak and Gilligan (1982) and Ullian (1976; 1981) have proposed that sex role development can be interpreted in terms of cognitive developmental stages. These interrelationships suggest that structural development may be a crucial factor in identity development in adolescence, affecting sex role identity, self definition, future expectations and the real process of decision making across a period of socially demanded important life decisions. Cognitive developmental theory has been most clearly deployed in the study of moral development. In the context of its historical development, this theoretical approach has also provided the most detailed analysis of adolescent development in Kohlberg's work. The study of moral development involves the exploration of not only how individuals develop as people, but also, and fundamentally, how they come to live with each other as social beings. This crucial focus necessarily signifies several related premises around the central tenet that the moral domain is comprised of human relationships: a social context defines human life; it consists of peoples' interrelationships; these relationships necessarily include conflict; the resolution of this conflict occupies a key operating role in universal moral concepts of should/ought, right/wrong, good/bad. This central feature and its necessary concomitants becomes an important tool and way of viewing alternative, but related, features of identity development.

These interrelationships have important implications. The integration of the different modes of moral reasoning and different conceptions of self, demand the exploration of alternative manifestations of the exertion of the individual's framework of thought and organization of ideas. The exploration of choice, reaction to conflict, and the specific applications of decision making which fall within the sphere of universal moral concepts, are also called into play in the key adolescent task of mapping the future. This process spans theoretical boundaries, it is central to identity development, it is crucially associated to a myriad of other real adolescent concerns, and it is located within a period when individuals are given a context for choice in education, in forming important relationships, and in organizing future alternatives.

The potential and strength of a cognitive developmental model of identity development in adolescence is, then, heightened by empirical findings on the relationship between sex role self-concept and future aspirations (Bem, 1974; Spence and Helmreich, 1978) and, as mentioned, by work relating sex role development and cognitive developmental changes (Pollak and Gilligan, 1982; Ullian, 1976; 1981).

Marcia has suggested that we can construe identity as: '. . . a self-structure — an internal, self-constructed, dynamic organisation of drives, abilities, beliefs, and individual history' (1980, p. 159). This constellation of an intricately woven set of personality variables and values has an important and often non-determined role in the process of career choice and work decision-making, for which we have a rhetorical expectation as a key task and an outcome of adolescence. This expectation is assigned to a system of education which has no framework realistic to girls' experiences, or means of achieving such a framework for its accomplishment.

Present developmental frameworks which, as one, explain growth in terms of differentiation, separation and increasing autonomy, ignore the view that adaptation is also concerned with integration, attachment and inclusion. In her work, Gilligan (1977) has exemplified how differentiation (a stereotypically male theme) is allowed, and even honoured with the language of growth and development; and integration (a stereotypically female theme) is denigrated as signifying dependency and immaturity. The implicit suggestion behind her work is that male bias has led to an ill-placed esteem for differentiation (and so growth), to the detriment of integration (and so dependency). Such a position importantly demands that a realistic model of development should not only be informed by both sides of this conflict, but also by the conflict itself.

The theories we have to inform these frameworks will be discussed below. Crucially, the theories do not adequately describe the experience of females because they are not based on that experience. If we are to accept and possibly rejoice in the breadth and significance of human experience, the theories do a disservice to our understanding of human development.

COGNITIVE DEVELOPMENTAL THEORY

The cognitive developmental approach is based on a rationale and empirical assumption that people have a mode of reasoning which comprises a constellation of their ideas. Individuals are held to organize their thinking in a variety of situations within a specific framework; a structural and complete form of reasoning with a consistent inner logic and coherence. Different frameworks are revealed in qualitatively different modes of moral reasoning. These frameworks impute to individuals the potential, the appetite and the need for the progressive construction of a rational and routine method of bringing their experience in the world into a sensible whole, a way of making sense. One way of making sense is assumed to prevail for an individual at any one time because of the qualitative difference between the inner logic of each mode.

The core of the moral domain is brought into focus by Gilligan's empirical identification of a conception of morality (the orientation of Care), not represented in the fifty years' work on cognitive developmental theory. The cognitive developmental model of morality has been based firmly within a Justice orientation. If any other orientation was seen, it was not heard and not represented theoretically. Two ethics, one of Justice and one of Care, have been portrayed in literary and philosophical conceptions of morality. Both orientations are concerned with how people learn to live with each other, but differ in their resolution of how this is made real. The ethic of Justice cites shared rules, principles, duties and rights as regulators for performance and how one person treats another. It has been translated as logical, rational and objective; a mode of moral thought. The ethic of Care urges that everyone will be cared for and no one hurt, by mutual responsiveness. It has been treated as a converse image, as illogical, irrational and subjective; associated with moral feeling.

Such differentiation is not made in peoples' consideration of different moral dilemmas, but the two different moral orientations, conceptually distinct frameworks which people use to organize their moral thinking, have been exemplified empirically (Gilligan, 1977; Gilligan and Murphy, 1979; Lyons, 1982; 1983). The orientations are revealed by the different concerns of the different conceptions of morality. They call on cognitive developmental theory to represent both.

Cognitive developmental theory, in its consideration of morality, has been concerned so far with the Justice orientation. The focus of this approach began with Piaget (1932/66) and has continued with Kohlberg's (e.g. 1966) theoretical and empirical work on the verification of an invariant sequence of hierarchically ordered stages of justice reasoning. Both Piaget's and Kohlberg's works were based on male data. Their expositions of the moral domain recognized, but 'ghetto-ized', the centrality of human relationships as an ethical assumption. Each focussed instead on the idea of Justice as a single concept of morality, as primary in defining the moral domain. This ethical assumption has not been empirically tested or proved by Kohlberg's research (Kohlberg, *et al.*, 1983, p. 162). Its implications, however, that all individuals use the Justice orientation as the major mode of moral reasoning, and that equity and reciprocity, inherent to the notion of Justice, form all human relationships, have been used to integrate the primacy of Justice in Kohlberg's research. Kohlberg presented Justice dilemmas to his sample, elicited Justice reasoning, and made coding provision only for statements meeting Justice-defining criteria. He then equated stages of Justice reasoning and developmental sequence. The cognitive developmental model of morality has been based firmly within a Justice orientation. A changing comprehension of the duties, rules and rights, intrinsic to the Justice orientation, has described development. It is worth reiterating that the theory-building samples which informed the model were all male.

A feminist perspective, typified by the work of Gilligan, has begun to inform cognitive developmental theory, just as it has begun to seriously challenge work on identity development. I would like to explore theoretical approaches to identity and to attempt to inform that exploration with Carol Gilligan's work.

IDENTITY DEVELOPMENT RESEARCH

The challenge to theories of adolescent identity development emerges specifically because of the limitations of those theories in coping with girls' real accounts of their experience. Real life portrayals of dynamics, which are other than those accounted for in current theoretical formulations, must signal the need for more powerful explanatory tools.

Erikson's (1968) account of identity development is probably foremost within psychology and within popular currency. Erikson described the process by which identity is developed, as one of differentiation, marked by the increasing inclusiveness of a widening circle of significant others. The self is separate and the aim of identity development is the larger scale embracing and accommodation of significant others.

Conversation with women about their lives reveals individuals not separated to begin with, but rather connected to and related with others. This connected self, encapsulated by a relational mode of discourse, has also been illuminated in the work of Ullian (1976; 1981). Women's discussions about their lives often focus on a central task of the building and achieving of a sense of self, not apart but separate from others. Separation for a self that is inclusive and connected is necessary to allow the individual to care for herself as authentically and reliably as she can care for someone else.

Studies looking at adult development (Levinson, 1978; Rubin, 1979; Sheehy, 1974) have described significant issues of self definition emerging from mid-life crises and have expounded on the nucleus of self definition. Rubin (1979) found that where women suffered depression in mid-life, it was not because their children had left them *per se*, but rather because this alteration in life style demanded that the individual concentrate on her sense of self as the centre of her definition. Chodorow (1978) has also discussed the vulnerability of women as they must define who and what they are.

Such a process of self-definition may not solely belong to mid-life. Consideration of related issues is also a feature of younger age groups. The process could be a developmental one (rather than age related) and could be associated with the societal factors which raise cognitive conflicts. Whatever the form, such an account begins to shape a different foundation underlying the path of development for women. It strikes a dynamic cast of identity development as the self seeks to understand and appreciate its own concerns. It also gives individuals the opportunity to explain their own reality.

An acceptance of individuals' right to portray their own reality leads to the recognition of a further contradiction in Erikson's outline of the development of female identity. This contradiction specifically eshews the crux of a feminist perspective and so enhances its importance:

> The stage of life crucial for the emergence of an integrated female identity
> is the step from youth to maturity, that state when the young woman, whatever

her work career, relinquishes the care received from the parental family in
order to commit herself to the love of a stranger and to the care to be given
to his and her offspring. (Erikson 1968, p. 265)

The nature of, and factors involved in, a commitment to another, and plans to
rear a family are the important issues here; however their presentation does not
adequately explore and expand upon the complexity of the process of connection.
Women, in their concern with caring for others which develops from their early
childhood years, do not emerge suddenly into a world of adulthood, marked by
care, commitment to care, and love. This has been a centrifugal reality from birth
onwards.

Marcia (1966; 1980) built on Erikson's theoretical approach and developed a
means of empirically testing identity formation, through identity statuses. Some
work has been critical of the identity status approach and its relation to womens'
lives (Miller, 1976), and Marcia (1980) has indicated that the construct itself and
its accompanying methodology may be at fault:

The identity status research was undertaken as a construct validity project
based on Erikson's theory. Thus at least the face validity of that theory was
accepted. Erikson's theory is one that accounts largely for identity development
in males. . . . The problem is that the implications [of the insights Erikson
has provided into feminine identity] have not been carried through into theory
and research in the same systematic for women as for men. Both Erikson's
theory and the identity status research began with a theoretical model
applicable to men and then extended that model to women. The results are
that both Erikson's theory and the identity status approach work only more
or less, when applied to women. (Marcia, 1980, p. 178)

The implications of this epistemological orientation to theoretical explanation
are important in evaluating the explanatory power of existing theoretical
approaches to real life experience.

The experiences of women have been treated with inadequate consideration
in the construction of models of development, which have focussed on the
experience of men. This is a clear assumption of gender difference and it has
been problematic for psychological understanding of both sexes. Carol Gilligan
has brought both points into sharp focus. Gilligan has sought specifically to outline
the dynamics of women's identity formation and provides a comprehensive model
of women's development, and a more distinct model of identity formation and
development *per se*.

The central focus of Gillligan's work is the analysis of changing conceptions
of self. From these perceptions, Gilligan has formed the portrayal of a
developmental sequence of a form of moral judgement, different to the one
typically voiced in cognitive developmental research. The form is one at the centre
of women's moral concerns. Gilligan invited women to discuss moral conflict
based on the identity conflicts they enunciated and the dynamic pattern of identity

development which emerged. Working within Kohlberg's framework of a cognitive developmental model of moral development, she used Kohlberg's model to study women's judgements in deciding between having an abortion or going through with a pregnancy. She found:

> . . . the sequence of women's moral development follows the three-level progression of all social developmental theory, from an egocentric through a societal to a universal perspective. (Gilligan, 1977, pp. 482–483)

However, she also found, not reasoning based on the considerations outlined in Kohlberg's model, but reasoning based on different considerations; and not the development outlined by Kohlberg on the basis of his longitudinal male data, but development based within a different and distinct moral conception. Kohlberg's model characterizes women's moral thinking as conventional in its interpersonal bias, and assigns women to the third stage of a five stage series:

> . . . herein lies the paradox, for the very traits that have traditionally defined the 'goodness' of women, their care for and sensitivity to the needs of others, are those that mark them as deficient in moral development. The infusion of feeling into their judgements keeps them from developing a more independent and abstract ethical conception in which concern for others derives from principles of justice rather than from compassion and care. (Gilligan 1977, p. 484)

This is to suggest, then, that an interpersonal bias is not the topic, but the structure, of women's moral voice, and that the exertion of choice could strengthen the relational mode of thinking. In the exercising of choice between self and other, Gilligan derived structures of thinking which she used to describe a sequence of moral development based on an increasingly complex arrangment of women's connected selves. This sequence outlines a progressively complex relationship between self and others in women's identity development. Furthermore, Gilligan suggests that Care is the pivotal influence on that development.

Gilligan has, then, called for an analysis of why the Care orientation has been left beyond the pale of cognitive developmental theory; why girls' and womens' thinking has not been included; and why the design of moral development research has not encompassed real (only hypothetical) moral dilemmas.

In analysing her data, Gilligan identified a mode of moral reasoning which was qualitatively different from the concern with Justice issues typically rendered in cognitive developmental theory. She found a consistent concern with issues of care and responsiveness in human relationships. She also found developmental changes in conceptions of care, as understanding of human relationships underwent a progressive reconstruction. Her work links modes of moral reasoning and different conceptions of self, it also suggests that, since females typically respond from within the Care orientation, that the different modes of moral reasoning are gender related.

Gilligan's arguments clearly show that epistemologically and ethically, the assumptions of cognitive developmental theory on the focus of the moral domain can be questioned; and that human relationships and concepts of self within relationships can be brought into primary rather than secondary import within moral concern. Gilligan urges us to consider both Care and Justice as distinct orientations and modes of moral reasoning. She also calls for an early consideration of the modes of moral reasoning, necessarily separate from, in the first instance, the assumption of developmental sequence. Her work has played a major role in reworking the assumptions of cognitive developmental theory, in order that they are more appropriate to real life, that they are informed by it, and can explain it. In building on her work, Lyons (1982; 1983) has developed an instrument to study identity and to specify a procedure which can identify the two different moral voices. It specifically and systematically permits analysis of the real life answers to a series of questions and offers a step towards putting the revision of the theory into practice. As a way of looking at the world and as a way of accounting for and explaining it in a more coherent and comprehensive way, this trend emerges from and typifies a feminist perspective.

A 'real life approach' demands that conflict and conflicting realities be encompassed and enthusiastically embraced within our theories. Women's reality is not just different from the narrow version of men's reality which has been passed into popular use. Women's realities are different from each other, as Nicolson, Chapter 8, also notes. It is an almost fatuous observation, but our theories do not see it. Lyons' work has demonstrated the existence of a small, if central, proportion of empirical tools available for the study of identity and its development. The nature of those tools, their epistemological assumptions and their explanatory powers, demand their revision. We require a unity in this revision. It should be responsive to peoples' experiences; it should be based within a questioning, inquiry-based demand mode; it should be shaped by the assumptions of a shared world view. The multiple meanings of men's and women's lives are important, their experiences mutually illuminate experience and development. This is the central feature of a feminist perspective and it is one which should revitalize psychological explanations of identity development.

MODELLING IDENTITY DEVELOPMENT IN ADOLESCENCE

As discussed, empirical evidence has linked sex role self-concept and career choice and paralleled sex role development and cognitive development. The theoretical issues explored in previous sections can now be mapped onto this empirical evidence and used specifically to inform issues of self-definition as they relate to future aspirations and definitions of potential future realities. I would like to attempt this process of mapping by presenting and discussing the themes which emerged from a series of conversations with 110 adolescent girls. The girls lived in Bristol and were aged between 13 and 19 at the time of the conversations. The ideas they expound therefore span some crucial years for psychological development, and the experiences they describe take place in the context of the decision making and planning expected of them during education and in the years immediately following it.

It is important to stress that the individuals who participated in this study were diverse, however, the issues which emerged as important to them as a group and the themes around which their considerations centred are intrinsically related to the previous sections of this paper.

The most important themes the girls elaborate focus on what is most immediate in their lives: homework, exams, friends, boyfriends, money, clothes and parents. Few of them are committed to an ideology of political values (which forms the centre of Erikson's concept of identity). The ideologies they have are mainly interpersonal. The general system of ideas with which they organize their lives gives emphasis to being a good person, and to values such as honesty, openness and caring for others. Occupationally they have chosen rather low aspiration careers, with few of those aged between 13 and 17 planning to go to university, although most see 'a good education' as being important, if only to keep the prospect of unemployment at bay. Many plan to work for a while, and treat study as a potential route should they be dissatisfied at work. With the exception of a small number, they wish to marry 'eventually'.

The majority of the girls see their life plans as a sequence of a few years' unmarried work involvement, several years of childless marriage, a period of full-time child rearing, followed by a return to some sort of involvement in work, a part-time job of some sort. The question of motherhood versus career seems, for the majority, to have been stably resolved in the direction of combining them. They seem to have made a unanimous and unconflicted choice to experience occupational involvement, marriage and motherhood.

This sort of planning appears to render an apparent flexibility in their sense of themselves and their futures; there is a certain readiness to deal with whatever might come. Most cannot imagine their future in five years time; asked about the future in ten years, most expected to have one or two children. The rest is less than clear. Asked about what they would like to be doing when they reached the same age as their mothers (at the time of the interview), they anticipate a life style identical in essence to their mothers, even where they express a certain amount of dissatisfaction with the content and quality of their mothers' lives.

The nature of feminine identity is often worked through in some way in their discussions. There is considerable cultural, conceptual and theoretical chaos with regard to the acceptable modes of being a woman. Much has been written on the importance of inner space, on the greater emphasis on interpersonal attributes over achievement in women (Erikson, 1968; Marcia, 1980). Certainly identity for these girls appears to centre more on what kind of person to be than on occupational or ideological choice; it also seems to depend on the responses of those who are important to them. It seems unwarranted, however, to reason on this basis that this emphasis on the interpersonal context is in the service of developing the skills necessary to become a wife and mother. Such a conclusion would miss the importance of a structural perspective. These girls seem to value interpersonal competence for its own sake. Getting along well with differet kinds of people brings an autonomous sense of satisfaction. They give the impression of enjoying closeness for its own sake and form relationships for the sake of the relationship rather than as a preparation for anything else. This organization of ideas itself suggests a different perspective to the one modelled in existing theories of identity development.

Nurturance is a shared ideal, which involves for individuals both affiliative and achievement needs. Many of the topics of their conversations concentrate on helping and working with others. Research on the achievement drive in women (e.g. Horner, 1972) has typically focussed on stereotypically masculine forms of achievement, such as competitiveness and aggression. Such traits are often at odds with ideals of nurturance and the girls seem to avoid such forms of achievement. However, it would be wrong to use this feature to negate the desire to achieve in the sense of being productive and making a positive contribution to society through personal achievements. It seems that as a group, they are less likely, but not unlikely, to think of their work in terms of getting ahead, or of being the best for the sake of competition. Instead, there is more of an emphasis on the less public achievements of helping and affecting the lives of others.

Identity does not seem to be a potentially plannable route for these girls. The future emerges more as a succession of phases, each with a different focus, but each integrating with the other phases. This represents a multifaceted portrayal of present and future self. The girls see themselves as being many things, but not necessarily at one time. Such flexible expectations have been translated as a vagueness of identity commitment. From a different perspective, however, it could be considered as a commitment to fundamentals and a willingness to accept accompanying detail as contextual and hence variable.

TOWARDS AN ALTERNATIVE MODEL OF IDENTITY DEVELOPMENT

The previous section outlines the content of a series of conversations, but begins to suggest that, in considering psychological processes, structural framework and individuals' own organization of their ideas should be analysed in addition to the content of individuals' answers. There is an important distinction to be drawn between content and theme, and this broader organization of ideas, which represents the individual's way of making sense of the world. This perspective is not marked by the existence of a theme or topic in someone's modelling of a problem. Underlying meanings and what they indicate are the markers. Such an analysis begins to acknowledge individuals' rights to define their own important categories, acknowledges the legitimacy of individual conceptions, and demands that real life data inform our theoretical models.

A network of relationships, offering connection and continuing connection to others is a consistent theme in the girls' elaboration of themselves and their lifestyles, as is the desire to map their surroundings through and to others. However, their ways of portraying these themes begin to take on and display a progressively complex way of operating within these circles of interdependence, and to represent an increasingly integrated and adequate understanding of their connection to others. There are coherent differences in the ways in which the girls describe themselves in relation to others. The strands of connection interweave the discourse and iterate the importance of existing within a relational mode. These strands are reflected in description of self in the future as well as current self.

Nichola (13 years old) describes herself:

> I get on well with some people. I got to try to get on well with other people, but if I can't get on well with them, then I try not to bother really. Me and my friend, we're always good out of school, but we're not very good in school. We don't get on well and we're always breaking friends. That upsets me. But when we're out of school, we're really good.

Asked, later in the interview, what she wants in the future, Nichola maintains the core significance of attachment:

> Important things is to get on well with people. If you don't get on, then it's not worth it. If you get on well with other people, then you'll be able to do a lot more things. They like you and you can go out more.

The theme of attachment and connection to others is clear and internalized, but this is not a complex mutual interaction of personalities, needs and response. Nichola grounds herself in 'having friends' and 'getting on' with them. Her rationale is fundamentally egocentric.

Tracey (15 years old) begins to explore these themes further:

> Well I think everybody says I can have a laugh. I got a sense of humour. I'd like to think that I got a good personality. I mean I'm not exactly good looking, but I'm not . . . I think to myself, you know, you're alright, you're okay, and if you think that, then other people might, if you got confidence in yourself. . . . I get on well with a lot of people. There's not very many people I don't get on with. I'd say I got on with quite a few people. I'm sort of an all-rounder. I don't mind who I'm with, what I'm doing. . . . I'm very close to my mum, my sister and my cousin. My boyfriend is to me. I was really infatuated with him first of all. But now the tendency is him all over me, sort of, I can't take it, it's too much for me. I'm only young, I want to meet a few people first. My family is close. I got a big family, and we're very close. That's why I talk to people.

Tracey also describes the most important things that will happen to her:

> I think getting a job is important to me. Because there are so many people
> out of work, I think it will be really nice to fulfil that. Meeting someone
> who really meant a lot to me would be nice. Somebody who liked me for
> the right reasons and I liked them for the right reasons. Sometimes you tell
> yourself it's for the right reasons, but you know that's wrong and you know
> their reasons are wrong, so you tend to be edgy and you don't feel right.
> It'd be nice to have the things and the people that you liked. It'd be nice
> to have a nice job, a nice family around you.

The themes of herself and her connection to others are further elaborated in her
consideration of the most important things that will happen to her. Tracey
sharpens her appraisal of herself by re-portraying the ways she thinks others see
her. Her concept of herself in the future has more strands of connection and
these are worked through in more complex ways. She has a clear notion of a
tradition to be maintained, as she works through 'right' and 'wrong' perceptions
of others and ways of understanding and being understood by them.

Seventeen year old Clare describes herself in the following way:

> A worrier. I don't know, I really would hope I care about people. I try to
> look more at what the person is than what they look like. Although if you're
> with friends you get caught up in that sort of thing. So I think your parents
> have got a lot to do with what you're going to be like. So I think you're a
> reflection of what they are. I think I'm a hard worker. That's the main bit
> of my description, but I don't like hurting people, their feelings are important
> to me.

Clare describes what will be important to her in the future:

> It'll be important that I'm happy. That whatever I've done in the previous
> years has been successful, I suppose that would be important to me, that
> I hadn't made a mess of everything. I hope that I've done everything in a
> way that I'd like to have done it, in a way that's not just pleasing to me,
> but everyone I've done it for. That's my aim. Suppose seeing my mum and
> dad happy would be a great satisfaction. Having known that I've achieved
> something somewhere with someone.

Clare demonstrates this more multifaceted sense of herself and her life in outlining
what she wants from the future. In describing herself, she begins, in outlining
her relationship to others, to consider notions of right and wrong as she defines
them, to differentially assess her own and her friends' values. Her future self
shows this growing importance of her own efforts and values, in the context of
those around her.

The contexts, outlined by these three girls, for thinking about the future
in adolescence do not appear to lend themselves to a model of a detached,

rule-governed, separate future, and the unravelling of a set path with set and discrete moments of rational choosing, towards its embodiment in a career and/or role as breadwinner. Such a route and pathway are mapped in career choice literature and are, implicitly, the set (if idealized and unrealistic) patterns which remain cogent for boys.

Girls often have difficulty in describing their futures in this way. Their typically connected, relational consciousness is not routed in a single moment of time. Their awareness and connection to others are necessarily associated with attending to others and responding to others. Who the others are may not be determined, but the self's responsiveness and interdependence is a central factor and a constant. It also becomes possible to project on future situations and potential conflict points. This centrality of response and care is heightened by the conflicts this perspective leads to. Caring for oneself and caring for others are often the bases for this conflict, such that, at one point a failure to care can be construed as a failure to be a 'good woman'. At another, events surrounding the conflict include considering the other's needs as a priority, maintaining a concern for others and the welfare of others. The maintenance of relationships can become the justification for a contextual choice.

In discussing an outlined situation of conflict, and relating the important things for a girl who has been offered the chance of promotion in a job she enjoys, to consider, when asked if she will move to the new job in a different city, Rachael (13) voices again the contextual elements of connection:

> I think I'd feel proud about it, but I think she wouldn't like going away. She'd like to stay really. She's got to leave her flat and she might have to leave her boyfriend for so many months and have to try to find a house to live in where she was going to find accommodation. She'll be alone. She'll have to find accommodation. She'd have to have a car to get there as well, leave all her friends behind her to find a new area to live. She should ask her mum and dad. I'd think about losing my friends mostly.

The context here is practical, and relational themes stretch towards significant others. She wants the attention, care and advice of others, but Rachael is not elaborating a complex perspective of self-investment. Within a more egocentric approach, fear of loneliness is the main thing to be avoided.

Trudy (15) explores more complex interrelations and outcomes posed by a work/family choice, into which she resolves the dilemma. She bases her solution in a traditional script of attachment:

> Work is very important to her because she just got promoted and everything and then there's a sense of achievement once again, because she knows she's worked hard to get to that place. Women don't work for the rest of their life like men, they get married and even if they don't get married . . ., I would hate that. So I'd like to work if I was in her place for as long as possible if I could. Like if I had a sudden illness, I'd want to work right up, as long

as I could. If her boyfriend cares about her that much, I think that he should propose. The engagement, that would stop them . . . it wouldn't break them apart. If he cared about her that much he might. I think they should get engaged.

Sarah (19) considers context, interdependence and a more complex sense of herself in her working of the problem. She presents and expects more multi-dimensional investments from herself and from those around her. Her own values clearly relate to her thinking about the future and she begins to bring them into focus:

How serious she is with her boyfriend, how serious she thinks the future prospects with him are, whether marriage is one of the positive outcomes of the relationship, how often is she going to see him, what her family is going to think. If she's thinking of getting married and settling down in the area, getting a house, then I might not take it because I'd think of him first. If the relationship is in a stalemate situation, I'd take the job and become independent from him. I think work would be very important, but I think it depends on what the situation with the boyfriend is . . . . A job is an object, friends and people are part of your life. Maybe work is as well, but it's a completely different attitude. It's still that I'd have a job and maybe in a few years' time a job would come up, like in Bristol. I wouldn't have to move. If I stayed where I was, hopefully a job would come to me, but I'd have him. I wouldn't have hurt him and I'd be happy.

The themes summarized in the first part of this section emerge in quite a different light from these fragments of much longer conversations. The themes are there, but the perspective of responsiveness emerges from the growing awareness of future alternatives, expanding appreciation of the complexities of interrelationships, and from the more complex understanding of self and others and real implications for the future. As the individuals increasingly grapple with the roles and rules which their experience informs, and the growing need for choice uncovers, they must find a way to countenance their changing relationships with others, and social *mores* and pressures.

This is a basis for a different conception of identity development: not a conception exemplified by a separate self, but one which reinforces the importance of inclusion and the need to explore real life descriptions of experience and ideas. The examples presented show how individuals' ways of describing themselves in relation to others differ. Their presentation together offers a basis for considering these differences as central to the construction of ways of exploring self-definition, and its importance in adolescence as a feature of making decisions about the future, which have far reaching implications.

CONCLUSION

This chapter has attempted to portray a dichotomy between the content of discourse and the perspective which results in discourse, by exploring how the meanings underlying discourse have been translated theoretically. The major thrust has been to argue that we need to re-examine carefully which meanings have been studied and the way in which they have been studied. An inextricably interwoven strand of this argument has been that feminist research has already begun to challenge existing paradigms and to signal the way ahead for future research.

Theories of identity development and models of career choice, because of their formulations on theories built on male data, do not and cannot cope with the real implications of a working future for adolescent girls. A framework and a context for the exploration of future aspirations and decision-making necessarily rests on an adequate theoretical model of identity development. Such a context is not provided by fragmented references to equal opportunities (particularly where girls may see no reality in those opportunities), or by encouraging achievement of a particular sort in the selection of a career (on a professional basis) and in autonomous self-maintenance, if there is no real life grounding for individuals' construction of these ideas separate from their identities and their construction of events.

Goals are given priority in a way which excludes future realities for girls by denying a validity to a different framework, and preventing full planning for an integrated and multifaceted future. The framework exists: it is revealed in the constructions individuals give to their self-definitions, to the problems they face and to the options they see themselves as having. Its development is revealed in the progression in structural complexity across individuals in their constructions of their own reality.

The research on which this chapter is based aimed at a better understanding of the process by which adolescent girls identify their options for the future. It has revealed that choices must be brought within a practical focus in order that individuals can undertake informed consideration of themselves and their lives and in order that they can broaden the parameters which are recognized as giving context to choice, by including interrelationships between self, identity, family, careers and work.

There is no one framework or account which will fulfil this aim; nor is there one method of data collection and analysis that will inform it. There is, however, an importance in the incorporation of different methodologies which can explore people's realities. It is the responsibility of feminist theory to acknowledge and integrate the authenticity of individuals' rights to define their own important categories, to define who they are in the world, and to operate from within a mode of enquiry rather than a mode of assessment.

The exploration of cognitive developmental theory as a tool for examining identity development in adolescence has illuminated the issues which are to the fore of the feminist mission. Significantly, the issues arise because the constructions at the heart of real life data are frequently different to those expounded theoretically. This anomaly itself leads to the four interrelated issues which have been traced in this chapter. They are issues central to Carol Gilligan's (1977) work: categories within existing theory building data have been drawn from all male samples; the all male sample is itself a basis for an unexplained hypothesis of gender difference; such a hypothesis is dangerously misleading when it allows the application of the model to women; such a form of model building does not question what might have been omitted, what a different sample might have achieved, and why the model does not apply to women.

I have argued *both* that theoretical approaches to adolescence would suggest that a cognitive developmental model could usefully expand our understanding of identity development *and* that the existing parameters of cognitive developmental theory are not accurate enough to yield an analysis rich enough to deal with both men and women.

Women's experience illuminates human experience, and, in the context of this chapter, it also illuminates development for both males and females. The key task now lies in fulfilling the demand that the *whole* domain be mapped. The purpose of that mapping is not simply to produce a new perspective, but to undertake a systematic exploration of human reality in order to empower psychology to deal with it.

NOTE TO CHAPTER 3

1. This chapter is based on a research project funded, as a postgraduate studentship, by the Economic and Social Research Council. The project was conducted at the University of Bath and supervised by Helen Weinreich-Haste.

REFERENCES

Bem, S. L. (1974). Measurement of psychological androgyny. *Journal of Consulting and Clinical Psychology* **42**(2), 155-162.

Chodorow, N. (1978). *The Reproduction of Mothering: Psychoanalysis and the Sociology of Gender*. Berkeley, University of California Press.

Cockram, L. and Beloff, H. (1978). *Rehearsing to be Adults*. Leicester, National Youth Bureau.

Erikson, E. (1968). *Identity: Youth and Crisis*. New York, W. W. Norton.

Gilligan, C. (1977). In a different voice: Women's conception of self and of morality. *Harvard Educational Review* **47**(4), 481-517.

Gilligan, C. and Murphy, J. (1979). Development from adolescence to adulthood: The philosopher and the dilemma of the fact. In: D. Kuhn (ed.), *New Directions for Child Development: Intellectual Development Beyond Childhood*, Vol. 5. San Francisco, Jossey-Bass.

Horner, M. S. (1972). Towards an understanding of achievement-related conflicts in women. *Journal of Social Issues* **28**, 157-175.

Kohlberg, L. (1966). Stage and sequence: The cognitive-developmental approach to socialization. In: D. Goslin (ed.), *The Handbook of Socialization Theory and Research*. Chicago, Rand McNally.

Kohlberg, L. (1969). Continuities and discontinuities in childhood and adult moral development. *Human Development* **12**, 93–120.

Kohlberg, L., Levine, C. and Hewer, A. (1983). Moral stages: A current formulation and a response to critics. In: J. Meacham (ed.), *Contributions to Human Development*, Vol. 10. Basel, S. Karger.

Levinson, D. (1978). *Seasons of a Man's Life*. New York, Random House, Inc.

Loevinger, J. (1966). The meaning and measurement of ego development. *American Psychologist* **21**, 195–206.

Loevinger, J. (1976). *Ego Development*. San Francisco, Jossey-Bass.

Loevinger, J. (1979). Scientific ways in the study of ego development. *The 1978 Heinz Werner Lecture Series*, Vol. 12. Worcester, Mass., Clark University Press.

Lyons, N. (1982). Conceptions of self and morality and modes of moral choice: Identifying justice and care in judgements of actual moral dilemmas. Unpublished doctoral dissertation, Harvard University.

Lyons, N. (1983). Two perspectives: On self, relationships and morality. *Harvard Educational Review* **53**(1), 125–145.

Marcia, J. E. (1966). Development and validation of ego identity status. *Journal of Personality and Social Psychology* **3**(5), 551–558.

Marcia, J. E. (1980). Identity in adolescence. In: J. Adelson (ed.), *Handbook on Adolescence*. New York, Wiley.

Miller, J. B. (1976). *Toward a New Psychology of Women*. Harmondsworth, Penguin.

Piaget, J. (1932/1966). *The Moral Judgement of the Child*. New York, The Free Press.

Pollak, S. and Gilligan, C. (1982). Images of violence in thematic apperception test stories. *Journal of Personality and Social Psychology* **42**(1), 159–167.

Rosenkrantz, P. S., Vogel, S. R., Bee, H., Broverman, I. K. and Broverman, D. M. (1968). Sex role stereotypes and self concepts. *Journal of Consulting and Clinical Psychology* **32**, 287–295.

Rubin, L. (1979). *Women of a Certain Age: The Midlife Search for Self*. New York, Harper and Row.

Sheehy, G. (1974). *Passages*. New York, E. P. Dutton.

Spence, J. T. and Helmreich, R. L. (1978). *Masculinity and Femininity*. Austin, University of Texas Press.

Ullian, D. Z. (1976). The development of concepts of masculinity and femininity. In: J. Lloyd and J. Archer (eds), *Exploring Sex Differences*. London, Academic Press.

Ullian, D. Z. (1981). Why boys will be boys: A structural approach. *American Journal of Orthopsychiatry* **51**(3), 493–501.

Chapter 4

Post-structuralist Theory and Everyday Social Practices: The Family and the School

Valerie Walkerdine

In this chapter I shall be concerned with understanding how assumptions about 'good mothers', 'sensitive teachers' and the 'nature of the child' operate and have effects in those domestic and pedagogic practices which make up the daily lives of many women and children. I shall be concerned primarily with the relationship between conceptions and truth, power and the construction of the subject. In this case, I want to explore the way in which post-structuralism may help us to understand the positioning of girls and women in these practices.

The discourses which define good teaching, child rearing and child development define for us what 'mother', 'teacher' and 'child' are taken to be. My argument will be that such definitions form part of a variety of 'regimes of truth' which have positive and powerful effects in regulating the modern order. I shall argue that these 'truths' are historically and socially specific and I shall suggest that while they define what is 'supposed to be', the relationship with 'what is' is problematic, and it is that which I shall explore in the second part of the paper. In order to understand the experience of what it means to be a woman, I shall argue, it is necessary to examine how the truths produced about us, and which we constantly struggle with, are themselves related to elaborate fears, desires and fantasies. What is 'seen' and what is 'believed' and what we struggle with and against in ourselves is not some *tabula rasa* femininity. On the contrary, we live out the effect of those fantasies and struggle with them every day of our lives. It is that engagement with those facts, fictions and fantasies which I take to be a central part of what a feminist engagement in and with psychological truths might be about. In this short sketch then, I want to explore briefly how some of the ideas that I have found useful from post-structuralism may help towards producing a way of approaching gender and sexuality and its relation to subjectivity. Here I am developing the use of the term subjectivity presented in Henriques *et al.* (1984). I want to suggest ways in which such an approach might take us forward beyond classic conceptions of the subject within social psychology. I want particularly to show the difference between the concept of 'truth' and 'veridicality' in the work of Michel Foucault and the concept of 'ideology'.

Let me begin by exploring certain formulations about 'women' and 'children' in primary schools and then go on to examine how the theoretical tools which I am involving might be useful in understanding the phenomena under interrogation.

PRIMARY SCHOOL PRACTICES AND THE UNIVERSAL CHILD

Modern pedagogic practices rely heavily on concepts derived from developmental psychology. I would argue that the way these concepts enter into the regulation of pedagogic practices helps constitute and position 'teacher' and 'child'. By this I mean that they 'define' and 'monitor' 'the child' such that when we examine the actuality of pedagogic practices we are not so much faced with an 'ideology of childhood' which distorts what children are 'really like', so much as a 'truth' which regulates what 'should be'. My argument is, therefore, that there is no simple matter of 'revelation' so much as a multiply constituted subject, for whom the interplay of signs produce conscious and unconscious struggle. Central to my formulation is a shift in the concepts of power and resistance.

Let me begin by examining a set of interrelated statements about the primary school, teachers and children.

> . . . the first essential for a teacher of young children is that she should have the right temperament . . . such work as this will demand wide and thorough theoretical knowledge and also the ability to apply this knowledge with particular children. Child Study — the study of children's mental and physical development — should form the basis of her training. Her studies in psychology should be connected directly with descriptions and observations of actual behaviour in children. The young teacher in training should study the stages in development of children up to the age of seven with due regard to every aspect of growth. (Consultative Committee of the Board of Education, 1933 (The Hadow Report), p. 153)

> When children are materially, intellectually or emotionally deprived, teachers must strive to serve as substitutes for parents, to make children feel that they matter, however little they are able to respond, and however unattractive they appear to be. Much is asked of teachers in these circumstances: to be patient when children develop slowly or regress, to provide experience rather than short cuts to it, to care tenderly for individual children and yet retain sufficient detachment to assess what they are achieving and how they are developing . . .

> Our study of children's development has emphasised the importance of maturation in learning. The corollary is not to make the teachers' role passive but to underline the importance of diagnosing children's needs and potentialities . . .

Teachers must support apathetic children . . .
They must challenge and inspire children . . .
They must sometimes recognise a child as being more gifted than they are themselves . . .

. . . (teachers) have to select an environment which will encourage curiosity, to focus attention on enquiries which will lead to useful discovery, to collaborate with children, to lead from behind . . .

To a unique extent English teachers have the responsibility and spur of freedom.
(Central Advisory Council for Education (England), Vol. 1, 1967 (The Plowden Report), p. 311. Emphasis added)

These two extracts from government reports are over 30 years apart, but they demonstrate clearly a set of relationships which I want to address. Let me summarize below the qualities which these quotations suggest that the teacher of young children should possess.

The right temperament;
A thorough theoretical knowledge of Child Study and psychology;
The ability to apply this knowledge;
A parent substitute;
The ability to make children feel they matter;
Patience;
Provision of experience;
Tender care;
Detachment;
Diagnosis of potentialities;
Challenge and inspire children;
Encourage curiosity;
Collaborate;
Lead from behind;
Responsibility and spur of freedom.

This is a formidable list, and yet a close reading of the texts of both reports would give us a far clearer picture of what is expected in the teacher. She forms part of a couple, the other half of which is 'the child'. She is the substitute mother. There is no father (unless he is the head teacher, or the psychologist waiting in the wings).

Notice how it is training and knowledge of the psychological aspects of children's development which, together with her capacities for nurturance, make the teacher of young children the 'trained' and 'detached' 'observer'. She is like a mother — but she is trained in the science of observation. Her detachment will therefore keep her from getting too caught up with desires.

Let us just note briefly some of the characteristics which she does *not* possess: she does not 'teach', but rather 'provides experiences'; she does not 'discipline', but 'cares', 'diagnoses', 'challenges', 'inspires', 'encourages'. We could develop a whole list of absences to counter the presences of the qualities which *she* is supposed to possess, and we would find that those absences would constitute a dangerous voice from the past, the spectre of authoritarianism, of the old ways, of overt power and regulation. Here there is apparently no regulation, only the 'responsibility and spur of freedom'.

Elsewhere, I have documented some aspects of a historical account of the development of pedagogic practices and the place of women in them (Walkerdine, 1983; 1984; 1985a). Here, let me simply signal some aspects of the constitution of the modern 'truth' about pedagogy. The development of modern psychology, and especially the study of children, is central to the possibility of this truth. It is this knowledge which, from the quotations alone, appears central to modern practices of regulation. That is, it is the 'facts of child development' which form the bedrock of modern pedagogy and which the teacher must know. It is these which form the basic monitoring devices of the pedagogy itself, and it is these which, as I aim to demonstrate, form the basis of a modern form of pedagogic government. It is the female teacher who is held responsible for this government and for the creation of a fictional space in which 'freedom' is to be assured. I want particularly, therefore, to examine the place of women as teachers in the ensuring of a 'rationally ordered and governed' social order, which claims to be about the maintenance of freedom. I want to examine aspects of the terrible burden placed on women. It is women as teachers who, in the words of the Hadow Report, have amplified their 'capacities for maternal nurturance'. We need to understand, therefore, how it comes to be the case that the present practices understand teaching and learning in the way that they do, how this came about and what effects this has for women and children in schools today.

In order to examine the current situation, therefore, I want to draw upon certain concepts about power, knowledge and truth which derive from Foucault; this will also illustrate how such concepts can be utilized to examine an issue such as this. Foucault is primarily concerned with power and in describing the relationship between shifts in forms of power and strategies of government which relate to the rise of the human sciences. The history which Foucault traces is not, in the classic sense, a 'social history'. It is rather what has been described as a 'history of the social' or a 'history of the present'. By that, what is meant is that it traces historically the 'conditions of possibility' of present social forms and practices, especially modes of government. It asks, for example, not 'how have women and children been controlled?' or 'how has the family been shaped?' but rather 'how are modern pedagogic and family practices themselves sites for the production of modern forms of government and modes of individuality?' Although Foucault has been concerned with the relationship of modern capitalism to those forms and practices, one of the aspects of his work on power and the human sciences is that it allows us to examine the *productive* power of psychological knowledge in the regulation of 'the social' itself. Psychology, in this sense, does not distort a set of real relations (or a real nature) which lurk beneath waiting to be freed; rather, because of its effectivity in the regulation of practices themselves, it helps to constitute what that nature means and how it is lived out and regulated. Central to my enterprise in this chapter, therefore, is the demonstration that psychology is productive of the social positions and identities through and by which subjectivity is created.

I would like to explore this a little further. Foucault demonstrates (1979a; Gordon, 1980), that an important shift in the form of government took place in association with the rise in a set of knowledges and technologies for the regulation of the population. Particularly important for my purpose is the shift from a form of government which relied upon sovereign and visible power, to an invisible power, itself invested in the very technologies designed to classify nature and regulate normality. For example, in relation to mental measurement, Nikolas Rose (1979; 1985) demonstrates the way in which the calibration of the normal distribution of certain capacities in the population provided the basis not only for techniques of classification, but also for the division of the population to be educated, into normal, subnormal, abnormal and so forth. On this basis, educational institutions and practices could be developed in which normal and subnormal children were produced as subjects of those pedagogic practices. That is, the knowledge of mental measurement itself was instrumental in providing a system of classification, and therefore regulation, which observed, checked and monitored the form of 'individual' itself. We can suggest, therefore, that what 'normal' meant was defined by the practices of measurement themselves. Technologies such as this acted powerfully to produce the very techniques and practices for the regulation of normality within the population.

The development of the human sciences was, in Foucault's terms, central to the possibility of the modern form of government, of bourgeois democracy and the notion of the bourgeois individual created as its object. The human sciences helped to produce methods of measurement and classification of the population newly contained in towns and cities (see also Hacking, 1981). It is these methods which were directly implicated in the new form of government which depended upon techniques of population *management*. This management had as its target a form of power which was not overtly coercive in the sense of a visible sovereign power vested in the person of the monarch, but was relatively 'invisible' and depended upon producing management techniques in which the people accepted the form of government (apparently of their own free will) and *did not rebel*. Therefore, I intend to demonstrate that the modern primary school forms an important place where this 'free will' is established. It is in this sense that we can begin to understand the position of the teacher as 'the responsibility and spur of freedom'. The freedom which she has to foster is, I would argue, the notion of bourgeois individuality. It is the fear of the 'rising of the masses', of revolution which necessitates a form of government which is *apparently* non-coervice.

The teacher, then, is responsible for freedom. Historically, it is possible to understand the position of compulsory schooling (introduced towards the end of the nineteenth century) as important in the aim to produce 'good habits' in the population (Jones and Williamson, 1979). These habits of thrift, industriousness, good living and so forth, would help prevent the possibility of criminality (the criminal personality) and poverty (bad habits) which would fuel the feared rebellion. However, while at the time of Empire, hard work and overt surveillance were seen as good methods of regulation, it was later felt that overt forms of government, for example practices in school based on coercion, were likely to precipitate rather than inhibit rebellion. This is because children might appear to learn their lessons but secretly harbour resistance. To counteract this resistance, a mode of 'covert' surveillance was introduced, based on 'love' and not 'fear' which meant that the lessons were to be learnt apparently by 'free will' this time. Two things are central here. The first is that it was the fear of totalitarianism — of the Russian Revolution for the Right, of the rise of Germany for the Left — which fuelled this enterprise. The second is that the centrepiece of the new pedagogy, with its love replacing fear, is the woman teacher. A scientific pedagogy based on objects, as in Robert Owen's mill school in Lanarkshire (Hamilton, 1981) was advocated. Originally, infant school teachers had been men (Clarke, 1985). But 'love' was felt to be the province of women as opposed to the stern and frightening authority of men. Thus women, with their capacities for maternal nurturance, began to be recruited into the teaching profession. Frances Widdowson (1983) notes that the rise in teacher training went hand-in-hand with the rise in middle-class women's education. Several things are important here. Firstly, until this point middle- and upper-class women had struggled to be allowed to enter higher education. However, their efforts were frequently countered on the grounds that education would damage their reproductive capacities, which would significantly damage the future of the race (Walkerdine, 1985a; Sayers, 1982):

> The deficiency of the reproductive power amongst upper class girls may reasonably be attributed to the over-taxing of their brains. An over-taxing which produces a serious reaction on their physique. This diminution of reproductive power is not only shown by the greater frequency of absolute sterility, nor is it shown only in the early cessation of child-rearing, but it is also shown in the very frequent inability of such women to suckle their infant. (Henry Maudsley, 1896, quoted in Sayers, 1982, p. 8)

Middle-class women, then, were not only considered fitted only for motherhood, but had a moral and political imperative to mother. After all, it was necessary for these women to breed in order to balance the known fecundity of the 'lower orders'. Educating women was a danger to the moral and political order. Women, therefore, had to be guardians of that moral order and the regulation of their sexuality and its channelling into nurturance was central to that regulation (Donzelot, 1980; Foucault, 1979b; Bland, 1981; Weeks, 1981). The responsibility for *correct* mothering, for producing the right citizens, was foremost. However, when love and nurturance became central concepts in the new pedagogy, higher education in the form of teacher training was opened to women. Thus women could be educated to 'amplify their capacities for maternal nurturance'. As the Hadow Report, quoted earlier, suggests, not only did the woman have to have the right temperament, but she also had to be trained in psychology to be able to observe, monitor, classify and regulate 'normal development'. The rise in teacher training therefore produced the possibility of an apparatus to ensure that the right kind of teachers would be produced. By regulating entry requirements and certificating teachers, social identities and positions could be produced in which teachers were created in the image of the desired 'good' pedagogy.

It was women, therefore, who formed the bedrock of the emergent 'caring professions' in which a certain level of education — training — combined with a sensitive, nurturant femininity, were the order of the day. We can look, then, to the practices to this date of producing women's education, and the positions open for girls, and we can find in schooling the necessary social identities created for girls to become carers. I shall return to this.

It is women, whose sexuality itself is regulated to produce 'normal femininity', who become the central prop of the new form of pedagogy. Teachers, trained in psychology, were to assume the entire responsibility for the 'freedom' of children, and for the continued maintenance of the bourgeois democratic order. I want, therefore, to demonstrate that women, positioned as teachers, mothers, carers and caring professionals (such as nurses, social workers, nursery workers and so forth) are held absolutely necessary for the moral order: they are responsible. This responsibility places women as at once safe, yet potentially dangerous (the bad mother). It places them as responsible for ensuring the possibility of democracy, and yet as deeply conservative. (Why else should classic studies of resistance — for example, Willis, 1977; Hall and Jefferson, 1976 — extol the virtues of masculine resistance, upholding women as politically conservative, passive and antithetical to resistance?) My argument is that, quite simply, women of all classes have been placed as guardians of an order from which it is difficult to escape. If you are told that you are totally responsible for the nature of the child and with it, therefore, the possibility of freedom, of democracy — how much guilt and pain is involved in resisting such a notion?

Such responsibility is a crucial issue for feminist engagement: the area of theory and practice which defines children's 'needs' and women's 'responsibilities' is often only contested by recourse to arguments about shared parenting. This approach seeks to take apart and to examine the claims to truth and positive effects of this truth about women and children. It therefore presents us with the basis of a far more powerful argument.

The 'truth' of women's sexuality is, then, constantly reproduced in the practices in which our identities are formed: as schoolgirl, mother, teacher, psychologist, secretary — whatever. The regulation of, and our identities in, those practices, makes us guardians of a fiction of autonomy and possibility. How then are we to go beyond such truth, which continually attempts to define us?

I have long been critical of a position in the psychology of women which would claim, in a liberal humanist tradition, that women have been denied 'independence' and 'autonomy', have been stifled and therefore need to be 'set free'. My criticism of such a position is that basically it denies the contradiction and doublebind of women's position in relation to child care. That is, we are held responsible for the autonomy and independence of others. Yet, that autonomy and independence is not, I would argue, the basis of any struggle for women, since it is precisely the basis of those qualities considered necessary for the maintenance of the liberal order. It is the form of 'covert regulation' which has us believe that 'freedom' is contained in the possibility of an illusion of choice.

It is this which I now wish to explore in several ways: firstly, by examining the practices through which children are regulated, in order to demonstrate how such practices operate; secondly, by examining how teachers are held responsible for a fictional freedom within the walls of the classroom as quasi-home; thirdly, by examining some aspects of the regulation of school girls as children.

'TEACHER' AND 'CHILD' AS POSITIONS

I have suggested that the power/knowledge relations produced in the modern form of government understand the school as an important site of social regulation. This means that the 'good teacher' and the 'normal' and 'natural' child are defined within the discourses and the practices that regulate their production. To explain what I mean by this I want first to discuss the term 'positioning in discourse' and then go on to exemplify how this works in relation to 'the child'.

The theoretical framework I am using differs in several important ways from an idea of 'social construction', which uses the idea of multiple roles, selves, or a structural functional model, for example. It is also different from other uses of the term 'discourse' (e.g. Potter *et al.*, 1984) and other similar usages such as 'accounting systems' (Shotter, 1984). Firstly, the concept of discourse utilized, especially in the power/knowledge relations of Foucault's later work, stresses the historical constitution of knowledge. It is therefore *post*-structuralist and in that sense can be seen as necessitating a shift beyond usages which rely on structural forms of linguistics and, for example, Althusserian formulations of ideology. It is precisely the historical effectivity of knowledge in forms of government which is central to this usage. We can thus suggest that such 'positionings' have powerful and 'real' effects, while at the same time acknowledging that their 'truth' is itself historically produced within certain specific conditions of possibility. In addition to this, 'social accountability' approaches tend to get trapped within a rather 'hollow concept of the human being (Henriques *et al.*, 1984; Ingleby, 1980). Foucault's post-structuralism does not address the problem of subjectivity directly, but rather skirts around it, offering instead an understanding of the 'subject' — or how we become 'subjected'. This still leaves an important area unexplored, as I have suggested elsewhere (Henriques *et al.*, 1984): subjectivity cannot be defined as a 'sum total of positions in discourse'.

In addition, we might also look to the critiques of structuralism which have emphasized that the social 'totality' is not a well-fitting and founded structure, but is more contradictory than some models of simple causality suggest. Understanding the social domain as a contradictory nexus of social practices (Hirst and Woolley, 1984) allows us to examine a way beyond a sense of a smooth and coherent identity. Rather, we can envisage a set of identities or positions, produced within the discursive relations of different practices which do not necessarily fit together smoothly. In this sense, then, we have a notion of 'conflict' or 'contradiction' between the different positions.

However, if we take as central to this account the mode of regulation of practices, it is the power of such regulation which is central. Regulation might take place through modes of signification, but it is more than this. It is not simply 'meaning', as in symbolic interactionism, for example. The model of power being utilized understands power not so much as a fixed possession (as in sovereign power), but as an aspect of the very regulative knowledge itself. For example, by defining what the 'nature of the child' is, certain behaviours are felt to be produced and regulated.

Foucault uses the term 'veridicality' to distinguish the 'effects' of 'truths' from an epistemological or empirical sense of whether something is real. I want to very briefly explore some of the veridicality, the truth producing effects, of modern pedagogic practices. If we can explore the possibility that 'subject-positions' do not create unitary or coherent identities, then subjection can take place within a variety of contradictory practices. This means that for women or girls, the designations 'teacher' or 'child' relate to the positionings within those specific practices, and are not co-terminous with 'woman' or 'girl'. That is, 'woman' is not itself a unitary category, but relates to different positionings as, say, 'teacher', 'wife', 'mother' etc. These different practices have different histories (Bennett *et al.*, 1980); and the effects in terms of power may well be differently lived (see, for example, Walkerdine, 1981, where I explore how a woman teacher is powerful as 'teacher', but rendered powerless as the object of young boys' sexist abuse.)

I have already briefly indicated the qualities ascribed to the 'teacher'. I want here to explore the practices for production of the 'child'. If we examine aspects of modern primary school practice, from the organization of time and space to the details of curriculum and pedagogy itself, it becomes clear that every aspect of schooling is premised upon a notion of 'the nature of the child'. The difference from the old pedagogy, with its overt regulation, is marked in a variety of ways. The architecture and arrangement of the school itself, as well as the seating arrangements in the classroom, are designed for flexibility and for a pedagogy centred upon a unique and individual child (Walkerdine, 1984; Bernstein, 1975).

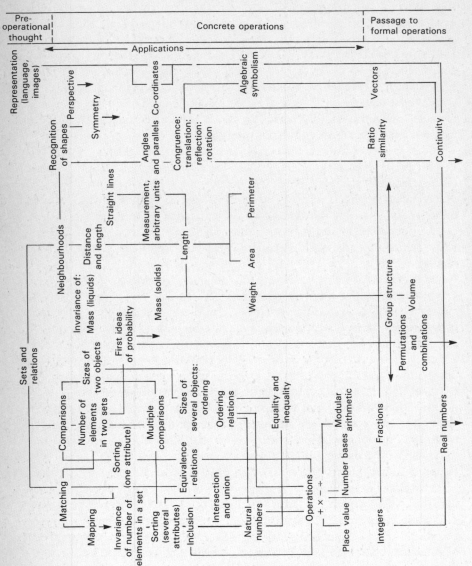

Figure 1. The concept tree (from Matthews et al., 1978, p. 14).

(1) Can sort a variety of articles, picking out sameness
    and difference.   ....
(2) Can sort a variety of objects into categories
    suggested by teacher.
     (a) colour   ....
     (b) size   ....
     (c) shape   ....
     (d) other   ....
(3) Can choose and explain his own sorting categories.   ....
(4) Understands some comparative words.   ....
(5) Can order three or more objects visually by size.   ....
(6) Understands:
     inside
     outside   ....
     on   ....
     in front of   ....
     behind   ....
     next to   ....

Figure 2. Sample record card (from Matthews et al., *1978, p. 18)*

The organization of time, too, permits and celebrates individual, and not class, activity. The division between work and play is reduced so as to build upon 'natural activity'. In other words, the whole pedagogy itself is designed to permit the possibility of certain things considered 'natural' and 'normal' to children. We cannot say in any simple sense that such a pedagogy and such modes of learning would exist in this way outside of those very practices designed to produce their presence. In this way it begins to be possible to examine how such accomplishments, behaviours and activities are *normalized*. The practices are set up to produce certain responses, based on a theoretical edifice which defines them as natural. Their presence, therefore, becomes normal, their absence pathological. This is ensured by a set of regulative devices which monitor, check and evaluate the presence and absence of such responses. Such devices as record cards, marking procedures and work cards all do this. For example, we might note what it is that is chosen to record: no longer knowledge as facts, but capacities or concepts, taken to be natural. There are many examples of such devices, and I reproduce here simply two aspects of one pre-school mathematics practice, *Early Mathematical Experiences* (Matthews *et al.*, 1978), to demonstrate what this implies.

The Concept Tree was devised especially with co-workers of Jean Piaget in Geneva and illustrates the way in which mathematical knowledge had become understood as concepts developing in a stagewise progression through a structural sequence of cognitive development. The record card then was to monitor such development. The Concept Tree provides the skeleton of those *concepts* which are to be the object of regulation and surveillance. The section on the Concept Tree in the General Guide is followed immediately by a section on 'Record Keeping'. The reader is advised on how to 'record' the conceptual progress of each child. For example, teachers are offered the following advice:

> A number of teachers have found it useful to make diary entries about children, noting their day to day activities.
>
> But what about the information that is passed on to another teacher? She may be in the next room or the next school, but will certainly want to know something about the group of children she is taking on. It has long been the practice to take groups of children to meet their new teachers and see their new classrooms. Some teachers think it would be just as helpful for the new teachers to meet their next classes while they are still in the nursery or kindergarten. In this way the teacher would see many of the activities that the children are being encouraged to take part in and make her own decisions about their capabilities (as a group). Children with particular interests or failings could be pointed out to her and the records that had been kept could be shown to her. Together, they could decide which information would be most helpful in providing continuity of experience for the children.
>
> If this personal contact is not possible, then written notes must be relied upon and many local authorities are experimenting with various cards and lists which will convey vital information in the most economical way. Although a lengthy personal record may give a better all-round picture of a child, the new teacher who wishes to find out which child is liable to have an asthma attack or can already count in twos and fives, really needs a quick reference chart. For this reason, as far as mathematics is concerned, it may be better to make a summary check list, which picks out some of the points which have already been recorded. The following is one that might be useful.
>
> It gives suggestions of activities that would demonstrate a child's progress in the acquisition of various concepts.
>
> (1) *Sorting*: can sort a collection of ten objects (not all alike) and discuss how.
> (2) *Ordering*: given five crayons or pencils of different lengths, can order them according to their length.
> (3) *Matching*: given five cubes in a line and a pile of toy cars, can match a car to each cube.
>
> (Matthews et al., 1978)

It is true that 'concepts' become reified as the objects of the regulative techniques themselves. Certain activities are set up in the classroom in the first place, and then particular behaviours are read as 'evidence' of development and become the basis of what is 'known' about each child—a process of normalization. Notice particularly that these records are taken to be important for transfer from one teacher to another, so that they become the basis on which 'normalizing judgements' come to tell the truth of what 'the child' is and then act as the basis of pedagogic practices. Therefore, they are in no sense the object of psychological debates which are simply 'applied' in practice. They become the basis of 'knowledge' in their own right.

What is important is the way in which such regulative practices, premised on nature, are developed in certain specific conditions of possibility. Although I have no space to do so here, we could chart the emergence of the concept of 'nature' which is utilized, and relate it specifically to the feared 'rising of the masses', especially with respect to primitive versus civilized behaviour; and aggression, understood as animal-like, and so forth. In respect of the new practices based on 'love', it is the recuperation of rebellion, resistance and aggression which is prominent. We can relate the entire emphasis on nature and activity to such concerns.

However, importantly, deviation from normality is not non-existent in this scheme. Of course children fail, but their failure is understood and potentially corrected through a variety of discourses and practice. One category of children who appear to exhibit behaviours which are 'abnormal' is that of girls. I shall argue that the regulation of girls' sexuality and their production as carers is in conflict with their positioning as children. It is this which produces difficult psychic struggles. But first, let me exemplify how we might understand the teacher as responsible for, and guardian of, a moral order in which rebellion is to be transformed into 'freedom'.

The classroom has become a space which is understood as an 'environment' which can 'facilitate' development. The model of an organism developing in interaction with an environment, which can be facilitating or not, is common to a variety of developmental accounts, from Piaget to Winnicott. It is within such a model, as we shall see, that the school is to become 'facilitating', specifically to counter the 'deprived' environment which may be particularly common in inner city areas and with working class mothers. So that 'when children are materially, intellectually or emotionally deprived, teachers must strive to serve as substitutes for parents . . .' (The Plowden Report, 1967, p. 311).

The notion of the school and the classroom, and indeed the teacher, as an environment to facilitate development, understands the pedagogic space as being set up for a set of individuals, whose development has to be monitored. In no sense, then, is such a space a *class* room—that is, one which has any sense of the class as a social unit. The teacher, as we have already examined, becomes facilitating; it is she who must be sensitive, watch, observe and monitor development. Certain qualities are required in her, which are different from, and yet complementary to, the child, whose freedom she is responsible for facilitating. My specific argument here is that the teacher is held responsible for facilitation through the provision of an environment. She is to become a mother-substitute to counter deprivation. This way, she is responsible for the possibility of 'freedom', that is the moral regulation of children, such that they grow to become democratic citizens. She is therefore both 'safety' as 'facilitator' and 'danger' as 'morality'. The classroom becomes a kind of fictional space where 'freedom' in a controlled environment is made possible.

It is my contention that the teacher, following the mother, is held responsible for the production of the democratic citizen by assuming a model of nature in which the process of birth and child development is primary, and primarily a process taking place between mother and child. Here, the house (and in this case the school) becomes like an enclosed space, away from the 'outside world', and in which a controlled environment is possible. In this environment (at once natural and highly synthetic) a child can develop potentially free from aggression and passion which might cause antisocial behaviour. The family and the school are seen as causal, a baseline, and themselves placed within a social and historical framework. It is this which, I suggest, places an incredible and impossible burden upon women to be 'teacher' and 'mother', to be nurturant and caring. In his presidential address to the British Association in 1916, William Temple described the *hope* contained in the school (and therefore in love, and in the teacher) in the following way:

> In the name of those who have died for the freedom of Europe, let us go forward to claim for this land of ours that spread of free education which shall be the chief guarantee of the freedom of our children for ever. (quoted in Selleck, 1972, p. 87)

Moral imperatives appear very strong as they relate to women's responsibilities with respect to the rearing of children. It will be remembered that the arguments against educating women related to child rearing, and were only lifted when such capacities for maternal nurturance were professionalized.

I would suggest that in this view of freedom, it is liberal humanism which places the 'teacher' as guardian of a terrible fiction: a fantasy of the 'freedom of our children forever'; the guardianship of a moral order which is only possible if childhood is checked and monitored in a specially controlled environment from the moment of birth (and even before). Although such accounts of liberation talk of the freeing of children, it is clear that never before have children been so monitored, so regulated (Rose, 1985). Mothering practices become the object of considerable intervention, and it is the mother's place herself to monitor development, while her own fitness itself is also the object of scrutiny (Donzelot, 1980; Riley, 1983; Urwin, 1985). While I am not describing mothering practices here, it is clear that pedagogic practices are devised specifically as an intervention in relation to these, and that the positioning of women as carers is paramount. I am suggesting that the classroom, then, can be understood, like the 'idealized' home, as a fictional space in which a fantasy of freedom is played out. This means not only constant monitoring, but also the centrality of concepts of (circumscribed) 'free' choice, which are ubiquitous in early education (Walkerdine, 1985b).

Now, none of this guarantees that all classrooms are copies of the textbook version. Indeed, recent work on primary school practices suggests that this is far from the case (Galton *et al.*, 1982). However, what is important here is that such practices have a clear moral and political imperative. The presence of such practices, therefore, has itself to be the object of constant monitoring (advice, inspection) to ensure that it exists, and teachers have to see themselves as responsible. I suggest that the 'facts' of child development have also to be constantly proved to exist in order to become the scientific basis of such practices. We might treat such proof, not as a mark of a certain truth, but of an uncertain desperation to demonstrate that it is so (Walkerdine, 1985a; BhaBha, 1983).

The teacher who is taken to be totally responsible is faced with an impossible task, the management of an idealist dream, an impossible fiction. Such a position induces guilt at not being good enough. Such guilt is a constant feature of the discourse of primary school teachers. Such guilt has significant effects for women, which it is important that feminism confronts and examines.

How, then, might we characterize women's attempts to live out the contradictions and conflicts in such positions? To explore this I now wish to turn to the education of girls and their positioning as children, in order to demonstrate the way in which their pathology in one discourse is precisely what sets them up for the caring professions.

THE 'GIRL' AND THE 'CHILD'

Both the 'girl' and the 'child' are, in many ways, impossible positions. They set sanitized and idealized images of innocence and safety. There is a long tradition of empirical work in psychology and education which has attempted to prove the inferiority of girls in the sciences and mathematics. Such work hinges particularly on the association of masculinity and reason, and often suggests that girls' performance itself presents something of a problem. Although the mean performance of girls in most school subjects is higher than that of boys throughout their school careers, it is very common indeed to present this performance itself as in some way pathological. In particular, it is common to present girls as 'passive', 'hard working', 'helpful', 'rule following'. These qualities are felt to be antithetical to the 'active, enquiring' nature of childhood and therefore become a threat to the idea of a pedagogy set up to permit and facilitate activity. Consider some comments made by teachers about girls and boys; for example, the following remarks taken from work in the Girls and Mathematics Unit are all made about *girls* whose academic performance is good:

> Quiet. Gets on very well, sits down and gets on with it. Very rarely makes mistakes. Very tidy handwriting.
>
> Technically, she's very good and creatively she has the ideas . . . She's not outstanding, no . . . but always does her best . . . her behaviour is impeccable . . .
>
> Very, very hard worker. Not a particularly bright girl but everything she presents is very high. Her hard work gets her to her standards.
>
> She's not a high flier. But she plods along and does quite well—a very nice personality.

These girls are 'hard workers' with 'nice personalities'. Conversely, girls *can* be considered 'brilliant', but look what happens to the teacher's understanding of what that means:

> She's very good, she's very able. She's a madam, that's unfortunate. It's got to the stage where she thinks she knows it all and you really can't tell her, and she won't take any advice really . . . and she's got this unfortunate attitude that's rather domineering.

So, a 'very able' girl is referred to very pejoratively. Not only is her 'activity' considered 'domineering', but her sexuality is also implicitly the object of slur: she is called a 'madam'.

By comparison, note how boys' bad behaviour is excused and even to some extent felt to be the teacher's (or parents') fault:

> Damian . . . covered the work as well. He's been in Greece . . . He's interested because he comes up and says that he's bored . . . and that's the reason why he makes a lot of mistakes . . . he tells me that as well.

> I would say he is the brightest child in the class, but again is someone who needs to be encouraged. He can be very rude, and can be obstreporous with other children rather than the teacher. But he has a very good ability, very interested in everything, a very good general knowledge and has an all-round ability with a lot of potential.

> His parents have split up recently and since then his behaviour has gone downhill completely. Very difficult to settle . . . to accept reprimands or to be encouraged to get on with his work . . . he's in the second group and not very bright academically, above average mind you, but again his work has suffered because of the break up.

Girls' performance constantly places them as opposite to the qualities of 'real' children. In the regulation of pedagogic practices, therefore, it poses a constant threat and dilemma because here is good performance produced in apparently the 'wrong' way. This might suggest that given that 'activity' is 'natural', girls' performance must be the result of some pathology. However, it is precisely the kind of performance and behaviour which is considered appropriate to the regulation of the moral order: kind, helpful, nurturant. In many cases, the power of girls in the classroom is given precisely through their operation as sub-teachers (Walkerdine, 1981; 1985c). In displaying behaviour considered pathological with respect to childhood, they are at the same time displaying the requirements necessary to join the caring professions. After all, it is precisely the combination of high attainment *and* nurturance which is so desired in teachers.

It would be important to attempt to examine some of the ways in which girls come to take up such positions, but it is beyond the scope of this chapter. However, I would like to end by briefly examining the way in which the regulation of sexuality enters into the concept of childhood and the effect of this for girls.

That is, that sexuality, in playing no part in pedagogic discourses of childhood (except with respect to boys), makes displays of sexuality itself something which is forbidden, hidden and subverted.

CHILDHOOD SEXUALITY: THE SPECTRE OF THE 'BAD GIRL'

I have suggested that the fictional space of the classroom is a site for the embodiment and playing out of powerful fantasies which aim to produce the social order as known, calculable and safe. The sexual division of labour and the regulation of women's sexuality forms a central trope in this fiction. And it is here that sexual difference is also played out. However, in the fiction of 'the child', sexuality has been sanitized and has slipped from the account altogether. Although some accounts concentrated on the sexual expression and liberation of children (as for example in A. S. Neill's use of the work of Wilhelm Reich), the sexuality of girls generally becomes converted into maternal nurturance. Foucault has suggested that there was:

'A hystericization of women's bodies: a threefold process whereby the feminine body was analysed—qualified and disqualified—as being thoroughly saturated with sexuality; whereby it was integrated into the sphere of medical practices, by reason of a pathology intrinsic to it; whereby, finally, it was placed in organic communication with the social body (whose regulated fecundity it was supposed to ensure), the family space (of which it had to be a substantial and functional element), and the life of children (which it produced and had to guarantee, by virtue of a biologico-moral responsibility lasting through the entire period of the children's education): the Mother, with her negative image of 'nervous woman', constituted the most visible form of this hystericization'. (Foucault, 1979b, p. 104)

The 'universal and natural' child is one for whom sexuality is central but left behind on the path toward rationality. In later formulations, neither gender nor sexuality is mentioned and we are left with a de-sexualized, safe, self-disciplined child on the road to autonomy. But the de-sexualized child is constructed as a fiction in the fantasies and desires of adults for safety. In this fantasy, sexual desire of adults for children (Rose, 1984) becomes displaced on to an image of childhood innocence. It takes considerable denial to displace the desires of adults for children and produce a clean cut version of childhood. If the sexuality of girls and women constitutes a danger to the moral order, then it is precisely this sexuality which is lurking *outside* the sanitized space of the classroom, continually threatening to intrude. Although it is 'play' and 'action' which enter into the child-space, girls continually accompany their activities in school with discussions of television programmes and singing extracts from popular songs. It is popular culture, with its overt representations of the child-woman (the child as sexualized object of an adult gaze) which threatens to enter the classroom, and which is hidden and subverted at its margins.

I want to refer to one six year old girl, Janie, who was part of an intensive study of six year old girls undertaken by me (Walkerdine, 1985c). Janie was the archetypical 'good girl'. This meant that she was not so much 'active' as 'the hard-working girl destined to join the caring professions'. Indeed her stated ambition was to become a teacher. Yet, through the image of the 'good girl', hiding in the margins, we are presented not with a unitary identity, but a bad, sexualized child threatening to erupt through to the surface. We are faced with an image which attests to the failure of the pedagogic practices to constitute the innocent child as its object.

The pop song 'Oh Mickie' (recorded by American singer Toni Basil) was sung relentlessly by the girls in Janie's class in the summer of 1982, when I made the recordings. Toni Basil, on the promotional video of the record, is the epitome of the sexualized schoolgirl. She presents a romanticized 1950s image of the American cheerleader, complete with pigtails and heavy make-up. She sings to Mickie to 'give it to me, give it to me any way you can'. The song is angry and pleading at the same time. Not only was the song sung frequently, but six year old Rose held a talent competition in her garden in which 'Oh Mickie' was sung. Only that year nine year old Tracy Lee Jolleys had reached the final of Saturday Superstore's *Search for a Star* with her eroticized mime to the record.

But Janie does not only join in the singing. She is transformed in minutes from 'good' to 'bad' girl. She leaves the classroom and goes to pose in front of the mirror in the privacy of the toilets to sing her own private version of 'Oh Mickie'. And her 'positioning' is transformed—from child to woman, from virgin to whore. Indeed, Griffin (1983) and McRobbie (1978) have both remarked on the way in which secondary school girls overtly use adult heterosexuality (the wearing of make-up with school uniform, for example) to resist being 'children'.

I am suggesting, therefore, in this short sketch that the positions which I have set out are historically constituted and relate centrally to issues about power and government. However, the multiple positionings accorded to women are often in contradiction and themselves provide sites for struggle and resistance. The theoretical edifice that I have outlined is in no sense enough. It does not explain how we might move towards understanding the 'failure' of positions and the living out of struggle. It is to psychoanalysis that we might turn to explore such issues (see Sayers, Chapter 2, this volume and also, for example, Urwin, 1985; J. Rose, 1983; 1984; Mitchell and Rose, 1983; Irigaray, 1984); although it is object relations psychoanalysis itself which has been central to modern forms of regulation (for example, the incorporation of the ideas of Winnicott, Bowlby etc. into social work: see Urwin, 1985 and work in preparation). There is much work to be done for feminists working within psychology. This work is theoretical, historical, empirical and yet, and always, engaging with the very specificity and positively of present practices and the ways that they form us. For me, however, the specificity and historicity of our struggle with the fictional discourses which pronounce their truth and claim to 'know' us, is always a space for contestation and for hope.

REFERENCES

Bennett, F., Coward, R. and Heys, R. (1980). The limits to financial and legal independence: a socialist-feminist perspective on taxation and social security. *Politics and Power* 1, 185–202.

Bernstein, B. (1975). Visible and invisible pedagogies. In: *Class, Codes and Control*, Vol. 2. London, Routledge & Kegan Paul.

BhaBha, H. K. (1983). The other question: the stereotype and colonial discourse. *Screen* 24 (6), 18–36.

Bland, L. (1981). The domain of the sexual: a response. *Screen Education*, 39, 56–68.

Central Advisory Council for Education (England). (1967). *Children and their Primary Schools* (Plowden Report). London, HMSO.

Clarke, K. (1985). Public and private children. In: Steedman, C., Urwin, C. and Walkerdine, V. (eds), op. cit.

Consultative Committee of the Board of Education. (1933). *Infant and Nursery Schools* (Hadow Report). London, HMSO.

Donzelot, J. (1980). *The Policing of Families*. London, Hutchinson.

Foucault, M. (1979a). *Discipline and Punish*. Harmondsworth, Penguin.

Foucault, M. (1979b). *The History of Sexuality: Vol. 1. An Introduction*. Harmondsworth, Penguin.

Galton, M., Simon, B. and Croll, P. (1982). *Inside the Primary Classroom*. London, Routledge & Kegan Paul.

Gordon, C. (ed.) (1980). *Power/Knowledge*. Brighton, Harvester.

Griffin, C. (1983). Young women and work: The transition from school to un/employment for young working class women. Paper presented at British Psychological Society Annual Conference, York.

Hacking, I. (1981). How should we write the history of statistics? *Ideology and Consciousness* 8, 15–26.

Hall, S. and Jefferson, T. (1976). *Resistance through Rituals*. London, Hutchinson.

Hamilton, D. (1981). On simultaneous instruction and the early evolution of class teaching. Mimeo, University of Glasgow.

Henriques, J. *et al.* (1984). *Changing the Subject: Psychology, Social Regulation and Subjectivity*. London, Methuen.

Hirst, P. and Woolley, P. (1984). *Social Relations and Human Attributes*. London, Methuen.

Ingleby, D. (1980). Review of A. Lock (ed.) *Action, Gesture and Symbol: the Emergence of Language*, London, Academic Press. *European Journal of Social Psychology* 10, 319–28.

Irigaray, L. (1985). *Speculum of the other woman*. Ithaca, Cornell University Press.

Jones, K. and Williamson, K. (1979). The birth of the schoolroom. *Ideology and Consciousness* 6, 59–110.

McRobbie, A. (1978). Working class girls and the culture of feminity. Unpublished MA thesis. CCCS, University of Birmingham.

Matthews, G., Matthews, J. *et al.* (1978). *Early Mathematical Experiences*. Addison-Wesley (General Guide) Schools Council.

Mitchell, J. and Rose, J. (1983). *Jaques Lacan and the Ecole Freudienne: Feminine Sexuality*. London, Routledge & Kegan Paul.

Potter, J., Stringer, P. and Wetherell, M. (1984). *Social Texts and Context*. London, Routledge & Kegan Paul.

Riley, D. (1983). *War in the Nursery: Theories of the Child and the Mother*. London, Virago.

Rose, J. (1983). Femininity and its discontents. *Feminist Review* 14, 1–26.

Rose, J. (1984). *The Case of Peter Pan: or the Impossibility of Children's Fiction*. London, Macmillan.

Rose, N. (1985). *The Psychological Complex*. London, Routledge & Kegan Paul.

Rose, N. (1979). The psychological complex: mental measurement and social administration. *Ideology and Consciousness* **5**, 5-68.

Sayers, J. (1982). *Biological Politics*. London, Methuen.

Selleck, R. J. W. (1972). *English Primary Education and the Progressives: 1914-1939*. London, Routledge & Kegan Paul.

Shotter, J. (1984). *Social Accountability and Selfhood*. Oxford, Blackwell.

Steedman, C., Urwin, C. and Walkderdine, V. (eds) (1985). *Language, Gender and Childhood*. London, Routledge & Kegan Paul.

Urwin, C. (1985). The regulation of mothering: the persuasion of normal development. In: Steedman, C., Urwin, C. and Walkerdine, V. (eds), op. cit.

Urwin, C. (In prep.). *On the Regulation of Mothering*. Cambridge, Policy Press.

Walkerdine, V. (1981). Sex, power and pedagogy. *Screen Education* **38**, 14-21.

Walkerdine, V. (1983). Girls and mathematics: a reflection on theories of cognitive development. Paper presented at International Society for Behavioural Development, 7th Biennial Meeting, Munich.

Walkerdine, V. (1984). Developmental psychology and the child-centred pedagogy. In: Henriques, J. *et al.*, op. cit.

Walkerdine, V. (1985a). Science and the female mind: the burden of proof. *Psych. Critique* **1** (1), 1-20.

Walkerdine, V. (1985b). On the regulation of speaking and silence: sexuality, class and gender in contemporary schooling. In: C. Steedman, C. Urwin, and V. Walkerdine, (eds) op. cit.

Walkerdine, V. (1985c). Processes in the development of gender and mathematics at home and at school. Unpublished final report to the ESRC on grant no. HR 8268/1.

Weeks, J. (1981). *Sex, Politics and Society*. Harlow, Longman.

Widdowson, F. (1983). *Going up to the Next Class: Women in Elementary Teacher Training*. London, Hutchinson.

Willis, P. (1977). *Learning to Labour*. London, Saxon House.

Chapter 5

Linguistic Repertoires and Literary Criticism: New Directions for a Social Psychology of Gender

Margaret Wetherell

The question this chapter addresses is how to analyse femininity and masculinity or construct a social psychology of women and men. Is femininity a set of traits — narcissism, dependence, communion and so on — developing naturally from biological differences, a set of psychological states fixed by the different experiences, limitations and potentialities of being a woman; or is it a set of stereotypes basic to roles and taken up by the people who adopt those roles?

All of these perspectives seem to obscure the main point about gender. I want to suggest that femininity and masculinity are ideological practices all the more effective because they appear as natural and inevitable results of biology or experience. The appearance of something coherent which could be explained as a property of the individual is precisely the effect of this ideological movement.

Habitual practice assigns children to one category or other. Name, identity and, later, type of occupation and access to resources become fixed by that sexual category. The symbolic and excessive importance of a sexual differentiation which seems vital only for the continuation and preservation of a certain kind of *status quo* is established and reinforced by family, media, and education. Actions and self-descriptions become, as a result, genderized, associated with just female or male, and then universalized so that the categories become homogeneous as well as separated, superordinate to other identities. As feminists appreciate, what in this way, becomes, taken for granted, and thus completely 'obvious', is also often the most difficult to penetrate and criticize.

Femininity and masculinity, examined closely, reduce to a set of codes or conventions and devices used to produce categorical difference. Gender, it will be argued, is not a matter of consistent unitary single identities, 'male' and 'female', but develops from contradictory and frequently fragmentary pieces of

77

discourse, repertoires, and accounting systems available to individuals to make sense of their position, and which historically and contingently have come to be marked as feminine or masculine responses.

In turning this way to language and cultural practices of representation we will be following a track which may not be familiar to social psychologists but which will be to many others. The analysis developed here is an extension of earlier work (Potter *et al.*, 1984) and builds upon the concept of a linguistic repertoire (Potter and Mulkay, 1985). Help will be sought from literary critics and other cultural critics who have attempted to deconstruct the images of women and men offered in fiction, advertising, and more generally (Abel, 1982; Coward, 1984; Ellmann, 1979; Heath, 1982; Williamson, 1978), and from a recently elaborated model of the human subject as positioned ideologically (Adlam *et al.*, 1977; Coward and Ellis, 1977; Henriques *et al.*, 1984).

Initially, however, the argument will develop negatively through a critique of some standard socio-psychological approaches to gender, looking particularly at the definition and measurement of femininity and masculinity, themes of agency versus communion, or animus and anima, in the psychology of women and men. In order to argue for a reconceptualization of gender in social psychology, it is first necessary to see the problems with the existing framework.

COMMUNION AND AGENCY: THE EXIGENCIES OF GENDER MEASUREMENT

> It might seem quite a simple matter to obtain a measure of someone's feminity and masculinity, at least on the face of it. All that we require is some way of determining the degree to which people think that they conform to the characteristics typically associated with women and men, respectively. (Smith, 1985, p. 92)

The difficult part, indeed, is the definition of these characteristics and their status. Measurement then supposes that these traits will be enduring or displayed consistently across situations and are thus a meaningful attribute of the person.

In psychology, feminine and masculine have usually been understood in terms of a communion/agency, or alternatively expressivity/instrumentality, distinction. This distinction has been proposed in many guises from Jungian psychotherapy (de Castillejo, 1973; Johnson, 1976) to Bakan's (1966) dualities of human existence and Parson's and Bales's (1955) division of tasks in the household or group, and it is referred to in a number of chapters in the present volume. Bakan maintains, for instance, that:

> . . . a fundamental polarity underlies human existence at all levels from the cellular to the societal—the constructs of agency and communion . . . agency and communion are male and female principles, differentiating the aggregate

of males from the aggregate of females . . . in psychological functioning, agency is seen in differentiation of self from the field, in intellectual functions involving separating and ordering, and in interpersonal styles involving objectivity, competition, exclusion, and distance; communion is seen in the merging of self with the field, in intellectual functions involving communication, interpersonal styles involving subjectivity, co-operation, acceptance and closeness. (quoted in Carlson, 1971, p. 271)

Thus, to put it more bluntly:

> Big boys are made of—independence, aggression, competitiveness, leadership, task orientation, outward orientation, assertiveness . . .
> Big girls are made of—dependence, passivity, fragility, low pain tolerance, non-aggression, non-competitiveness, inner orientation, interpersonal orientation, empathy, sensitivity, nuturance . . . (back cover publisher's blurb for Bardwick's *Psychology of Women,* 1971)

Jung claimed that two complementary but opposed principles, the anima (feminine) and the animus (masculine), of archetypal and mythical status, could be identified in the human psyche. Anticipating the modern emphasis on psychological androgyny, he argued that men not only contained animus aspects but also a smaller element of anima functions which would emerge from time to time, and similarly women were not only anima but also to some extent animus.

Precise specification of the nature of anima and animus is rare but a sense can be gained if we put together a pastiche of terms used by authors such as de Castillejo and Johnson. The animus-like agency is thus 'focussed consciousness and separation' of an 'impersonal collective character' involving 'reflection, deliberation and self-knowledge', not to mention 'active achievement, cool reasonableness, mastery, penetration and the overcoming of the obstacles of nature'; the anima is more 'primaeval and oceanic, more closely tied to the original instinctive pattern' and manifested in 'diffuse awareness, natural contact with the living springs in the unconscious, values of life, unity, relationship and relatedness'. The anima is represented too by the following traits: 'waiting, passive, artistic, sense of the unbroken connection of all things, suffocating, inarticulate, raging vanity, conniving lust, pettiness'.

Unfortunately, women seem to benefit little from their animus side. Witness the following:

> . . . (femininity) expresses an attitude of spiritual waiting, and tending, and readiness for the meeting with its opposite which is a prerequisite for inner wholeness. Without this she becomes prey to the masculine within herself, a raging spirit of intellectual or physical activity to which no man can be related, and to which she can in no way relate herself. (de Castillejo, 1973, p. 57)

Although animus and anima are tied to the myths and tales told to make sense of the environment and human relations, by sleight of hand they also become more than that: as constitutive, biologically inevitable, patterns of consciousness. Developed in this form, de Castillejo and Johnson's anima and animus can quickly be rejected as semi-mystical ramblings, but, nonetheless, the more general agency and communion concepts to which they conform have become a powerful common sense in psychology, an implicit background knowledge which is never deconstructed but built upon as a foundation and correspondingly taken for granted.

Bem's (1974) Sex Role Inventory (the BSRI), for example, probably the most popular modern socio-psychological method for measuring gender identity, is clearly prey to this. Bem's aim in the inventory was to identify several gender options (feminine, masculine, or an androgynous combination of both) and operationalize these in questionnaire form. People completing the questionnaire could then determine their psychosexual identity. They were to read a list of traits presented then decide on the suitability of each trait as a self-description.

To select the items for inclusion in the inventory, Bem asked student judges to rate each of 400 personality characteristics in terms of its desirability for a woman or a man. Students were instructed not to think in terms of their own criteria for desirability but to intuit the kinds of criteria 'American society' would use. The complete inventory consists of 20 highly desirable feminine characteristics, 20 highly desirable masculine characteristics and 20 neutral or filler items. It is clear from examination of the BSRI that the agency/communion framework has been replicated by this procedure (feminine traits, for example, include warm and tender; masculine traits, aggressive and analytical).

In Bem's inventory, however, femininity and masculinity need not be tied to biological sex. Masculine females and feminine males are potential outcomes along with the androgynous (equally high in positive feminine and masculine traits) and the undifferentiated (equally low in positive feminine and masculine traits).

In this tradition of gender measurement, agency and communion have been linked to a much more modern set of assumptions about sex role stereotypes and the socialization process (Bem, 1974; 1975; 1976; Bem and Lenney, 1976; Bem et al., 1976). Bem states that 'the BSRI was founded on a conception of the sex-typed person as someone who has internalized society's sex-typed standards of desirable behaviour for men and women' (1974, p. 155, my emphasis). Despite being conventional and stereotypical this does not mean that these standards are not psychologically real for those who are sex typed. On the contrary, Bem maintains that people's behaviour can be predicted from their endorsement of stereotypes on the inventory; the other key word in the previous quotation, therefore, is 'internalized'.

Bem has gone on to institute a body of research which demonstrates this psychological reality, developing a programme of experiments which confirm that the psychologically feminine, for example, not only endorse the appropriate stereotypes on the inventory but behave in other situations in 'typically feminine' ways; and, moreover, that androgynous women and men are psychologically superior, in the sense of being better adjusted, more capable, human beings.

The conclusion arrived at by Bem *et al.* (1976) from one set of experimental results illustrates this trend:

> . . . only androgynous males were high in both instrumental and expressive domains; that is, only androgynous males were found to stand firm in their opinions as well as cuddle kittens, bounce babies, and offer a sympathetic ear to someone in distress. In contrast, the feminine male was low in independence, while the masculine male was low in nuturance. (p. 1022)

Empirical proof, apparently, that people live out the agency and communion scripts set out for them.

The social psychology of gender identity is thus characterized, first, by the need to find meaning in a feminine/masculine divide, and, second, by the desire to find the definitive content of those categories. These are usually understood in terms of some version of the agency/communion distinction and then fixed as a property of the individual across context and time.

As Smith (1985) points out, in many respects the BSRI and similar instruments are a considerable advance over earlier measures, representing the transition from a sex difference method to a more flexible stereotype or self-categorization approach. Sex differences are no longer assumed *a priori*, the inventory depends on willingness to categorize oneself in terms of a social consensus about what females and males should be like. It is not my aim in this chapter, however, to demonstrate the positive aspects of Bem's work in terms of the history of psychological research in this area, or indeed to criticize the methodological problems with the actual measurement procedure (cf. Smith, 1985, Chapter 5; Eichler, 1980); rather, my intention is to examine the more global assumptions which underlie this tradition of work.

There seem to be three main grounds for suspecting that this kind of approach impedes the analysis of human relations and, in fact, may be more actively retrogressive. First, it seems probable that the force of femininity/masculinity discourse lies in the very assumption of a meaningful categorical difference rather than in the specific content identified through research as constitutive of that difference. Second, for this reason, Bem's inventory and others like it reinforce one set of 'imaginary identities', strengthening their ideological potential and legitimacy. Finally, there are problems with the model of the subject implicit not only in biologically inherent accounts but also in socialization notions of gender adoption.

Clifton *et al.* (1976) have demonstrated, with respect to the BSRI, that if people are asked to generate descriptions of various types of women (career woman, bunny, woman athlete, housewife, clubwoman) then only the image for 'housewife' matches the image of femininity or communion in the inventories. This not only illustrates the narrow realm from which Bem's gender stereotypes are drawn but points to a more fundamental problem.

Women athletes may rarely be seen by others as affectionate, gullible, tender, yielding, etc. or as 'feminine females' on Bem's scale, yet they are hardly immune from the ideological momentum of femininity discourse, as becomes apparent from even a cursory acquaintance with the traditions of sports broadcasting. For the woman athlete, it is the fact that she can be marked as 'feminine', whatever her attributes, and thus diminished, that is important. The possibility of categorization is more powerful than the content usually attributed to the categories.

Spender (1980) has called the general tendency for 'masculine' attributes and occupations to be valued and 'feminine' derogated and downgraded, the 'plus male, minus female' phenomenon. She documents cases where a certain type of linguistic construction (the tag question) becomes an indicator of control over a conversation when used by men, but where the same type of construction tends to be seen as a sign of weakness and hesitancy when used by women. We don't need to assume for one moment that there is only one correct interpretation of the meaning of the linguistic construction in question to see that in this case femininity and masculinity have become moveable categories. They have come to resemble the two possible readings that make up some well known visual illusions, either it is an old woman or it is a vase, either it is a dalmation dog or a pattern of leaves against a white background: the prior conceptualization or choice of reading determines the content and what can be seen. The content becomes shaped to the category.

The substance of femininity/masculinity categories may, in this way, be surprisingly flexible; women and men may be described in all kinds of ways, but what is vital for social reproduction is the possibility of difference and its value marking. It must be more useful, therefore, for the social scientist to examine how femininity/masculinity labels work to define situations and discourse, in combination with the power to have those labels accepted, i.e. creating content and organizing value; rather than identifying, as Bem does, the feminine or masculine as an inherent fixed property of certain states. Social psychologists could begin to investigate, for instance, how particular versions of sexual identity are adopted for characterizing one's own and others' actions in specific situations. Attention could be fruitfully directed to what is achieved by these different kinds of accounts.

A great deal seems to be missed that is crucial to the understanding of the social position of women and men, if we assume that the content of femininity or masculinity is unvarying and can be unproblematically 'discovered' once and for all, as one might discover what is inside a box. In this case the contents of the box could be constantly changing and can always be renegotiated; the important issue is how they are negotiated and often, to continue the analogy, the agreement that there are two boxes in the first place.

Paradoxically, in her most recent writings, Bem seems to have grasped parts of this point, although at the same time she continues to struggle to fix femininity and masculinity, but in a new guise as 'gender schema'. She writes:

> Even more importantly, however, the concept of androgyny is insufficiently radical from a feminist perspective because it continues to presuppose that there is a masculine and a feminine within us all, that is, that the concepts of masculinity and femininity have an independent and palpable reality rather than being themselves cognitive constructs derived from gender based schematic processing. A focus on the concept of androgyny thus fails to prompt serious examination of the extent to which gender organises both our perceptions and our social world. (Bem, 1981, p. 383)

Critics like Eichler (1980; cf. also Johnston, 1985) argued that androgyny was a meaningless ideal. As Eichler demonstrated, if our society was actually androgynous, the concept of androgyny itself could not exist, because sex (apart from in a strictly biological sense) would be considered an irrelevant variable and defunct as a term of reference for social organization (1980, p. 70). It is illogical to aim towards androgyny but to regard it at the same time as the combination of highly desirable feminine and masculine qualities. While conceding the point on androgyny, Bem, unfortunately, continues to maintain that gender identities can still be unilaterally defined, albeit as 'cognitive constructs'. Once again the implication is that gender conventions persist because they are internalized by individuals. But do they not persist because of their role in the reproduction of patriarchical social forms and because of their potential for flexible application?

All this goes to show that this type of social psychology has effectively decontextualized sex. Gender identities in the BSRI are viewed in the abstract, quite independently of the situations to which they might relate. In effect, a set of 'imaginary identities' is produced. The stereotypes or social consensus reflected by a small group of students become, in the inventory, reified into a normative standard, invariant across contexts, culture, and history, which constrains personality description.

Bem's attempt to discover gender as a literal state rather than to treat it as a metaphorical device could thus serve to bolster up the very ideological practice she hoped to defuse (through the concept of androgyny). This is the second problem with the BSRI. The gender identities produced results in ideological products (agency/communion) acquiring a tangible, measureable and constant reality through their representation as psychological, character variables. What, for instance, do the people who complete the BSRI learn? As Eichler and Johnston point out, they learn that their disposition is open to scientific test and, moreover, here is evidence that what people seem to believe about femininity is actually the case. 'Sex role stereotypes, as established, serve as a gauge for reality, rather than reality serving as a corrective for the stereotypes' (Eichler, 1980, p. 68). The otherwise highly tendentious and clearly reactionary fantasies of Jung, Bakan, etc. are in this way perpetuated. Their claim to be neutral descriptions of what is the case about women and men remains effectively unchallenged.

Following the general trend in social psychology as a whole, there has been little consideration of the power relationships or access to resources implicated in women as communion, men as agency schemes. In short, little feminism. The implications are clear, but seen as unproblematic or merely accepted as a given.

Carlson, for instance, notes in her discussion of a more psychoanalytically orientated version of agency and communion:

> Central to Gutmann's formulation is the contrast between two kinds of 'maturational milieus' of men and women. Men inhabit an impersonal milieu — whether of business, battlefield, or prairie — a milieu governed by impersonal laws of nature, of economics, of the political order. Women inhabit the personal world of family, neighbourhood, community — a milieu governed by familiar forces of feelings, shared expectancies, predictabilities. (1971, p. 268)

Beware the woman who steps outside her ecological niche! It seems unfortunate, to say the least, that such admirable personal qualities should lead women into subjugated and oppressed positions.

Finally, we should examine the model of the human subject which underlies the social psychology of gender and accounts for some of its difficulties. It is unquestioned, as a central presupposition of psychometrics, that the human subject is unitary, coherent and consistent across situations, also in some way an 'individual' separated from, but influenced by, the rest of society (cf. the critique of socialization by Adlam et al.; 1977). Bem's inventory, for example, encourages the view that androgyny, femininity, and masculinity are traits which one either has or does not have. As an individual with a specific psychosexual identity you enter into relationships with other individuals with their own identities, producing and sustaining the social matrix.

This impression, however, is an illusion fostered by a method of measurement or style of investigation. Variability, contradiction and the construction of mental life through interaction, are carefully edited out of the record. A snapshot of a constrained either/or type of response at one moment in time is generalized to become a permanent psychological feature. Other methods of study, such as the collection of discourse for analysis, clearly demonstrate that variability and inconsistency are exactly the principal characteristics of any naturally occurring human justification, explanation or self-analysis (Potter, 1984; Potter and Litton, 1985). There seems no reason to believe that discourse about gender will prove an exception.

That is, if we look at how people talk about gender and sexuality and draw upon received notions to account for their own and others' behaviour, we might well find fragmentary rather than coherent references to 'femininity' and 'masculinity'. A multitude of contradictory and inconsistent self-characterizations depending on context might emerge, as opposed to one stable identity. A rapidly shifting discursive construction or creation of subject positions and group memberships might appear, acting as options to be taken up or rejected, by the interlocutor: far removed from an ordered intercourse between two fixed, 'already created', individuals.

How could social psychology cope with the possibility of people who are alternately 'androgynous', 'feminine' or 'masculine', and with a 'femininity' of ambiguous content outlined at one moment as expressive communion, but at another as instrumental and personal? Or a situation where, also, the repetition of these terms may signify more about the nature of divisions and power relations within a society, than the built-in character and temperament of the individual member?

Before making any suggestions, however, in answer to this question, it might be helpful to pause and consider a similar debate within feminist literary criticism. The terms of reference for this debate and method of resolution, although they may initially appear irrelevant, clarify the problem for the social psychologist, and further indicate the complexity of the dilemma.

WOMEN READING WOMEN

The development of feminist literary criticism has in many respects paralleled the investigation of femininity in social psychology (cf. Potter *et al.*, 1984, Chapter 1) but with the exception that a much more confident and sophisticated analysis of ideologically potent images has emerged. It is ironic that literary criticism, through its dealings with fictional constructions, could advance the methods and theoretical analysis required to understand the regularities of gender operation in prosaic everyday life.

One of the first achievements of feminist critics was to bring to the foreground the social location of the author, displaying the consistent bias and distortion in male writers' descriptions of women. Critics like Ellmann (1979) and Millett (1969), in particular, have ensured that authors like Mailer, Miller and D. H. Lawrence can no longer be read with the same innocence. Their descriptions of women now appear contingent, questionable, risible and embarrassingly misogynist.

Ellmann claimed that four meta-principles govern the stereotypes of women found in literature and, by extension, have also influenced the critical assessment of female authors. First, sexual difference in texts is often achieved by a nature/art distinction. Rather like communion and agency, female functions are portrayed in literature as natural, unthinking, unself-conscious, while the male principle is assertive against nature, struggling rationally and self-consciously to improve and progress. Both can be seen as an ideal but the association with nature also demotes the female. Typically, says Ellmann, 'when the (male) observer reconsiders his own condition, and experiencing a revived gratification on its account, finds the same supposed thoughtlessness of others contemptibly naive' (1979, p. 62). Similarly in psychology, agency and communion are held up as equally ideal states, but it seems also that male agency just happens to fit men for high status and the exercise of power.

Second, there is the principle that female and male qualities are complementary; rather than covering the same spheres, they advantageously and, somehow, miraculously balance out. Third, there is the different base/superstructure notion of progress for women and men:

> Every feminine virtue implies a vice . . . women unfortunately are women, and their ideal is attained by rising above themselves . . . On the other hand, men are not men without effort and their ideal condition is attained by their becoming, and (with luck) remaining, simply men. (Ellmann, 1979, pp. 66–68)

Defective woman to supersexual ideal, versus subsexual male to proper sexual male, in 23 chapters.

Finally, Ellmann, unlike the social psychologist of gender, notes the fluidity of modern stereotypes, so that while the ascription of sex differences remains constant, the perceived content and evaluation varies widely. ('It is impossible for women to believe so much about themselves', 1979, p. 59). As argued in the last section, femininity and masculinity appear (it seems in fiction too) as highly unstable, contradictory states. The creation of difference and the organization of material which this allows, is the central achievement, even though the sense of the categorization may vary widely. A broader deconstruction of the mechanisms of gender labelling, following on from feminist critics' treatment of literature, must help the understanding of this process.

Feminist critics, besides their interest in the transmission of images of women, have principally sought to analyse the social position of the female author, and female experience, as a basis for writing. Novels written by women and subsequently displaced or forgotten have been rescued and re-evaluated. Attempts have been made to specify what has been seen as the unique and particular nature of women's writing style and the female literary tradition. Showalter (1982) has called this activity 'gynocritics' and sees it as combined with the 'androcentric criticism', illustrated by Ellmann and Millett's scholarly work, which deconstructs and reanalyses the presentation of women in the male literary tradition.

It is with the self-conscious development of androcentric and gynocentric criticism in feminist literary studies that the relevance to the social psychologist emerges. These activities immediately question the nature of sexual production and difference. Feminist literary critics cannot avoid deciding on the status, for instance, of the woman writer and reader, and the basis for the 'experience' or 'essential nature' she draws upon to produce or decode fiction. Different kinds of response have prevailed, but in some cases it seems clear that, as in social psychology, in deconstructing images of women, another image has often been privileged and left unexamined.

Gardiner (1981), for example, has claimed that the female psyche and social identity lead naturally to the choice of specific forms of literature (auto-biographical, fluid, escaping traditional narrative genres). We almost seem to be back again to 'oceanic' femininity, formless and tidal, but strangely at the same time personal and intimate. Other critics, (e.g. Burr-Evans, 1972) have asserted that women readers can learn unproblematically from women authors. Self-knowledge or 'the real experience of being a woman' follows from reading as though modern female authors were simply a more sophisticated version of the agony aunt.

Like Bem, these critics assume a common experience and essentially different psyche which separates women from men. It is on this basis that a female literary tradition has frequently been constructed. In the short term this has proved, as in psychology, to be no bad thing. In counterposing the dominance of male experience as the arbiter of taste with a feminine tradition, these critics reveal the contingency of male comment. What seemed a natural and obvious relation to the world, when contrasted with a different emphasis, can be seen as self-interested and exclusive. However, like the psychologist, the literary critic is still left with the problem of explicating the status of this feminine experience, confirmed or otherwise by texts, and with the suspicion that a woman-centred approach may ultimately fail to identify the reasons for the potency of textual images.

Culler puts this dilemma succinctly: 'Feminist readings,' he writes, 'are not produced by recording what happens in the mental life of the female reader as she encounters the words of *The Mayor of Casterbridge*' (1983, p. 49). That is, experience will not do as a ground for literary discovery, and, it is possible to add, if the reading is to be feminist or politically competent, just any woman's experience will not do either.

The difficulty with an appeal to experience, in particular a distinctively feminine experience, which female authors represent in their texts and which is recognized by the female reader as psychologically true, seems to be that the function of the text itself as a linguistic system or set of codes and patterns of signification becomes overlooked. Language is not a neutral reflection or representation of reality, it is *constitutive* of that typical experience, creating 'woman's nature', etc. As Furman (1980) puts it, in her argument for a genuinely textual feminism, the social and psychological significance of images cannot be sought in the personality behind the text which produces or reads it, but in the analysis of the language itself.

Literature becomes best viewed as a conglomeration of conventions for creating versions of reality. They are effective to the extent that the reader recognizes that reality as natural and unquestionable. The moment of recognizing 'a truth' about oneself in a novel (true because it appears to correspond with a current version of what one's experience was) should not, therefore, be the moment when analysis stops and knowledge is presumed to have been gained, but should become the starting point for another investigation of why that sense of recognition occurs in relation to the organization of the language itself, and the immediate questioning of the desirability of what has become 'obvious'.

It is in this sense that Coward (1980) has argued that properly feminist novels cannot be equated with just any woman-centred novel, or feminist criticism with the rescue of just any works based on women's experience. Not only, she argues, is there no common experience of womankind to refer to (otherwise how does one analyse the response of women of differing political orientations?) but many novels claiming to be based on archetypally female experience, (capable of 'changing women's lives' as their back covers maintain), have more in common with the narrative structures and expectations of that other class of 'woman-centred' novels, the popular romance.

A feminist criticism, according to its proponents, must thus be politically resonant, working effectively with a concept of ideology. Androcentric criticism must appreciate not only that women have been excluded and the images are unflattering, but also how entire structures of metaphor, unnoticed linguistic habits and genre demands have legitimated female marginality. Culler neatly draws this conclusion together by reproducing Showalter's argument. The feminist critic, Showalter notes, is concerned 'with the way in which the hypothesis of a female reader changes our apprehension of a given text, awakening us to the significance of sexual codes' (cited in Culler, 1983, p. 50). An integral activity, therefore, is investigating how the woman reader might have or could read 'as a man', endorsing and welcoming anti-female versions, and misogyny. Reading 'as a woman', becomes an acquired status, not a given one.

The position textual feminist literary criticism seems to have got to, then, is first, an emphasis on femininity/masculinity as shifting states, either in the encoding or decoding; and second, the view that these states are produced through language rather than being fundamentals which texts merely describe. This, incidentally, is what most distinguishes this approach from that taken by Bem and her contemporaries. Bem too sees femininity and masculinity as shifting, not necessarily linked to biological sex, but, as we saw, this displacement from physiology has not produced a social or political analysis of their function, only a retrenchment of individualism.

As a corollary to the two points above must go the recognition that human psychology and self-consciousness can no longer be seen as private, idiosyncratic realms, cut off from social relations. They are open to analysis through their material signs — the linguistic systems of which novels are simply one form. These systems subtly work to create and circulate a set of subject positions or identities which become the currency of human interaction and self-understanding.

As a logical extension of this frame of thought, recent feminist analyses have moved beyond the evaluation of 'great works' to the everyday: television programmes, advertisements and magazines (cf. Coward, 1984; Williamson, 1978; Winship, 1978). But how might the social psychology of gender become similarly feminist, and thus critical of, rather than subservient to, the social order? How might it become similarly sensitive to the organization and achievement of feminine and masculine subject positions in everyday speech, action and reaction?

THE SOCIO-PSYCHOLOGICAL STUDY OF 'FEMININITY' DISCOURSE

Although the argument cannot be developed extensively here, I want to suggest that through the concept of a 'linguistic repertoire' (cf. Potter and Mulkay, 1982; 1985; Potter and Litton, 1985) and the careful attention to discourse that this presumes, a progressive social psychology of gender might arise. This approach will necessarily assume that what is accessible for study, and thus its foundation, is the relatively autonomous ideological practices of a culture.

The function of an ideology is assumed here to be the elimination of the awareness of contradictions in material circumstances or perception of exploitation; mainly through the presentation of relationships (which seem important only for a particular kind of social arrangement) as natural or common sense. In this way sectional vested interests become general. In the case of gender, the analysis of ideology involves researching the construction of women as certain kinds of consumers, reproducers and agents/non-agents in the workforce (cf. Centre for Contemporary Cultural Studies, 1978): an outcome which requires the production of specifically 'female desires' (Coward, 1984) and 'appropriate' representations of ambition and place. This, then, is the frame of reference for our study of gender.

What, however, is meant by a linguistic repertoire? Within a cultural system, as Coward (1984), Winship (1978) and others have demonstrated, it is possible to identify meta-patterns or broad regularities in an ideology. For example, the pervading femininity/masculinity ideology has as a perennial feature the representation of male as norm and female as deviation, so that, to take one case, 'progress' for women (and for society as a whole) is viewed unproblematically and as occurring when women are able to incorporate more and more 'masculine' tasks and roles. There is much less impetus for men to incorporate 'feminine' tasks. Spender's (1980) 'plus male, minus female' phenomenon would count as another type of organizing principle. Linguistic repertoires are the substance which constitute these broad meta-themes. They may engage femininity/masculinity directly through concerns with motherhood, child rearing, sexuality, breadwinning, etc., or through various different subjects which may from time to time come to be specifically marked out separately for women or for men (e.g. Coward's, 1984, analysis of food pornography, ideal homes or 'our songs').

A repertoire consists of a set of recurrent and coherently related stylistic, grammatical and lexical features, including seminal metaphors and tropes or figures of speech. Just as one can point to the phonological, intonational and accent patterns that make up the distinctive 'voice' attributed to a particular social group, so one can also identify consistent linguistic patterns in terms of content and mode of explanation. People, we have noted, are familiar with a wide range of repertoires for a given topic and are quite capable of producing discrepant and contradictory versions. Flexibility and variability of this kind can be helpfully understood if the use of repertoires is related to functional differences in the contexts in which they are produced and in interactional goals. Repertoires can be characterized in terms of the guiding principle they elucidate and the identification of stylistic regularities: what is consistently omitted, for instance; the relation of subject to consequences; passive grammatical form, etc., define their boundaries.

A good illustration of the material discovered through this kind of discourse analysis can be found in a recent unpublished interview study conducted by Hilda Stiven (1985, in collaboration with myself and Jonathan Potter), which looked at female and male undergraduates' representations of children, careers, employment and achievement.

In general terms, first of all, Stiven found that whereas both women and men students were what is usually described as 'career orientated', for women this vision of their future could only be sustained for a limited time. Their image of themselves in their 30s/40s, say, was comparatively blank and uncertain. There was some response, in other words, to the likely institutional barriers to come. However, unfortunately, the inadequate set of repertoires available to most respondents to make sense of their working lives would only admit individual solutions. For example, for some women happiness came from 'just being a housewife'; for others such domesticity was not a positive state of affairs but individual circumstances made it the only 'practical' outcome; alternatively, still other women might become, through their own efforts and talents, 'superwomen', combining career and family. They would provide a demonstration for men that it was possible to be a woman and succeed as well. This demonstration was thought a necessary step before women as a whole could be taken seriously.

A great many of these women, that is, could only account for failure to achieve, or for the *status quo* for women, in terms of individual characteristics, or through instincts and a natural order which made domestic life inevitable and desirable. Their accounts, in fact, paralleled the traditional psychological analysis (Horner, 1972) which has it that women 'fear success' and this personality trait explains their low profile. In both cases explanations in terms of the structure and organization of society are obscured.

The particular repertoires which sustained this pattern fell into several categories. With regard to employment, for instance, a familiar repertoire was presented which has it that women are a problem for employers; or, adopting a phrase used by a number of respondents, they are 'a risk not worth taking'. The guiding principle here is that the employers' concerns are reasonable and the problem needs to be worked out by women within existing social structures. Through 'proving themselves equal' or 'being good at their job', women might persuade employers that they personally are a risk worth taking. The general impression gained from the interviews is that few of the women doubted their own ability to prove themselves as exceptions in this way; and perhaps as a result, if they fail to find an accommodating niche, they will be less likely to question the system within which they work, and more likely to attribute failure to contingent accidental factors.

This accounting system was generally combined with a repertoire concerning social change, which construes change and progress as natural and inevitable processes. The history of women, therefore, could be represented as a story of gradual improvement up to the present day. This repertoire has several functions. First, it legitimates a positive view of society, as willing to solve problems and slowly combatting injustice; it rules out the necessity for 'drastic steps', particularly feminist movements which might 'go too far'; it renders personal intervention or action unnecessary; and it maintains the view that even though social change is potentially disruptive and negative, it can be contained, accommodated and diffused through slow progress.

The most notable internal contradictions revealed by Stiven's research concerned the tension between 'equal opportunities' and 'practical necessities' repertoires. Briefly, equal opportunities to work, freedom of choice and mutual decision making were claimed by most to be desirable ideals and a *sine qua non* of good relationships between husband and wife. Nonetheless, it was also understood that practical necessities and the 'nature of things' would result in the woman taking the primary responsibility for child rearing and that her career would be subordinate to her partner's. The equal opportunities repertoire satisfied one function, allowing for one kind of self-presentation expounding the ideal, while appeal to what usually must be the case, or to unfortunate realities, recognized and contributed to the actual *status quo*. It is not suggested that this contradiction is cynically proposed by, say, the male respondents. On the contrary it is a more general feature of the organization of discourse about female/male, both repertoires are sincerely held and one equally sincerely regretted. However, the contradiction is rarely noted by respondents. Although difficult to substantiate without a more extensive exposition, it was a case where inconsistency in response could very obviously be related to interactional goals and the context.

Stiven's findings could be understood as exemplars of what Tajfel (cf. 1981) has called *status quo*, social mobility, and social change belief structures. Williams and Giles (1978), for example, have argued that, as for other oppressed groups, distinct sub-groups of women can be identified according to their choice of strategy or perception of their social identity. Thus some women accept the *status quo* as legitimate; others seek to move as individuals into the more valued group, separating themselves as different from other women and adopting 'masculine' styles and norms. This may be typified by accepting training to become assertive, for example. Yet others attempt to change the very basis on which evaluation of superiority/inferiority is based through actively promoting social change. Parts of the repertoires described above (and others which emerged) could be understood in these terms. (See also Chapter 6 for a fuller discussion of the intergroup relations perspective.)

However, one difficulty with this application, which immediately becomes apparent, arises from Williams and Giles' assumption that identity must be coherent and single so that their sub-groupings of women appear homogeneous and distinct. Stiven notes that many of her respondents showed mixtures and pieces of different repertoires, some of which appeared unambiguously *status quo* in orientation, others perhaps more reminiscent of a social mobility belief structure, and so on. Ultimately, they escaped easy categorization in terms of a global social identity.

This result highlights the very different model of the subject which would underlie a discourse approach to the study of gender. The unit of study is not the person but the linguistic repertoire or accounting system and its ideological implications. This emphasis allows us to make sense of diversity and contradictions in a manner prohibited by psychological analyses based on traits, biologies, or internalized sex role identities. We can respond to the variability and inconsistency evident in natural discourse which has in the past had to be repressed through a retreat to yes/no format questionnaires or strictly applied content analysis.

To the methodologist, this might seem a gain at the expense of the empirical certainty derived from neatly ordered response categories. However, it is normal practice with this type of discourse analysis (cf. Potter, 1985; Potter and Mulkay, 1982; Gilbert and Mulkay, 1984) to present the data or discourse on which any description of repertoires is based. This makes the process of interpretation manifest and allows for the reader to substantiate any disagreement. The method of construction is laid bare in a way not encountered in conventional presentation of results. It would, of course, also demonstrate the recurrent stylistic, grammatical and lexical features which distinguish repertoires and allow for their identification.

Finally, we should note that many of the repertoires identified through this kind of process will appear mundane and obvious. This is not surprising given that the aim is to examine the structure of everyday thought. But it is precisely at these points that society is reproduced and justified as people rationalize and make sense of their apparent place within it. By making the banal and commonsensical strange through analysis, it is possible to see in a new way something of how ideologies operate. This takes place at the level of individual understanding and explanation that social psychologists must consider their prime domain.

To summarize and conclude, the intention of this chapter has been to try and demonstrate why the socio-psychological study of gender is at an impasse. Social psychologists, it was suggested, have failed to capture the richness and subtlety of everyday conceptions of femininity and masculinity and, moreover, they have supported one kind of ideology in lieu of a critical examination. But, on a more positive note, it is clear that feminist literary critics have actively and productively confronted a similar dilemma about the definition and status of femininity. This debate clarifies the tools and emphases that a new social psychological approach might adopt and suggests that we can begin to learn from the upheavals and questionings in other disciplines. One thing is obvious: any new perspective such as the discourse analysis sketchily outlined in this section must be unavoidably political and thus in some way engaged with feminism.

REFERENCES

Abel, E. (ed.) (1982). *Writing and Sexual Difference*. Brighton, Harvester Press.
Adlam, D., Henriques, J., Rose, N., Salfield, A., Venn, C. and Walkerdine, V. (1977). Psychology, ideology and the human subject. *Ideology and Consciousness* 1, 5–56.
Bakan, P. (1966). *The Duality of Human Existence*. Chicago, Rand McNally.
Bardwick, J. (1971). *Psychology of Women: A Study of Bio-Cultural Conflicts*. New York, Harper & Row.
Bem, S. (1974). The measurement of psychological androgyny. *Journal of Consulting and Clinical Psychology* 42, 155–162.
Bem, S. (1975). Sex-role adaptability: One consequence of psychological androgyny. *Journal of Personality and Social Psychology* 31, 634–643.
Bem, S. (1976). Probing the promise of androgyny. In: A. G. Kaplan and J. P. Bean (eds), *Beyond Sex-Role Stereotypes*. Boston, Little, Brown and Co.
Bem, S. (1981). Gender schema theory: A cognitive account of sex-typing. *Psychological Review* 66, 354–364.
Bem, S. and Lenney, L. (1976). Sex-typing and the avoidance of cross-sex behaviour. *Journal of Personality and Social Psychology* 33, 48–54.

Bem, S., Martyna, W. and Watson, C. (1976). Sex-typing and androgyny: Further explorations of the expressive domain. *Journal of Personality and Social Psychology* **34**, 1016–1023.

Burr-Evans, N. (1972). The value and peril for women of reading women writers. In: S. K. Cornillon (ed.), *Images of Women in Fiction: Feminist Perspectives*. Bowling Green, Ohio, Bowling Green University Press.

Carlson, R. (1971). Sex differences in ego functioning: Exploratory studies of agency and communion. *Journal of Consulting and Clinical Psychology* **37**, 267–277.

Centre for Contemporary Cultural Studies. (1978). *Women Take Issue*. London, Hutchinson.

Clifton, A. K., McGrath, D. and Wick, B. (1976). Stereotypes of women: A single category? *Sex Roles* **2**, 135–148.

Coward, R. (1980). Are women's novels feminist novels? *Feminist Review* **5**, 53–65.

Coward, R. (1984). *Female Desire*. London, Paladin.

Coward, R. and Ellis, J. (1977). *Language and Materialism*. London, Routledge & Kegan Paul.

Culler, J. (1983). *On Deconstruction*. London, Routledge & Kegan Paul.

de Castillejo, I. (1973). *Knowing Woman: A Feminine Psychology*. London, Hodder and Stoughton.

Eichler, M. (1980). *The Double Standard*. New York, St. Martins Press.

Ellmann, M. (1979). *Thinking About Women*. London, Virago.

Furman, N. (1980). Textual feminism. In: S. McConnell-Ginet, R. Borker and N. Furman (eds), *Woman and Language in Literature and Society*. New York, Praeger.

Gardiner, J. K. (1982). On female identity and writing by women. In: E. Abel (ed.), *Writing and Sexual Difference*. Brighton, Harvester Press.

Gilbert, N. and Mulkay, M. (1984). *Opening Pandora's Box: A Sociological Analysis of Scientists' Discourse*. Cambridge, Cambridge University Press.

Heath, S. (1982). *The Sexual Fix*. London, MacMillan.

Henriques, J., Holloway, W., Urwin, C., Venn, C. and Walkerdine, V. (1984). *Changing The Subject*. London and New York, Methuen.

Horner, M. (1972). Toward an understanding of achievement-related conflicts in women. *Journal of Social Issues* **28**, 157–176.

Johnson, R. A. (1976). *She: Understanding Feminine Psychology*. New York, Harper & Row.

Johnston, E. (1985). The feminist challenge to psychology: sex-role stereotyping. Unpublished Manuscript, University of St Andrews, Scotland, UK.

Millett, K. (1969). *Sexual Politics*. London; Rupert Hart-Davis.

Parsons, T. and Bales, R. (eds) (1955). *Family, Socialisation and Interaction Process*. Glencoe, Illinois, Free Press.

Potter, J. (1985). Testability, flexibility: Kuhnian values in scientists' discourse concerning theory choice. *Philosophy of the Social Sciences* **14**, 303–330.

Potter, J. and Litton, I. (1985). Some problems underlying the theory of social representations. *British Journal of Social Psychology* **24**, 81–90.

Potter, J. and Mulkay, M. (1982). Making theory useful: Utility accounting in social psychologists' discourse. *Fundamenta Scientiae* **3**, 259–278.

Potter, J. and Mulkay, M. (1985). Scientists' interview talk. In: M. Brenner, J. Brown and D. Canter (eds), *The Research Interview: Uses and Approaches*. London, Academic Press.

Potter, J., Stringer, P. and Wetherell, M. (1984). *Social Texts and Context*. London, Routledge & Kegan Paul.

Showalter, E. (1982). Feminist criticism in the wilderness. In: E. Abel (ed.), *Writing and Sexual Difference*. Brighton, Harvester Press.

Smith, P. (1985). *Language, The Sexes and Society*. Oxford, Blackwell.

Spender, D. (1980). *Man-Made Language.* London, Routledge & Kegan Paul.

Stiven, H., Wetherell, M. and Potter, J. (1985). Women in employment: an analysis of social representations. Unpublished Manuscript, University of St. Andrews, Scotland, UK.

Tajfel, H. (1981). *Human Groups and Social Categories.* Cambridge, Cambridge University Press.

Williams, J. and Giles, H. (1978). The changing status of women in society: An intergroup perspective. In: H. Tajfel (ed.), *Differentiation Between Social Groups.* London, Academic Press.

Williamson, J. (1978). *Decoding Advertisements.* London, Boyars.

Winship, J. (1978). A woman's world: 'Woman' — an ideology of femininity. In: Centre for Contemporary Cultural Studies, *Women Take Issue.* London, Hutchinson.

Chapter 6

Sex Role Beliefs and 'Traditional' Women: Feminist and Intergroup Perspectives

Susan Condor

INTRODUCTION

Pioneering attempts to document 'the feminine mystique' (Friedan, 1963), 'patriarchal attitudes', (Firestone, 1970; Millett, 1970) and 'women's consciousness' (Rowbotham, 1973) established the analysis of social ideology as an essential aspect of feminist activity. Although contemporary theorists have largely rejected Friedan's (1963) original supposition that social representations of femininity actually constitute 'the problem', they continue to demonstrate concern over the subjective aspects of the sex role system, often borrowing Freudian perspectives on the development of self and social consciousness (see Sayers, 1982, and Chapter 2, this volume), and Althusserian premises concerning the relative autonomy of the ideological state apparatus (e.g. O'Brien, 1982). These concerns obviously correspond to social psychologists' enduring preoccupation with stereotypes (e.g. Miller, 1982), and attitudes (e.g. Cooper and Croyle, 1984). It is, therefore, hardly surprising that the academic union between the women's movement and social psychology has proven a fecund source of research into 'sex stereotypes' and 'sex role attitudes' (see, e.g. Ashmore and Del Boca, 1979; Deaux, 1985; Wetherell, Chapter 5, this volume).

In this chapter I will be examining the actual and potential impact of feminism on social psychological analyses of sex role related beliefs, focussing in particular on the opinions and attitudes of non-feminist ('traditional') women. I will be using the term 'traditional' simply to refer to women who do not wish for change in the sex role *status quo* (cf. Fowler *et al.*, 1973). The term 'feminist' will be used in a similarly broad sense—simply to denote ideas and actions directed towards ending female social subordination. I will argue that although current social psychological formulations owe much to the premises of feminism *as a* belief-system (considering women as a low status social group and emphasizing the deleterious effects of traditional stereotypes and role attitudes), the potential contribution of a feminist perspectives *on* social beliefs (emphasizing the need to understand women's subjective experience in their own terms) has yet to be optimized.

SOCIAL PSYCHOLOGICAL CHARACTERIZATION OF TRADITIONAL WOMEN: THE IMPACT OF FEMINISM

The issue of sex role attitudes was originally broached by social psychologists as a corollary to their interest in racial prejudice. The suggestion that the psychological processes underlying a predisposition to antisemitism would also involve elements of misogyny (Adorno *et al.*, 1950) inspired some early research into the personality correlates of sex role related beliefs (e.g. Allen, 1954; Nadler and Morrow, 1959). Remnants of this perspective are still apparent in research which attempts to relate sex role attitudes to authoritarian or dogmatic personality structures (Bowker, 1981; Sarup, 1976; Whitehead and Tawes, 1976), and to examine the correlation between sex role beliefs and attitudes towards racial groups (Woudenberg, 1977). Social psychologists' present interest in sex role related attitudes and stereotypes is, however, largely attributable to the development of feminist concerns in the social sciences (see Ashmore and Del Boca, 1981; Beere, 1979).

The women's movement may be seen not only to have influenced the popularity of sex stereotypes and role attitudes as a subject of research, but also to have affected the way in which these topics are discussed in the social psychological literature. In the following pages I will be concentrating on social psychological approaches to the attitudes and beliefs of women who generally support existing sex role arrangements. From the perspective of feminism, women are regarded as a low status social group and 'traditional' images of the characteristics and roles appropriate to men and women are regarded as forms of 'ideology' (Keohane *et al.*, 1982) underlying and reinforcing female social subordination. Social imagery which ultimately serves the male purpose (e.g. Bernard, 1978; Figes, 1970; Millett, 1970), is seen to have become generalized, with the consequence that 'women [like] other objectified groups define their own realities through the perspective of their oppressors' (Brittan and Maynard, 1984, p. 204). Women who accept the *status quo* are hence sometimes seen to be suffering from a form of 'false' consciousness, (cf. e.g. Barrett, 1980; Spender, 1985).

These premises may be seen to have influenced social psychological theory and research in three ways. The first of these is an awareness of the way in which psychological theories may themselves constitute part of the patriarchal 'superstructure' (e.g. Weisstein, 1973). This has led to some now well accepted theoretical reformulations; for example, questioning the biological determination of sex roles (e.g. Mednick and Tangri, 1972), or the association of 'appropriate' sex typing with mental health (Bem, 1974; Kaplan and Bean, 1976).

Second, feminist ideas have influenced how social psychologists interpret the attitudes and stereotypes held by their 'subjects'. With the development of feminist perspectives, social psychologists came to regard established sex roles as constituting a 'social problem' similar in some respects to racial discrimination, with the consequence that indications of change in popular beliefs about the sexes are considered optimistic (e.g. Petro and Putnam, 1979), and programmes have been designed to accelerate the process of attitude change (e.g. Kilmann and Auerbach, 1974). One theoretical consequence of feminism has been the (often implicit) tendency to consider sex role attitudes in terms of models of intergroup relations (Condor, 1983). The impact of feminist perspectives on social psychological approaches to sex role traditionalism is perhaps most explicit when women are discussed as a 'minority' group (e.g. Bird, 1970; R. J. Dworkin, 1976; Kalmuss et al., 1981; Williams and Giles, 1978; cf. Hacker, 1951; Myrdal, 1944). In this, the influence of feminism has not generally extended to the development of new theoretical perspectives, but rather has led social psychologists to adopt theory and research methodology already developed in the field of race relations. It is suggested that women, like other low status social groups, may fail to display the 'norm' of ethnocentrism (Williams and Giles, 1978; cf. Sumner, 1909), but may rather 'identify with the aggressor' (Hacker, 1951; cf. Allport, 1954), sharing with men negative stereotypes of their own sex (Rosenkrantz et al., 1968), and displaying 'prejudice' toward other women (Goldberg, 1968).

The third way in which social psychological analyses have been influenced by the women's movement is in the use of feminist premises as a basis for speculation. I will be arguing later in this chapter that much of the 'data' interpreted as illustrating 'group self-hatred' or 'false consciousness' on the part of traditional women may represent a product of research methodology rather than a valid description of the way in which women actually perceive the sexes. For the moment we may note how social psychologists have speculated on the debilitating consequences of sex role traditionalism for women's identities (see, e.g. Whitehurst, 1979). Following the common assumption that, 'self hatred and feelings of worthlessness tend to arise from membership in underprivileged or outcast groups' (Cartwright, 1950, p. 440), it is suggested that negative social images of women will lead women to suffer negative *self-images*:

> Women, like—in some cases—Blacks and other ethnic minorities, have internalized the 'inferiority' of their group into a kind of 'self-hate' phenomenon. (Williams and Giles, 1978, p. 431)

In line with the suggestion that 'minority group' movements may result in new, more favourable, identities for members of historically oppressed groups (see, e.g. Tajfel, 1978a,b), it is suggested that developing feminist perspectives will bring in their wake new, more positive, self-imagery for women:

> Self-esteem and self-confidence are characteristics that one might expect to be associated with women's nontraditional goals and attitudes, since traditional 'feminine' personality is devalued in our culture. (Zuckerman, 1980, p. 150)

There is, however, no consistent evidence that women have generally lower measured self-regard than men (see, e.g. Wylie, 1979), nor that sex role attitudes covary with self-esteem (e.g. Albright and Chang, 1976). Apart from these empirical considerations, the suggestion that women's identity problems may be resolved by the development of feminist consciousness on the part of the individual clearly reflects an adherence to the idea that stereotypes and attitudes are, themselves, 'the problem'.

It seems likely that one reason why these representations of pre-feminist womanhood have been accepted so readily is due to their correspondence with existing theory, not only concerning 'minority groups' in general, but also concerning the nature of womanhood. Psychologists have long suggested that women may be negatively disposed towards their own sex (see Epstein, 1980) and to themselves as women (see, e.g. Tauer's 1979 discussion on Freudian theory) and may hence suffer from problems in identifying with their sex (Lynn, 1961). The distinctive aspect of the new 'feminist' perspective lies not so much in a critical re-examination of the existing literature as in the promise of the liberating effects of widespread attitude change.

Although social psychological approaches to sex role attitudes may thus be seen to have been influenced by feminist views, it is important to note that feminism not only constitutes a form of social consciousness but has also developed a *theory* of social consciousness. Perhaps the most influential aspect of the developing feminist perspectives *on* social beliefs has been the opposition to attempts to objectify experience, in particular demanding that women be understood in their own terms (e.g. Stanley and Wise, 1983), with a consequent emphasis on qualitative research methodology (e.g. Mies, 1983). In line with recent attacks on the concept of ideological hegemony in both Marxist and sociological theory (e.g. Abercrombie *et al.*, 1980), feminists stress how the social world may be regarded in different ways by different perceivers (e.g. Spender, 1980), in particular emphasizing the distinction between male and female experiential 'worlds' or 'cultures' (e.g. Bernard, 1978; Stockard and Dougherty, 1983). The feminist analysis does not stop with the assertion of the relativity of social perception, but also raises the issue of the role of power in determining the codification of social knowledge. In particular, it is argued that whereas both men and women may be able to construct sex-distinctive meanings or 'truths', the ability to represent these in linguistic forms remains the perogative of dominant social groups, with the consequence that language tends to embody the experience of men rather than women (Spender, 1980). Social theorists have long argued that members of low status social groups may be capable of perceiving the same world in more than one way. Gramsci (1971, p. 33), for example, speaks of the 'two theoretical consciousness' of the worker, 'one which is implicit in his [sic] activity . . . and one, superficially explicit or verbal, which he [sic] has inherited from the past and uncritically absorbed'. Similarly, feminists suggest that women may possess 'double consciousnesses', sharing a distinctive world-view whilst simultaneously recognizing the world as presented to them by the dominant male culture (e.g. du Bois, 1983; see also Itzin, Chapter 7, this volume). Men, in contrast, are seen to be more likely to perceive a 'monodimensional reality', failing to recognize the existence of alternative *weltanschauung* (Spender, 1980).

Whilst social psychological formulations concerning sex role related beliefs may have been influenced by feminism *as* a belief-system, the implications of a feminist perspective *on* social beliefs remain almost unexplored. Despite Friedan's (1963) pioneering efforts to study women's attitudes by qualitative methodology and subjective interpretation, social psychological research has tended to adopt existing theoretical formulations and methodological procedures associated with intergroup attitude research (see Beere, 1979), leading to an emphasis on the construction of scales to measure individual differences in valency and strength of 'attitudes toward women' (Spence and Helmreich, 1972); 'sex role ideology' (Kalin and Tilby, 1978); 'feminism' (Dempewolff, 1974); or 'sex role orientation' (Brogan and Kutner, 1976; see also Condor & Brown, in press, for a similar discussion with respect to the intergroup literature). Although social psychologists often use factor analytical techniques in an attempt to analyse the multi-dimensional nature of sex role related beliefs (e.g. Adamec and Graham, 1978; MacDonald, 1974), the comparison of the responses of different individuals to the same scale illustrates a commitment to the concept of an 'attitude universe' in which social perception differs quantitatively rather than qualitatively. Factor analysis is also based on the assumption of within-subject 'consistency', and hence overlooks the possibility of 'double consciousness', as, indeed, does the concern over establishing 'reliability' in attitude scale construction and stable 'individual differences' in response to these scales.[1]

The possibility that social psychological research may have failed to reach an adequate understanding of the experience of non-feminist women occurred to me when conducting pilot research for a study on female identity (Condor and Abrams, 1984) in which I asked some women to 'talk through' some existing psychometric instruments. It became apparent that many of the women who did not wish for widespread change in sex role definitions were experiencing difficulties answering the sex role attitude scale (the AWS; Spence and Helmreich, 1972). Several women became quite aggressive, claiming that the questions were unanswerable. Others who placed their answers towards the 'appropriate' poles of the dimensions provided appeared to feel the need to qualify their responses; in fact, women who scored towards the 'conservative' pole of the AWS were nearly three times as likely to qualify their responses as were the women who scored towards the 'liberal' pole.

A review of the literature (Condor, 1983) suggested that, in their haste to produce prestigious 'hard' data (cf. Bernard, 1973), researchers have largely overlooked the need for documentary research concerning the nature of those sex role beliefs which individuals may hold more or less strongly. In particular, remarkably little interest has been shown in the qualitative nature of attitudes supporting the sex role *status quo*. Social psychologists often concentrate on the extent to which individuals accept 'feminist' beliefs (e.g. Dempewolff, 1974; Smith *et al.*, 1975; Welch, 1975), and even when constructing scales supposedly reflecting both feminist and non-feminist positions, the original item pool has seldom been based on the responses of 'traditional' women. In particular, several well known scales — including the AWS — have been based wholly or partly on Kirkpatrick's (1936) Attitudes Towards Feminism scale, the items of which were drawn from the resolutions of feminist organizations. Taking this observation together with the common use of feminist 'known groups' in validating attitude scales (e.g. Kilpatrick and Smith, 1974), it appears that traditional attitudes have been defined largely by default; simply as a disagreement with the stated aims of the women's movement, or as statements which feminists do not endorse.

In the following pages I will present a qualitative account of women's sex role traditionalism, based largely on the results of an open-ended questionnaire survey conducted in Bristol in 1982 (Condor, 1984). In this I will concentrate on the responses of 77 women who described themselves as supporting 'the existing roles of men and women' (whom I will refer to as 'traditional' women), although I will also refer to the responses of the 39 women who expressed a desire for a change in sex role definitions, for comparison purposes.[2]

WOMEN'S SEX ROLE TRADITIONALISM: A QUALITATIVE ACCOUNT

As a form of 'contraculture' (cf. Yinger, 1960), feminism might be defined in contrast to traditional social arrangements and the ideological forms supporting them. However, it need not follow that individuals who support the *status quo* articulate this in opposition to feminism.[3] Social psychological research has, however, often been based on the assumption that traditionalism may be regarded as the logical antithesis of feminism or liberalism: 'sex role ideology [is] conceived as a system of sex role beliefs forming a dimension with a traditional and a feminist pole' (Kalin and Tilby, 1978, p. 731). Even when not stated explicitly, the use of 'Likert type' summated rating scales implies that traditional beliefs may be simply conceptualized as 'less than' liberal attitudes. Such suppositions obviously conflict with feminist formulations which stress qualitative distinctions between forms of social consciousness, and with the personal experience of many feminists whose own sex role 'attitude change' was experienced in terms of a subjective paradigm shift (the so-called 'click' phenomenon, Bernard, 1975) rather than an increasing liberalization of their existing beliefs.

A particular distinction between the perspectives of the traditional and non-traditional women who answered my open-ended questionnaire was apparent in the extent to which they regarded men and women as comparable social groups. Non-traditional women tended to compare the sexes spontaneously, particularly in terms of economic factors, (fourteen (36%) of the non-traditional women compared the sexes in terms of economic factors, as compared with nine (12%) of the traditional women); and of social prestige, (twenty-five (63%) of the non-traditional women, as compared with fourteen (17%) of the traditional women). Traditional women were more likely to describe the male–female social dichotomy in terms of 'complementarity' (a concept which many of the respondents used spontaneously) and being interdependence:

> Men and women have different roles to play, society needs both and one is incomplete without the other.

> I feel that both sexes should be equal but realize that their equality stems from the balance of their different qualities.

> Men should dress and behave like men and women like women. That way they can complement each other instead of competing with each other.

If we are to understand traditional women's beliefs in their own terms, it may be preferable to regard this communal perspective on male–female relations as *qualitatively* distinct from the agentic perspective apparent in the responses of the non-traditional women, and characteristic of feminism, in which men and women are compared on like dimensions.

The assumption that traditionalism may be conceived as the opposite of feminism may have encouraged the tendency noted earlier for social psychologists to interpret traditionalism from the perspective of feminism. Thus, for example, it has been suggested that since feminists regard the subordination of women as unjust, traditional women accept their inferiority as legitimate (e.g. Williams and Giles, 1978). However, since traditional women may fail to compare the sexes on sociological dimensions, they may not *recognize* the existence of status and power differences between the sexes. Even in response to the direct question: 'Who do you think are respected more in society, men or women?', forty-nine (63%) of the traditional women failed to answer or replied that they did not know, and thirteen (13%) perceived their own sex to be the more highly respected. In contrast, only six (14%) of the non-traditional women failed to answer this question, and none of them suggested that females are more highly respected than males. Such findings are, of course, consistent with feminist analyses which have long suggested how traditional ideological systems may be 'sex blind' (Firestone, 1970) and prevent women from recognizing how their sex constitutes a social or economic 'interest group' (Hole and Levine, 1971; Kahn, 1976). It is, of course, only recently that *social scientists* have regarded males and females as distinct, comparable, sociological categories! (Bell and Newby, 1976; Delphy, 1981).

Regarding women's traditional attitudes within their own terms of reference may be particularly important if we are to appreciate the value associated with sex roles and stereotypes. Since feminism is concerned with the 'liberation' of women from family and domestic roles, traditionalism has, in contrast, been characterized as 'relegat[ing] women to the roles of housewife and mother' (Kalin and Tilby, 1978, p. 732). The image of traditionalism as restrictive is often reflected in attitude scale items, for instance, it is notable that the 'conservative' statements in Parry's (1983) modified version of the shortform AWS for British samples generally emphasize those things which women either *cannot* or *should not* do, behaviourally ('It is all right for men to tell dirty jokes, but I don't think women should tell them') or outside the home ('Women should not be bosses in important jobs in business and industry'). More generally, opinion statements which supposedly reflect traditional orientations tend to focus on the inability of women to perform male roles, or to hold powerful positions outside the home. For example, 13 of the 18 'traditional' items in Brogan and Kutner's (1976) SRO scale are concerned with 'career', as are 11 of the 17 items on Mason's and Bumpass's (1975) SRI scale.

It appears that a concentration on the way in which traditional sex roles restrict women's participation in the political and economic 'world of men' may reflect the interests of men and the concerns of liberal feminism rather than the preoccupations of traditional women. Rather than regarding their sex as inadequate, or unable to succeed in 'men's' roles, the traditional women who took part in my study appeared to regard the roles allocated to women as generally preferable to those allocated to men, and tended to express their support of the *status quo* from the perspective of the 'world of women', focussing on what women *can* and *should* do:

> Women should certainly have the same chance to 'do their own thing' as men, but they miss out on so much if they try to be like men in all ways.
>
> Disband women's lib. and the whole stupid concept of women's lib. It is time that women had some pride in themselves and got on with being women. Who wants to be 'equal' with men when we have it so much better?

If anything, it was men's roles which were regarded as restrictive. More than half ($n=43$; 56%) of the traditional respondents at some stage mentioned what they regarded as the limitations associated with men's roles, in particular, the pressures associated with breadwinning ($n=27$; 34%); lack of chivalrous attentions ($n=18$; 22%) and missing the fulfillment of motherhood ($n=29$; 37%). In contrast, less than a fifth ($n=7$; 18%) of women who expressed a desire for change in sex role definitions spontaneously alluded to the limiting aspects of the male role.

It was interesting that women who supported existing sex roles did not necessarily reject social change on all levels—nearly all the 'traditional' women ($n = 69$; 89%) articulated some support of 'women's rights' to equal pay, education and employment. This may reflect a general trend towards the liberalization of social norms (Deaux, 1985), perhaps indicating a 'new sexism' similar to the 'new racism' (Barker, 1981). However, it was notable that traditional women tended to regard 'liberation' as desirable only to the extent that a woman could be regarded as *an individual*:

> I think that a woman's place is in the home, if she has children, until they are 16. Then, if she wants to take up a career good luck to her. If she has no children she can be quite as capable of holding the same position as a man, and should have the same opportunities to do so.

> I feel very strongly that if more mothers stayed at home to look after their families, there would be a lot less juvenile crime. But it is obvious that if a woman is a career woman she should be allowed the same opportunities as men.

> I feel that women who perhaps have no instinct to be a homemaker should be able to pursue a chosen occupation without prejudice.

It was noted earlier how social psychologists often regard pre-feminist women as holding negative attitudes towards their own sex and hence themselves as women. However, when allowed to describe the sexes in their own terms, rather than displaying evidence of 'group self-hatred', traditional women tended to express a very positive attitude towards their own sex. Those women who expressed a wish for social change tended to evaluate the sexes equally (only seven (18%) of the non-traditional women spontaneously expressed evaluative favouritism for their own sex). In contrast, more than a third (thirty; 39%) of the traditional women stated a preference for women over men ('women are, on the whole, more civilized than men'; 'women have more of a sense of responsibility than men'). In particular, these women demonstrated a positive attitude towards traditionally defined 'feminine' characteristics:

> I would like to see women develop their feminine attributes, within them is security and strength.

> Women have intuitive strengths partly associated with their traditional roles of wives and mothers and it will be sad if these are diminished in the search for material advantage. We in the west lay too much stress on materialism, work, power, aggression, and not enough on spiritual values in the widest sense. It would be good to see more men shift towards women's caring, feeling, intuitive attitudes so there is an acceptance of our common humanity and peaceful co-existence throughout the world.

The observation that women may *value* the characteristics associated stereotypically with their sex is, of course, consistent with recent research which has questioned the established assumption that the feminine stereotype may be regarded as evaluatively negative (e.g. Ashmore, 1981; Williams and Best, 1977). The roles and characteristics traditionally associated with women may, of course, be regarded as essentially misogynous *from the perspective of feminism* which recognizes their role in excluding women from the 'world of men' and thereby maintaining an inequitable social system. However, the fact that, to feminists, traditional attitudes and 'woman-hating' are

> . . . empirical synonyms, inseparable, often indistinguishable, often interchangeable; and any acceptance of the exploitation of women in any area, for any reason, in any style, is both, means both and promotes both (A. Dworkin, 1983, p. 198)

should not mislead us into assuming that women who do not wish for change in established sex roles are necessarily unfavourably disposed towards their own sex.[4]

It was also interesting that the 'traditional' women articulated a high level of antipathy towards men and 'male' characteristics. The general image that I received was that of men as alien intruders, threatening to sully the hygenic, harmonious world of feminine concerns. The most common themes mentioned when describing the male sex were physical or psychological 'dirt' ($n = 18$; 23%), aggression, ($n = 24$; 31%) and immaturity ($n = 16$; 20%), and many women suggested that men ought to develop feminine qualities:

> [Men should be more like women . . .] in sensitivity, gentleness, not so independent and unfeeling . . .

> Men shouldn't be so concerned with winning and beating other people. They should try to learn something about tenderness and caring for others from their mothers and wives.

However, it was notable that many of the respondents excluded the male members of their own family from their description of 'men in general':

> Men like my husband and sons who are courteous and caring seem to be in the minority.

> When I consider my father and now my sons, it is quite clear that many men can be caring. It is a mother's duty to develop these qualities in her sons.

Hence, it appeared that the women who took part in this study regarded men as a category very negatively, but saw their own men as 'tame' (or, possibly, 'tamed' by feminine influence).

To borrow the terminology of the intergroup relations literature, it appears that women who support existing sex roles tend to differentiate between the sexes in favour of their own group, hence demonstrating 'ingroup favouritism' (e.g. Tajfel, 1978a) rather than 'group self-hatred'.[5] However, although it is tempting to suggest that it is this perceived favourability of the female sex role and stereotypic personality characteristics which lies behind traditional women's acquiescence with a social system which acts against their 'objective' interests (cf. e.g. van Knippenberg, 1984), it is also possible to sense an element of fear of undertaking the roles traditionally associated with men. To liberal social psychologists, undertaking a 'career' may appear a valued responsibility, source of income and potential arena for self-actualization (e.g. Chaftez, 1974). To many women the responsibility of wage 'earning' may appear merely a potential source of additional pressure and oppression.

The possibility that traditional sex roles and stereotypes may be regarded as favouring women leads to interesting questions concerning the 'negative identity' often imputed to non-feminist women by social psychologists. In suggesting that traditional women may perceive their sex favourably, I do not wish to deny that women often experience severe identity problems. It may well be that the positive evaluation of their sex as an abstract category may allow women to experience their womanhood as a positive 'political' or social (cf. Turner, 1982) identity, whilst this very over-idealization of women in general (together, perhaps, with a recognition of an alternative perspective on the part of their male significant others), may encourage women experience themselves, as individuals, to be failures. The phenomenon which Friedan (1963, p. 9) described as the 'strange discrepancy between the reality of our lives as women and the image to which we [are] trying to conform' was apparent in the responses of many of the women. It appeared that women's 'political' attitudes supporting female dependency in general were relatively unaffected by their own personal experience. For example, one young housewife expressed great dissatisfaction with her own life. She had been hospitalized for depression, and felt confined by her mothering role, being tied to the house with little adult company. Her husband refused her money for books and would not allow her to travel from the small village in which they lived to Bristol to meet friends or to attend evening classes. However, in failing to generalize from her particular experience to beliefs about women in general, this woman was simultaneously able to value women's traditionally defined role:

> In making women a better place in society we are in danger of throwing out a lot of the good things. There is a difference and long may it vive [sic].

In summary, it appears that, in adopting the perspective of feminism *as* a belief-system, social psychologists have incorporated into their theory and methodology certain assumptions concerning the nature of sex role traditionalism; for example, that it is somehow the 'opposite' of feminism, supporting the continuation of female subordination and hence, by fiat, reflecting prejudicial attitudes on the part of women against their own sex. On the basis of my, albeit speculative, discussion of my qualitative data, I would argue that whilst these suppositions may be 'true' in their own terms, to the extent that it is suggested that they characterize the way in which non-feminist women actually perceive the sexes, this constitutes an unwarranted objectification. Obviously, I would not wish to suggest that the responses of my small sample of 'traditional' women should be considered representative of female sex role traditionalism more generally. However, regarding the responses of this particular group of women in their own terms does indicate how the adoption of feminism as a belief-system may have, paradoxically, worked against the development of a feminist perspective in social psychological analyses *on* sex role attitudes. In the final section of this chapter I will attempt to outline briefly some of the implications that a development of a feminist perspective on social beliefs might have for our understanding of sex role traditionalism in particular, and social attitudes in general.

TOWARDS A FEMINIST PERSPECTIVE ON SEX ROLE ATTITUDES

On the basis of the preceding discussion, it is possible to outline a number of ways in which a feminist perspective might be distinguished from established social psychological attitude research. It should be noted that although my discussion has constituted something of a critique of social psychological analyses which consider women's sex role attitudes within the framework of existing models of intergroup perception, it is important to stress that a feminist perspective of sex role representations and attitudes would necessarily incorporate a model of men and women as (high and low status) social groups. I would, however, anticipate that a feminist approach to sex role related beliefs would differ from most existing social psychological analyses of intergroup attitudes in being based on the perspective of a subordinate rather than the dominant social group (cf. Zavalloni, 1973).

It seems likely that social scientific interest in the 'dominant ideology' (in sociology) and 'attitude universals' (in psychology) themselves represent what Spender (1980) terms the 'tunnel vision' of dominant social groups. As a perspective developed by members of a subordinate group, a feminist approach might, in contrast, reduce the emphasis on a hierarchical view of individuals in terms of acceptance of 'attitude universals', in favour of an increased consideration of social beliefs in terms of, possibly, 'incommensurable' paradigms (cf. Kuhn, 1962). A feminist perspective might also counter the current emphasis on measuring a single 'reliable' attitudinal position characterizing a particular individual in favour of an increased consideration of the concept of 'double consciousness'. This would demand a greater commitment to qualitative research research methodology, since simple quantitative measures of 'strength' of attitude generally reflect an attempt to 'reduce the diversity of human experience and the creativity of human meaning to one solitary sediment' (cf. Spender, 1983, p. 29).

Most social psychological analyses of intergroup representations fail to consider adequately the issue of power relations determining the formation and use of intergroup imagery in particular social contexts (Condor and Brown, in press), a perspective which might, again, be attributed to the fact that social psychology tends to be written by members of dominant social groups (cf. Deschamps, 1982). A major problem facing an attempt to develop a feminist perspective on social beliefs is that of incorporating feminist premises concerning the power discrepancies between the sexes without necessarily reifying these in the consciousness of others. I will argue that one consequence of the development of a feminist perspective towards social beliefs would be the need for social psychologists to recognize the distinction between the experienced knowledge of the 'subject' and codified knowledge (such as that presented in standard attitude scale items and the adjectives provided on stereotype adjective check-lists). Attitude scaling procedures were originally developed on the assumption that unobservable cognitive and emotional states of an individual may be measured by agreement or disagreement with verbal belief statements (e.g. Thurstone, 1931). However, it is important to note that since attitude scale items are *statements* they thus, presumably, share the characteristics of linguistic forms in society generally, which, as feminist linguists inform us (Spender, 1980), tend to reflect the meanings of men rather than women. On the basis of the earlier discussion, I would suggest that many existing sex role attitude scales have been codified from the perspective of equal rights 'feminism', which often adopts male standards (Duelli Klein, 1983). This would explain why the 'traditional' women in my pilot study felt the need to qualify their responses to the AWS. Since the English language has been constructed to embrace male meanings, women may find it easier to express their ideas conversationally (e.g. Ardener, 1975). Standard attitude scale statements, and stereotype adjective lists are, of course, not negotiable. However, the possibility of multiple sex role consciousnesses (including an awareness of sex roles as presented via the media, 'male' linguistic forms, the beliefs of significant others etc.), may mean that many women are able to fill in a quantitative attitude scale 'appropriately' whilst simultaneously aware, maybe on an ill-articulated level, that these statements only partially reflect their own opinions.

Regarding sex role opinion statements as a form of codified knowledge (rather than a 'pure' reflection of underlying psychological states) has interesting implications for what is often regarded as the 'basic' presupposition of attitude research, namely that evaluative orientations towards a social object or event may be inferred reliably from opinion statements (Thurstone, 1931) or measures of 'belief strength' (see Fishbein and Ajzen, 1975; but cf. e.g. Brogan and Kutner, 1976; Likert, 1932).[6]

The problems associated with attempting to deduce attitudes to social change from belief statements are well illustrated by the difficulties which may arise in trying to distinguish between 'traditional' and 'feminist' women on the basis of statements of opinion. The statements made by traditional women quoted above are often echoed in the early 'radical feminist' literature:

> We are proud of the female culture of emotion, intuition, love, personal
> relationships etc as the most essential human characteristics (Burris, 1973,
> p. 355)

and by 'second wave' feminist activists (cf. Eisenstein, 1984):

> The nuclear holocaust can only be averted by making men abandon their
> aggressive posturings and instead develop the emotional, 'caring' nurturing
> qualities which are usually labelled 'feminine' and, therefore, 'inferior'.
> (Riddel, 1982, p. 19)

In consequence, many attitude scale items supposedly indicative of traditionalism
might well be articulated by women who wish for social change:

> Aggression is naturally a male characteristic. (Kirsch *et al.*, 1976)

> A love for competing and winning is basically a male trait, even though some
> women may possess it. (Villemez and Touhey, 1977)

This correspondence is not only attributable to the fact that feminism genuinely
embodies aspects of 'female consciousness' (Kaplan, 1982), but also the fact that,
acknowledging the power of dominant groups to define and label reality, feminists
often consciously adopt the images and rhetoric of traditionalism in order to
promote their own ends: 'ideological weapons that men use against women can
be turned around and used as a collective means of self-affirmation against men'
(Jassen-Jurreit, 1982, p. 318). Such considerations emphasize the need to go
beyond the usual procedure of regarding opinion statements as indicators of
subjective 'attitude', to a consideration of them as aspects of rhetoric which cannot
be fully understood apart from the context in which they are articulated.

   In the earlier discussion I suggested that the attitudes of traditional women may
have been misrepresented partly because traditionalism has been identified as a
'male' perspective. This, of course, begs the question of whether there may be a
distinctively 'female' form of traditionalism. Although feminists often suggest that
there may be a qualitative distinction between the experiential 'worlds' of women
and men, very little research has compared the attitudes of the sexes qualitatively.
Most existing sex role attitude scales are intended for use by both males and females
(see Beere, 1979), and numerous investigations have established that women, on
average, tend to display quantitatively more liberal attitudes than their male
contemporaries (e.g. Albright and Chang, 1976; Spence and Helmreich, 1978).
Since in my qualitative study I was aiming to reach an understanding of women in
their own terms, I did not attempt to approach potential male respondents.
However, I did distribute some questionnaires to men (most of whom were work
colleagues or husbands of the women whom I questioned). It was notable that *all* of
these men ($n = 27$) at some stage used gender stereotypes or traditional sex role
prescriptions to express a negative evaluation of women's characteristics and roles:

Women are too emotional. Some are OK, but most you can't rely on. You can usually trust a man.

It's only natural for women to want to look after babys [*sic*] and the home etc. After all, they're not likely to be much good working on a building site or in a garage. There are lots of jobs that women just aren't [*sic*] suited to.

It is interesting to note the correspondence between such statements and the way in which sex role traditionalism is often encoded in social psychological attitude scales.

Again, we should be aware that the meaning of adjectives and belief statements cannot be understood apart from the wider context in which they are articulated (e.g. Asch, 1952; Merton, 1957). It is possible that even when men and women display the same measured 'level' of sex role traditionalism and articulate what, on the surface, appear to be very similar stereotypes and sex role prescriptions, these may, in fact, imply very different things to the people who hold them. It may be the case that whereas men may use traditional sex role stereotypes to articulate misogyny and a positive evaluation of the 'world of men', women, denied the ability to express their beliefs in their own terms, may use the same rhetoric to express ingroup favouritism towards their sex and the 'world of women'. As Rosaldo (1974, p. 39) concluded on the basis of her anthropological evidence, 'the very symbolic and social conceptions which appear to set women apart and to circumscribe their activities may be used by women as a basis for female solidarity and worth'.

Of course, it is the case that valued images of female roles and characteristics may be imposed on women by dominant groups in order to encourage their acquiescence to subordination (cf. van Knippenberg, 1984). However, rather than regarding women as suffering from 'false consciousness', and constituting passive victims 'brainwashed' (Friedan, 1963) by dominant belief systems, we should at least recognize the possibility that women may also be active in constructing their own realities, albeit with conceptual and linguistic resources (at present) limited by male rhetoric.

CONCLUDING COMMENTS: MODELS OF WOMAN IN FEMINIST SOCIAL PSYCHOLOGY—POLEMIC AND PARADOX

My aim in this chapter has been a modest one. I did not wish to embark upon a thorough review of the social psychological literature on sex role related beliefs, and I do not claim to have contributed significantly to this literature in the way of new data. Rather, my intention in presenting piecemeal data supplemented by speculative interpretation has been to illustrate what I feel to be an important problem facing social psychologists who, like myself, wish to develop 'feminist' perspectives in their work. This is the possibility that regarding individuals and social events from the perspective of feminism as a world-view may itself encourage the very tendency to objectify our 'subjects' which feminism opposes so forcefully. From my own past research I can outline at least three ways in which, in endeavouring to conduct 'feminist' social psychology, I have come to objectify other women.

First, psychology, as an academic discipline, often encourages objectification covertly through the concept of the 'unconscious': since our 'subjects' are not necessarily aware of why they act as they do, we should not take their statements at face value. In this way, the psychologist is elevated to the role of expert who 'knows' more than the actor. This problem is similarly associated with the adoption of feminist premises concerning 'levels' of consciousness: the conceptualization of feminism as 'raised' consciousness brings with it the implicit suggestion that feminists 'know best' (see, e.g. Spender, 1985).

Second, the desire to use social psychology to make 'feminist' statements (see e.g. Wilkinson, 1984), may present a danger in that, in drawing attention to the 'pervasive patterns of subordination, limitation and confinement that have hampered and crippled the development of the female half of humankind' (Keohane *et al.*, 1982, p. x), we may present an objectified, pathologized image of women as passive victims of social forces (see Zavalloni, 1973, for a similar discussion with respect to the 'race' relations literature). In particular it appears that, as a rhetorical device adopted in order to promote social change, feminist social psychologists have often accepted existing stereotypes of female psychology (see above, and Duelli Klein, 1983; Eichler, 1980 for similar points). In this way, in directing their efforts towards women's future interests, feminist social psychologists may propagate a derogatory image of women *as they are now*. To borrow Zavalloni's (1973, p. 68) words, 'even if it is seen as the result of oppression, the imputation that [low status group members] possess a damaged identity is an additional derogatory social representation thrown into the field of social interaction'.

Finally, and perhaps most paradoxically, the process of objectification may be encouraged by 'feminist' methodology. As feminists we are encouraged to interpret the world in terms of our own consciousness (e.g. Spender, 1985). Opposing the duality between the knower and the known (du Bois, 1983) which pervades the 'social cognition' literature (Condor and Henwood, 1985), we are encouraged to develop techniques of 'intersubjectivity' with the women 'for' whom we are conducting our research (e.g. Duelli Klein, 1983). The problem is, of course, that since not all women share our own feminist consciousness (yet!) there is a conflict between using our experience as data and considering (other) women's definition of a situation as valid in its own right.

NOTES TO CHAPTER 6

1. For the moment I am confining the discussion to the 'sex role attitudes' literature. Research concerned with 'sex stereotypes' has differed in format, being primarily concerned

with documenting the characteristics associated with men and women by aggregates of individuals (see, e.g. Ashmore and Del Boca, 1981).

2. I will refer to these women as 'non-traditional' since many of them appeared to embrace a liberal-individualist belief system and would not necessarily consider themselves to be 'feminists'.

3. In analysing traditional beliefs, may American researchers have concentrated on the members of *anti-feminist* organizations (e.g. Arnott, 1973). The present discussion concerns the beliefs of women who support the sex role *status quo* and who may, but do not necessarily, regard themselves explicitly in opposition to the women's movement.

4. It is, of course, well recognized that an individual's own attitudes may affect the way in which he or she regards other attitudinal positions. Within social psychology this issue has been examined in terms of the scaling of opinion statements according to valence and intensity (e.g. Eiser, 1984; Hovland and Sherif, 1952; Upshaw, 1962), and in terms of beliefs about the generality of one's own attitudes (see Judd and Johnson, 1981, for a specific consideration of feminist attitudes). I would wish to extend this primarily cognitive-judgemental analysis by suggesting that the characterization of traditionalism present in the feminist literature represents a rhetorical device rather than illustrating cognitive 'bias'.

5. Psychological studies which have documented how women 'discriminate against' their own sex have typically used male dimensions of comparison (in particular, academic achievement, e.g. Goldberg's 1974; 'misogyny test'). In contrast, research which has allowed women the ability to do so, has found that they may favour their own sex in terms of positive feminine stereotypic characteristics (e.g. McKillip *et al.*, 1977).

6. With respect to feminist hypotheses concerning women's recognition of 'multiple realities', and sociological theories of 'dual consciousness' it was interesting that traditional women did appear to be, to some extent, aware of the fact that men do not necessarily share their own positive evaluation of feminine roles. However, this was situated within a wider belief that in this way women may maintain their distinctive advantage. This was particularly apparent amongst the younger women, who often suggested that allowing men to think that they were 'the boss' was a small investment for the return of being paid for on 'dates'.

7. The relationship between sex role attitudes and stereotypes is generally poorly articulated in the literature. On one hand, stereotyping researchers often assume that descriptive images of men and women also embody evaluative orientations towards the sexes (e.g. Rosenkrantz *et al.*, 1968); that 'opinion statements' may be used to measure sex role attitudes (cf. Brogan and Kutner, 1976), and that stereotypes may, themselves, be prescriptive (Stoppard and Kalin, 1978). On the other hand, social psychologists continue to distinguish between the cognitive (stereotypic) and affective (attitudinal) aspect of sex role beliefs, suggesting that the two do not necessarily covary (Nielsen and Doyle, 1975).

REFERENCES

Abercrombie, N., Hill, S. and Turner, B. S. (1980). *The Dominant Ideology Thesis*. London, George Allen & Unwin.

Adamec, C. S. and Graham, M. (1978). The complexity of attitudes toward women. *International Journal of Women's Studies* 1, 503–516.

Adorno, T. W., Frenkel-Brunswick, E., Levinson, D. J. and Sanford, R. N. (1950). *The Authoritarian Personality*. New York, Harper & Row.

Albright, D. and Chang, A. (1976). An examination of how one's attitudes toward women are reflected in one's defensiveness and self esteem. *Sex Roles* **2**, 195-199.

Allen, D. (1954). Antifemininity in men. *American Sociological Review* **19**, 591-593.

Allport, G. W. (1954). *The Nature of Prejudice*. Cambridge, Mass., Addison-Wesley.

Ardener, S. (ed.) (1975). *Perceiving Women*. London, Dent/Malaby.

Arnott, C. (1973). Feminists and antifeminists as 'true believers'. *Sociology and Social Research* **57**, 300-306.

Asch, S. E. (1952). *Social Psychology*. New Jersey, Prentice-Hall.

Ashmore, R. D. (1981). Sex stereotypes and implicit personality theory. In: D. Hamilton (ed.), *Cognitive Processes in Stereotyping and Intergroup Behavior*. Hillsdale, N.J., Erlbaum.

Ashmore, R. D. and Del Boca, F. K. (1979). Sex stereotypes and implicit personality theory: toward a cognitive-social psychological conceptualization. *Sex Roles* **5**, 219-248.

Ashmore, R. D. and Del Boca, F. K. (1981). Conceptual approaches to stereotypes and stereotyping. In: D. L. Hamilton (ed.), *Cognitive Processes in Stereotyping and Intergroup Behavior*. Hillsdale, N.J., Erlbaum.

Barker, M. (1981). *The New Racism: Conservatives and the Ideology of the Tribe*. London, Junction Books.

Barrett, M. (1980). *Women's Oppression Today: Problems in Marxist Feminist Analysis*. London, Verso Editions.

Beere, C. (1979). *Women and Women's Issues: A Handbook of Tests and Measures*. San Francisco, Jossey-Bass.

Bell, C. and Newby, H. (1976). Husbands and wives: the dynamics of the deferential dialectic. In: D. L. Barker and S. Allen (eds), *Dependence and Exploitation in Work and Marriage*. Harlow, Longman.

Bem, S. L. (1974). The measurement of psychological androgyny. *Journal of Consulting and Clinical Psychology* **42**, 155-162.

Bernard, J. (1973). My four revolutions: an autobiographical history of the ASA. In: J. Huber (ed.), *Changing Women in a Changing Society*. Chicago, University of Chicago Press.

Bernard, J. (1975). *Women, Wives and Mothers: Values and Options*. Chicago, Aldine.

Bernard, J. (1978). Models for the relationship between the world of women and the world of men. In: L. Kriesberg (ed.), *Research in Social Movements, Conflicts and Change*, Vol. 1. Greenwich, Connecticut, JAI Press.

Bird, C. (1970). *Born Female: The High Cost of Keeping Women Down*. New York, David McKay.

Bowker, L. (1981). Racism and sexism: hints toward a theory of the causal structure of attitudes toward women. *International Journal of Women's Studies* **4**, 277-288.

Brittan, A. and Maynard, M. (1984). *Sexism, Racism and Oppression*. Oxford, Blackwell.

Brogan, D. and Kutner, N. (1976). Measuring sex role orientation: a normative approach. *Journal of Marriage and the Family* **38**, 31-40.

Burris, B. (1973). The fourth world manifesto. In: A. Koedt, E. Levine and A. Rapone (eds), *Radical Feminism*. New York, Quadrangle Books.

Cartwright, D. (1950). Emotional dimensions of group life. In: M. L. Reymert (ed.), *International Symposium on Feelings and Emotions*. New York, McGraw Hill.

Chaftez, J. S. (1974). *Masculine/Feminine or Human?* Ityasca, Peacock.

Condor, S. (1983). Toward a qualitative understanding of women's 'traditional' sex role attitudes. Paper presented at the BPS (Welsh Branch) student conference, UWIST, Cardiff.

Condor, S. (1984). Women's traditional sex role attitudes: 'identification with the aggressor' or 'ingroup favouritism'? Paper presented in symposium: Feminist research in social psychology: extending the perspective. British Psychological Society (Social Psychology Section) annual conference, Oxford, September.

Condor, S. and Abrams, D. (1984). Womanhood as an aspect of social identity: group identification and ideology. Paper presented at the international conference on Self and Identity, Cardiff, July.

Condor, S. and Brown, R. (In press). Psychological processes in intergroup conflict. In: W. Stroebe, A. Kruglanski, D. Bar-Tal and M. Hewstone (eds), *The Social Psychology of Intergroup and International Conflict: Theory, Research and Application*. New York, Springer-Verlag.

Condor, S. and Henwood, K. (1985). Stereotypes and social context. Unpublished manuscript, University College, Cardiff.

Cooper, J. and Croyle, R. T. (1984). Attitudes and attitude change. *Annual Review of Psychology* **35**, 395–426.

Deaux, K. (1985). Sex and gender. *Annual Review of Psychology* **36**, 49–81.

Delphy, C. (1981). Women in stratification studies. In: H. Roberts (ed.), *Doing Feminist Research*. London, Routledge & Kegan Paul.

Dempewolff, J. (1974). Development and validation of a feminism scale. *Psychological Reports* **34**, 651–657.

Deschamps, J-C. (1982). Social identity and relations of power between groups. In: H. Tajfel (ed.), *Social Identity and Intergroup Relations*. Cambridge, Cambridge University Press.

du Bois, B. (1983). Passionate scholarship: notes on vales, knowing and method in feminist social science. In: G. Bowles and R. Duelli Klein (eds), *Theories of Women's Studies*. London, Routledge & Kegan Paul.

Duelli Klein, R. (1983). How to do what we want to do: thoughts about feminist methodology. In G. Bowles and R. Duelli Klein (eds), *Theories of Women's Studies*. London, Routledge & Kegan Paul.

Dworkin, A. (1983). *Right Wing Women: The Politics of Domesticated Females*. London, The Women's Press.

Dworkin, R. J. (1976). A woman's report: numbers do not a majority make. In: A. G. Dworkin and R. J. Dworkin (eds), *The Minority Report: An Introduction to Racial, Ethnic and Gender Relations*. New York, Praeger.

Eichler, M. (1980). *The Double Standard: A Feminist Critique of Feminist Social Science*. London, Croom Helm.

Eisenstein, H. (1984). *Contemporary Feminist Thought*. London, Unwin.

Eiser, J. R. (1984). *Attitudinal Judgement*. New York, Springer-Verlag.

Epstein, C. F. (1980). Women's attitudes towards other women: myths and their consequences. *American Journal of Psychotherapy* **34**, 322–333.

Figes, E. (1970). *Patriarchal Attitudes*. New York, Stein & Day.

Firestone, S. (1970). *The Dialectic of Sex: The Case for Feminist Revolution*. London, Jonathan Cape.

Fishbein, M. and Ajzen, I. (1975). *Belief, Attitude, Intention and Behavior: An Introduction to Theory and Research*. Reading, Mass., Addison-Wesley.

Fowler, M. G., Fowler, R. L. and Van De Riet, H. (1973). Feminism and political radicalism. *Journal of Psychology* **83**, 237–242.

Friedan, B. (1963). *The Feminine Mystique*. New York, Norton.

Goldberg, P. (1968). Are women prejudiced against other women? *Transaction* **5**, 28–30.

Goldberg, P. (1974). Prejudice toward women: some personality correlates. *International Journal of Group Tensions* **4**, 53–63.

Gramsci, A. (1971). *Selections From the Prison Notebooks*. (ed. & trans. Q. Hoare and G. Nowell-Smith). London, Lawrence & Wishart.

Hacker, H. (1951). Women as a minority group. *Social Forces* **30**, 60–69.

Hole, J. and Levine, E. (1971). *Rebirth of Feminism*. New York, Quadrangle Books.

Hovland, C. I. and Sherif, M. (1952). Judgemental phenomena and scales of attitude measurement: item displacement in Thurstone scales. *Journal of Abnormal and Social Psychology* **47**, 822–832.

Jassen-Jurreit, M. (1982). *Sexism: The Male Monopoly on History and Thought*. London, Pluto Press.

Judd, C. M. and Johnson, J. T. (1981). Attitudes, polarization and diagnosticity. *Journal of Personality and Social Psychology* **41**, 26–36.

Kahn, V. S. (1976). Purdah in the British situation. In: D. L. Barker and S. Allen (eds), *Dependence and Exploitation in Work and Marriage*. Harlow, Longman.

Kalin, R. and Tilby, P. (1978). Development and validation of a sex-role ideology scale. *European Journal of Social Psychology* **11**, 131–147.

Kalmuss, D., Gurin, D. and Townsend, A. (1981). Feminist and sympathetic feminist consciousness. *European Journal of Social Psychology* **11**, 131–147.

Kaplan, A. and Bean, J. (eds) (1976). *Beyond Sex Role Stereotypes: Readings Toward a Psychology of Androgyny*. Boston & Toronto, Little, Brown and Co.

Kaplan, T. (1982). Female consciousness and collective action: the case of Barcelona, 1910-1918. In: N. O. Keohane, M. Z. Rosaldo and B. C. Gelpi (eds), *Feminist Theory: A Critique of Ideology*. Brighton, Harvester.

Keohane, N. O., Rosaldo, M. Z. and Gelpi, B. C. (eds) (1982). *Feminist Theory: A Critique of Ideology*. Brighton, Harvester.

Kilmann, P. R. and Auerbach, S. M. (1974). Effects of marathon group therapy on self-actualization and attitudes toward women. *Journal of Clinical Psychology* **42**, 607–612.

Kilpatrick, D. and Smith, A. (1974). Validation of the Spence-Helmreich Attitudes Toward Women Scale. *Psychological Reports* **35**, 461–462.

Kirkpatrick, C. (1936). The construction of a belief-pattern scale for measuring attitudes toward feminism. *Journal of Social Psychology* **7**, 421–437.

Kirsch, P., Shore, M. and Kyle, D. (1976). Ideology and personality: aspects of identity formation in adolescents with strong attitudes toward sex-role equalitarianism. *Journal of Youth and Adolescence* **5**, 387–401.

Kuhn, T. S. (1962). *The Structure of Scientific Revolutions*. Chicago, University of Chicago Press.

Likert, R. (1932). The method of constructing an attitude scale. *Archives of Psychology* **140**, 44–53.

Lynn, D. (1961). Sex differences in identification development. *Sociometry* **24**, 372–383.

MacDonald, A. (1974). Identification and measurement of multidimensional attitudes toward equality between the sexes. *Journal of Homosexuality* **2**, 165–184.

McKillip, J., DiMiceli, A. and Luebke, J. (1977). Group salience and stereotyping. *Social Behavior and Personality* **5**, 81–85.

Mason, K. and Bumpass, L. (1975). U.S. women's sex role ideology, 1970. *American Journal of Sociology* **80**, 1212–1219.

Mednick, M. S. and Tangri, S. S. (1972). New social psychological perspectives on women. *Journal of Social Issues* **28**, 1–16.

Merton, R. (1957). *Social Theory and Social Structure*. Glencoe, Ill., Free Press.

Mies, M. (1983). Towards a methodology for feminist research. In: G. Bowles and R. Duelli Klein (eds), *Theories of Women's Studies*. London, Routledge & Kegan Paul.

Miller, A. G. (ed.) (1982). *In the Eye of the Beholder: Contemporary issues in Stereotyping*. New York, Praeger.

Millett, K. (1970). *Sexual Politics*. New York, Avon Books.

Myrdal, G. (1944). *An American Dilemma*. New York, Harper.

Nadler, E. and Morrow, W. (1959). Authoritarian attitudes toward women and their correlates. *Journal of Social Psychology* **49**, 113–123.

Nielsen, J. and Doyle, P. (1975). Sex role stereotypes of feminists and nonfeminists. *Sex Roles* **1**, 82–95.

O'Brien, M. (1982). Feminist theory and dialectical logic. In: N. O. Keohane, M. Z. Rosaldo and B. C. Gelpi (eds), *Feminist Theory: A Critique of Ideology*. Brighton, Harvester.

Parry, G. (1983). A British version of the attitudes towards women scale (AWS-B). *British Journal of Social Psychology* **22**, 261–263.

Petro, C. S. and Putnam, B. A. (1979). Sex role stereotypes: issues of attitudinal change. *Sex Roles* **5**, 29–37.

Riddel, S. (1982). Hell no—we won't glow. *Spare Rib* **119**, 22–33.

Rosaldo, M. Z. (1974). Woman, culture and society: a theoretical overview. In: M. Rosaldo and L. Lamphere (eds), *Woman, Culture and Society*. Stanford, California, Stanford University Press.

Rosenkrantz, P., Vogel, S., Bee, H., Broverman, I. and Broverman, D. (1968). Sex-role stereotypes and self-concepts in college students. *Journal of Consulting and Clinical Psychology* **32**, 287–295.

Rowbotham, S. (1973). *Woman's Consciousness, Man's World*. Harmondsworth, Pelican.

Sarup, G. (1976). Gender, authoritarianism and attitudes toward feminism. *Social Behavior and Personality* **4**, 57–64.

Sayers, J. (1982). *Biological Politics: Feminist and Anti-Feminist Perspectives*. London & New York, Tavistock.

Smith, E., Feree, M. and Miller, F. (1975). A short scale of attitudes toward feminism. *Representative Research in Social Psychology* **6**, 51–56.

Spence, J. and Helmreich, R. (1972). The Attitudes Toward Women Scale: an objective instrument to measure attitudes toward the rights and roles of women in contemporary society. *JSAS Catalog of Selected Documents in Psychology* **2**, 66.

Spence, J. and Helmreich, R. (1978). *Masculinity and Femininity: Their Psychological Dimensions, Correlates and Antecedents*. Austin & London, University of Texas Press.

Spender, D. (1980). *Man Made Language*. London, Routledge & Kegan Paul.

Spender, D. (1983). Theorising about theorising. In: G. Bowles and R. Duelli Klein (eds), *Theories of Women's Studies*. London, Routledge & Kegan Paul.

Spender, D. (1985). *For the Record: The Making and Meaning of Feminist Knowledge*. London, Women's Press.

Stanley, L. and Wise, S. (1983). *Breaking Out: Feminist Consciousness and Feminist Research*. London, Routledge & Kegan Paul.

Stockard, J. and Dougherty, M. (1983). Variations in subjective culture. *Sex Roles* **9**, 953–974.

Stoppard, J. and Kalin, R. (1978). Can gender stereotypes and sex role conceptions be distinguished? *British Journal of Social and Clinical Psychology* **17**, 211–217.

Sumner, G. A. (1909). *Folkways*. New York, Ginn.

Tajfel, H. (1978a). *Differentiation Between Social Groups*. (European Monographs in Social Psychology). London, Academic Press.

Tajfel, H. (1978b). *The Social Psychology of Minorities*. London, Minority Rights Group.

Tauer, C. A. (1979). Freud and female inferiority. *International Journal of Women's Studies* **2**, 287–304.

Thurstone, L. L. (1931). The measurement of attitudes. *Journal of Abnormal and Social Psychology* **26**, 249–269.

Turner, J. C. (1982). Towards a cognitive redefinition of the social group. In: H. Tajfel (ed.), *Social Identity and Intergroup Relations*. Cambridge, Cambridge University Press.

Upshaw, H. S. (1962). Own attitude as an anchor in equal-appearing intervals. *Journal of Abnormal and Social Psychology* **64**, 84–96.

van Knippenberg, A. (1984). Intergroup differences in group perceptions. In: H. Tajfel (ed.), *The Social Dimension: European Developments in Social Psychology*. Cambridge, Cambridge University Press.

Villemez, W. and Touhey, J. (1977). A measure of individual differences in sex stereotyping and discrimination: the 'Macho' Scale. *Psychological Reports* **41**, 411–415.

Weisstein, N. (1973). Psychology constructs the female: or the fantasy life of the male psychologist. In: A. Koedt, E. Levine and A. Rapone (eds), *Radical Feminism*. New York, Quadrangle.

Welch, S. (1975). Support among women for the issues of the women's movement. *Sociological Quarterly* **16**, 216–227.

Whitehead, G. and Tawes, S. (1976). Dogmatism, age and educational level as correlates of feminism for males and females. *Sex Roles* **2**, 401–405.

Whitehurst, C. (1979). An empirical investigation of women's self-attitudes. *International Journal of Women's Studies* **2**, 76–86.

Wilkinson, S. (1984). Feminist research: ethogeny revisited? Paper presented in symposium: 'Feminist research in social psychology: extending the perspective,' British Psychological Society (Social Psychology Section) Annual Conference, Oxford, September.

Williams, J. A. and Giles, H. (1978). The changing status of women in society: an intergroup perspective. In: H. Tajfel (ed.), *Differentiation Between Social Groups*. (European Monographs in Social Psychology.) London, Academic Press.

Williams, J. E. and Best, D. (1977). Sex stereotypes and trait favorability on the ACL. *Educational and Psychological Measurement* **37**, 101–110.

Woudenberg, R. A. (1977). The relationship of sexual attitudes, attitudes about women and racial attitudes in white males. *Sex Roles* **3**, 101–110.

Wylie, R. C. (1979). *The Self Concept*. Nebraska, University of Nebraska Press.

Yinger, J. M. (1960). Contraculture and subculture. *American Sociological Review* **25**, 625–635.

Zavalloni, M. (1973). Social identity perspectives and prospects. *Social Science Information* **12**, 463–477.

Zuckerman, D. (1980). Self-esteem, self-concept and the life-goals and sex-role attitudes of college students. *Journal of Personality* **48**, 149–162.

Chapter 7

Media Images of Women: The Social Construction of Ageism and Sexism

Catherine Itzin

SEX ROLE STEREOTYPING

In a survey of 16 national newspapers conducted in 1983 the Trades Union Congress found:

> 53 pictures showing women in glamour poses emphasising female sexuality. There were 58 news and feature stories which portrayed women in terms of their sexuality, appearance and domestic relations, concentrating on women as housewives, prostitutes, rape victims or divorcees. There were 17 overtly sexist cartoons providing images of women which were denigrating and degrading e.g. nagging mothers-in-law, simple minded housewives, 'silly blondes', or women as sex objects with no other role or function in society. There were seven advertisements which portrayed women in traditional domestic roles, or taking a 'back seat' to the men in their lives, whether husbands, sons or colleagues. (TUC, 1984)

Only 47 stories portrayed women as workers and professionals with a contribution to make to society.

The TUC survey identified certain key sex role stereotypes: women as the sex symbols of a consumer society (in advertisements and in the emulation of pop and film stars), 'women whose only concerns are the welfare and needs of their immediate families', and a systematic concentration on 'appearance, sexuality and domestic relations'. The TUC also noted the press preoccupation with women as victims of rape and violence.

A similar pattern of sex role stereotyping was documented by the Women's Media Action Group (WMAG) when they too monitored the media over the years from 1981 to 1983 and found:

(1) 'blatant depiction of naked or semi-naked women, generally in a seductive pose, suggestive of availability, purely for titillation' (as in pin-ups or on page 3 of the *Sun*);

119

(2)   'wholly gratuitous and irrelevant use of female bodies' (as in advertising potato snacks or snooker);

(3)   'unnecessarily frequent use of women, usually scantily clad, to advertise products used equally by men and women' (showers, cameras);

(4)   'advertising of women's products using women in an unnecessarily titillating manner' (underwear);

(5)   'trivialisation of women, emphasising their sexuality rather than achievements';

(6)   'women as possessions, capable of being bought or portrayed as available';

(7)   'blatantly sexual portrayal of women in cartoons';

(8)   'art as an excuse for soft pornography';

(9)   'the use of parts of women's bodies, disembodied, therefore objectified and dehumanised';

(10)   'the desirability of slimness, hairlessness, odourlessness, beauty, youth in the "Ideal Woman" ';

(11)   'advertising of pornography in general magazines, with explicit pictures and descriptions of the sexual violence in them'.

They also found the following sex role stereotypes: women at home, in the kitchen or in bed, or with children; at work in servicing jobs; as a fantasized ideal woman; as perfectly feminine (caring, nurturing, sensitive, home-loving and passive); incompetent at manual or technical jobs; in submissive or dependent relationships with men in jokes. In the reporting of violence against women, they found:

> lurid headlines designed to catch the eye, rapes and sexual assaults described in excessive detail, a pretence of moral indignation, with a real motivation to titillation, the whole issue manipulated with the aim of selling newspapers. (WMAG, 1983)

An Equal Opportunities Commission survey of sexism and advertising produced an armoury of statistics on the sex role stereotyped portrayal of women in advertisements and concluded that in TV commercials women are 'predominantly portrayed in the traditional roles of housewife and mother'. They also concluded that:

> magazine and television advertising still tend very much to portray women in traditional and now largely out-of-date roles, as 'kitchen sink' caretakers reluctant to make (or incapable of making) important decisions — particularly outside the home, and as being essentially dependent or in need of men's protection or, of course, simply as sexual objects. (EOC 1982)

These are the kinds of misrepresentations of women that appear constantly in media directed at a mass and mixed-sex audience where the communication is apparently 'from people to people about people'. Documentation of this sexism in the media is now substantial and there is an increasing acknowledgement of it and awareness of its negative and inaccurate portrayal of women (Courtney and Lockeretz, 1971; Millum, 1975; Scheibe, 1979; Tuchman *et al.*, 1978; Wasner and Banos, 1973).

The majority of women do not live at home with their children in economic dependence on a male breadwinner. The reality is that 15% of households (in London) are single parent households — according to statistics from the National Council for One Parent Families (1983); 20% of households have a sole female breadwinner, and women are 40% of the workforce according to the EOC (1982). Of married women, 60% (or 73% depending on source) work full-time or part-time outside the home (EOC, 1982). Women do 80% of the domestic work; 98% of men have never cleaned the lavatory. Men seldom scrub the kitchen floor, iron, spring-clean or scour the cooker. And surveys in Britain, France and the USA all agree that in the vast majority of homes it is still women who take overall responsibility for running the household — even when each partner has a full-time job (see Segal, 1982; Kenny, 1983).

As the TUC Report concluded:

> women are workers and providers, exercising professional responsibilities and skills. They are the heads of families, householders and mortgage holders. They have bank accounts and are members of pension schemes. They do not spend the greatest portion of their lives getting married and divorced, seducing vicars, lying around semi-nude or even staying at home. (TUC, 1984)

Sex role stereotyped images of women in the media obviously do not reflect the reality of women's lived experiences and women's role in society. So what is their purpose? To look for an answer feminist sociologists have turned to images of women in women's magazines — where the audience is primarily women and the communication is apparently 'woman to woman'.

In a content analysis of the three best selling women's magazines (*Woman, Woman's Own* and *Woman's Weekly*), covering the years 1949–1974 and 1979–1980, Marjorie Ferguson identified the major themes, roles, values and goals represented to women. Well over half of the themes were concerned with getting and keeping a man and maintaining a happy family (67%). Just under half (46%) of the roles represented for women were that of wife and mother — or women trying to get married (the would-be wives). The other major themes were overcoming misfortune (28%), achieving perfection (17%), the problems of the working wife (3%), 'head triumphing over heart' (9%), how to be mysterious (the feminine mystique), youthful, successful, happy and more beautiful. The other main female roles were 'the beautifier' (11%), daughters and sisters (9%), the 'female female' (9%), the girl friend (5%), the careerist (7%), and the 'respectable woman' (4%).

The main values represented (not surprisingly, given the roles) were duty and self-control (26%), romantic love (16%), positive self-image (13%), social control, i.e. conformity (6%), family life (6%), good looks (5%), and wealth (4%). Only 6%

of the content covered female friendships and only 13% valued work. The major goals held out as desirable for women were personal happiness (23%), finding and keeping a man (16%), physical attractiveness (16%), having a happy marriage and family (15%), personal triumph over suffering (13%), and social conformism (4%). Only 12% of the content held out achievement in society as a goal for women.

The audience for women's magazines is enormous. They are read by 16 million women every week in the UK (1981 statistics). Forty-nine per cent of the female population read a women's weekly and 45% a women's monthly in 1981. The messages directly reach a female audience of millions and

> to the extent that their female readers accept their messages, the influence of those messages can be multiplied many times through a mother's influence on her children, a wife's influence on her husband, a lover's influence on her partner, and women's influence on one another. (Ferguson, 1983)

Ferguson believes that women's magazines are about femininity. What she calls the 'cult of femininity' (with its connotations of 'naturalness' and implications of 'passivity') is now understood by feminist sociologists to be the very 'active' social construction of femininity. According to Ferguson, 'the fact that women's magazines exist at all makes a statement about the position of women in society'. Feminist sociologists see this 'position' as one of women's subordination. Women's magazines teach women 'what to think and what to do about themselves' and their relationships. The lesson is in passivity and submission to men who are portrayed as 'dominant, active and authoritative' (TUC, 1984).

Women's magazines are based on the assumption that:

> a female sex which is at best unconfident, and at worse incompetent, "needs" or "wants" to be instructed, rehearsed or brought up to date on the arts and skills of femininity, while a more powerful and confident male sex already "knows" everything there is to know about the business of being masculine. (Ferguson, 1983)

Ferguson concludes that women's magazines act as 'agents of socialisation'.

Janice Winship, in an analysis of the same women's magazines for the Open University's 'The Changing Experience of Women' course, also recognized the influence of the magazines in 'moulding women's experiences'. According to Winship:

> women's magazines provide what can be described as "mirror images" for women, i.e. public images of femininity against which women, measure themselves, men judge women, and which are, therefore, formative in actually shaping women's experiences. (Winship, 1983)

AGE ROLE STEREOTYPING

While awareness of sexist images is almost taken for granted now, awareness of ageist images and attitudes is a more recent phenomenon. Alex Comfort is one authority who has popularized (1977) the distinction between biological ageing and what he called 'sociogenic ageing': 'the role society imposes on people as they reach a certain chronological age, the arbitrary rolelessness of retirement'. This includes the negative experience of poverty and the negative attitude of being regarded as redundant to life.

Though stereotyped images of old people in the media have not been so well documented as the sexist stereotypes of women, there is an increasing amount of concern about ageism in the media. In a paper delivered to the British Society of Gerontology annual conference in 1984, Penny Webb (of Medicus Productions) reviewed the research and discovered that, on television for example, there was a very small number of characters in the 65 and over age group (on average about 3%), and a distinctly male bias in the portrayal of the elderly. She cites four studies in particular: one (Arnoff, 1974), had analysed TV drama and found that older people comprised 5% of male and 5% of female characters. Another study (Francer, 1973) sampled 100 TV commercials for age content and found only two commercials with older characters; while a third study of 30 commercial network half-hours in the USA (Petersen, 1973) found only 32 old people, three of whom were women. Yet another study (Bradly, 1974) analysed 3500 characters over three years and found fewer than 100 (3%) in the 65-plus age range.

As with women, when older people are present in the media, they are usually portrayed in a stereotyped or caricatured way—as incapacitated or incompetent or pathetic. Writing about British television, Tony Ward (1983) describes how the old are 'either made to look feeble, senile and ridiculous, or aggressive and interfering'. Old people are frequently presented as asexual—without sexuality, sexual feelings or sexual activity, or they are stereotyped as dull or demented, rigid and reactionary. Contempt and ridicule are common attitudes.

As with sexism, the ageist images and attitudes are based on myths, misinformation and misrepresentation of reality. Old people are a significant and increasing proportion of the population—nearer to 20% (10 million) than the 3% portrayed on television. The age range of 20–49 may constitute two-thirds of all TV characters, but it represents only one-third of the population.

The publication *Against Ageism* (1983) isolates seven of the most commonly occurring but inaccurate assumptions about old people that lie behind the individual attitudes and the institutionalized practices of ageism:

   the myth of chronology;
   the myth of ill health;
   the myth of senility and mental deterioration;
   the myth of inflexible personality;

the myth of rejection and isolation;
the myth of misery;
the myth of unproductivity.

The reality is that there are enormous differences in the rates of ageing, so that there may be little difference between individual 50 and 60 year olds or 60 and 70 year olds.

There is no fixed age at which people become old. Though there are certain chronic medical problems that occur in old age (such as dementia, strokes and mobility disorders), elderly people suffer from few acute illnesses and research has shown that the health of people aged 65–74 is not much different from that of the age group before it. The reality is that ill health is not an inevitable consequence of old age, though the stereotype perpetuates this notion.

Likewise, though 'senility' is so much associated with old age that it (like the term 'geriatric', which literally means a branch of medical science) has become a term of ageist abuse, the reality is that the human brain does not 'shrink, wilt, perish or deteriorate with age'. Senility in the old is often confused with depression which affects people of all ages. The stereotypes which portray old people as wanting to cut themselves off ('disengage') from society are really a rationalization of an ageist society's separation of itself from old people—their compulsory exclusion from employment, and isolation into residential homes and hospitals (though again the *reality* is that this applies to only 5% of old people!). Old people are often portrayed as inherently miserable, when in fact it is the oppressive conditions of their lives that make them miserable (on the occasions when they are).

The images of ageism, like the images of sexism, serve to construct the internalized attitudes of subordination and to maintain the institutionalized practices of inequality (the denial of economic and decision making power and social status), not only in old people, but people of all ages. According to Robert Butler who first coined the term:

> Ageism can be seen as a process of systematic stereotyping of and discrimination against people because they are old, just as racism and sexism accomplish this with skin colour and gender. Old people are categorised as senile, rigid in thought and manner, old fashioned in morality and skills . . . Ageism allows the younger generation to see old people as different from themselves, thus they subtly cease to identify with their elders as human beings. (Butler, 1975)

And as Penny Webb points out: 'Such messages may influence their notions of how older people think, talk, behave and act toward others and in turn their own actions toward older people may be affected' (Webb, 1984).

THE COMBINED EFFECT OF SEX ROLE STEREOTYPING AND AGE ROLE STEREOTYPING

Research on ageism in the media has pinpointed the male bias in representations of the elderly: that older women are even less visible than older men and that this could distort perceptions of reality (Webb, 1984). This is really an understatement of the devastatingly negative effect of the combination of ageism and sexism in media representations of women. Not only has there been virtually no research in this area, the analysis that there has been of sexism in the media has totally overlooked the pervasive ageism that is so intimately interconnected with the sexist representation.

The reality is that described by Adams and Laurikietis (1980):

> Many of the trials surrounding *growing older* are ones that women feel more than men. Women are actually ashamed of growing older before they're anywhere near old age. Once they've reached their mid twenties, women are generally reluctant to reveal how old they are . . . Growing older for the vast majority of women purely and simply means becoming less attractive. Ageing in a woman is seen as making her not only unattractive but repulsive and almost obscene to the world. Sexually women are considered less desirable, which is reflected in their chances of marrying or remarrying after they are forty . . . Fame, money, power — all make a man more sexually attractive, and these often increase with age. But they don't make a woman more attractive. What she has to do is to keep young.

The only documentation of the combination of ageism and sexism in the media has come from the WMAG who found, for example, in monitoring the nation's press, the following advertisement for a skin cream:

> Nobody minds if your husband looks his age. Men are lucky. They needn't look young to be still attractive. They often get better looking over the years. Unfortunately, the same can't be said for us women. From the first moment a tiny line appears, we need to take extra care of our skins, with the specialist moisturising treatment . . .

The picture with the text was of a middle-aged, moustached, wrinkled but handsome man in the foreground, smiling — and a woman, middle-aged (or similar-aged) in the background, alarmed. As well she might be, for 'her man' is talking to another younger, and implicitly 'more attractive' woman. Women's magazines are full of advertisements with headlines like: 'Look ten years younger'; 'Free yourself of ugly stretch marks from pregnancy, dieting, exercise, even ageing'; 'Ashamed of your appearance? Worried about wrinkles and lines? Worried by thinning hair? Lines around the mouth?'; 'How to look younger longer'; 'Do some parts of your body look older than the rest?'. If so, and physiology being what it is, the message of these advertisements is: buy this or that product, do this and do that in order to 'stay young and beautiful' (as the song goes).

Birthday card humour is even more crudely sexist and ageist. For example, 'Here's to women over 40, and why men love 'em: They never yell, they never tell, they never swell and they're as grateful as hell'. Or, 'To someone who looks 29, acts 29 and would like to be 29'. Adams and Laurikietis (1980) found humour in general to be sexist and ageist; they isolated the following stereotypes in jokes: 'silly old moo—the missis' (the nagging wife), the mother-in-law (the wife's mother), the scatterbrain (stupid young woman); the dumb blonde (the young sex object), and the Amazon (fantasized superwoman, a substitute man). They *might* have added the 'sour spinster'. In each case we have two stereotypes: an age stereotype and simultaneously a sex stereotype. It is as if the sex objectification and sex role stereotyping do not exist independently of their age role stereotypes—as if the age and sex stereotypes are inextricably interconnected in communicating the negative images of and attitudes towards women.

Certainly, when young women or girls are presented, they are portrayed as sexualized and sex role stereotyped. Age-graded birthday cards crudely present girls as feminine, boys as masculine, from baby's first birthday onwards: a five year old boy is digging in the sand, the five year old girl reading demurely; the 12 year old boy canoeing, the 12 year old girl actually 'wearing adult style clothes and make-up reflecting the contradictory expectations of woman as seductress and innocent child' (WMAG Report No. 4). Toy advertisements like the Fisher-Price Tool Kit ('give him his own tool kit just like dad's') and the Fisher-Price Kitchen Set ('just the thing for the little miss'), are the rule rather than the exception. The ageism is not just at the other—older—end of the life-span: it affects women from birth onwards, and is integral to the sex stereotypes from the beginning.

When older women are portrayed—on the few occasions when they are not invisible by complete omission—they are exhorted to stay young and beautiful, to do things to their bodies to achieve this, and to wear make-up, hair products and clothes to conceal their real age. They, much more often than men, are shown as weak and helpless. They are used to sell mood-changing medicines: anti-depressants and tranquillizers. A typical medical advertisement shows an older woman before treatment (haggard) and after treatment (slightly less haggard). Older women are wholly categorized by exclusion in relation to romance, sex and leisure; they are excluded from many holiday package deals; and are shown as having fun only as part of a (heterosexual) couple on wedding anniversaries. They are excluded from work: newspapers are full of advertisements that specify ages, often as young as 30 or 35, with a top limit of 40 or 45, for the employment of women. Older women are shown in dependent roles—as pensioners in clubs or dependent on a man. Or they are shown as victims of violent muggings, especially of 'granny-bashing'. Rarely are older women portrayed as capable and independent, never as sexually attractive.

These combined messages of ageism and sexism affect women of all ages. Young women are prepared for rigid heterosexuality, sexual availability as well as attractiveness (divided by competition with each other for men), and for their role (i.e. unpaid or low paid work) in the sexual division of labour—for reproduction, childrearing and domestic labour. Older women are deemed 'past it', good for little except possibly to be idealized as grandmothers. All women, at whatever age, are portrayed as subordinate to men: passive, submissive. This is the ageist/sexist message of the media images.

We can turn again to a study of women's magazines—but now with an awareness of the combined apparatus of age role and sex role conditioning we may find in them. For the six-month period from January to June 1983, I carried out a content analysis of *Woman* magazine. There was only one issue that did not make major reference to 'women and age' in some way; many issues had one or more feature articles. In addition, there were letters in almost every issue about ageing and attitudes to ageing, plus 'agony column' letters.

There were many articles about 'stars': the famous—Petula Clark, Cilla Black, even men like Tom Jones; the royals—Countess Mountbatten, Princess Michael; the rich. The emphasis editorially was on how good they still look at 40 or over (how sexually attractive they still are even though they are supposed to be 'past it'), or how long and happily they have been married. They are represented as ideal wives or widows or mothers, and it is implied that there is something unusual about them. In other words, ordinary people would have succumbed long ago to ageing and unattractiveness and divorce.

There were a number of articles on the theme of 'how to stay young and fit' (significantly, not just fit, but *young* and fit) with the focus at different times on weight or hair or skin or health. There were single one-off features such as one on five middle-aged (and fat) chorus girls who were making a success in their work, or one on the 'relatively youthful looking' 36 year old top make-up artist who had decided, at 36, that she would remain single for the rest of her life unless she met 'Mr Right'. Four 'serious' features were devoted to the issue of older women. One was on the 'young image of the WI', one was on the problem of 'granny-bashing' (note the designation of female though the victims of the abuse were equally male and female), one was on old people mistreated by their own children in the role of carers, and one was on whether 'grandma and grandpa' should be put in old people's homes. However ostensibly 'serious', all four feature articles played on stereotypes: the stereotyped WI woman as middle-aged and dull; the stereotype of happy old age as being surrounded by a devoted family.

The precise breakdown of age references in editorial matter was revealing. Out of 21 issues (*Woman* is a weekly), all but one had significant editorial reference to age or ageing (usually reinforcing the stereotypes). Eleven editions had one major feature article, four editions had two, one edition had three, and two editions had four. This was in addition to the column 'You and Us' at the front, the regular two pages devoted to readers' letters and anecdotes, and Virginia Ironside's 'agony column' at the back, which included such age-related dilemmas as what to do with nagging mother-in-law, and whether an older woman should have a relationship with a younger man. Significantly, the only place where the stereotypes were questioned or contradicted was in the readers' letters and the 'How I Coped' column within that section — about women acting powerfully and presenting a positive image. These were derived from and based on the real experiences of women, and were very different from the stereotypes.

HOW THE STEREOTYPES FUNCTION

To be aware of the images and attitudes raises some important questions as to the meaning and purpose of this systematic misrepresentaton of women. What exactly is a stereotype and how does it function? A stereotype is really a representation of one aspect only of a human being (or rather a human being as a member of a group — women, children, old people, black people, Jewish people, people with disabilities): suggesting that this aspect represents the whole of those people, and creating the impression that it is characterizing those people in that group in an essential and significant way. Yet because it is only one aspect, a stereotype is a distorted or exaggerated or misleading representation of a human being or a group of human beings. A stereotype is thus a source of partial information, at best, and thus of misinformation. A stereotype is less a representation of 'real' human beings (of the 'humanness' of humans) than it is a representation of a particular idea about human beings. Basically, a stereotype represents a set of ideas or a set of beliefs about people — an ideology — rather than people as they are. Stereotypes are deliberately misleading; they perform the function of creating attitudes which, by their very nature, are negative attitudes. They function as a form of propaganda; they are the language of ideology — the way it is communicated.

In one sense, stereotypes in advertisements (and other media) are real. They are not, however, representations of real women, but rather representations of women's oppression. This — the oppression of women — is real. The material conditions of oppression are real, as is the ideology (and its armoury of stereotypes) which sustains the oppression. The message of the media representations is thus a message about the oppression of women, not about women themselves. Stereotypes reflect the oppression and assist in its construction.

The way in which stereotypes teach oppression or enable oppression to be learned (internalized) is the subject of Janice Winship's essay on the function of ideology in women's magazines. She concludes that what is taught to women is their (our) 'work' — of beauty, femininity, domesticity and consumption (Winship, 1983).

What the stereotypes provide is an education for women (and men, on the other end of the oppression) about their place in the social structure. They are tools for teaching subordination (and to males, dominance). They inform women of what their uses are. The important new perception is that they also inform women of *when* they are useful and at *what ages*. There are two agendas, a double message: one of sex stereotyping and control of sexuality, the other of age stereotyping and age control. Goffman (1979) comments on this: 'Gender, in close connection with age-grades, more than class or other social divisions, lays down an understanding of what our ultimate nature ought to be and how and where this nature ought to be exhibited'. The reality (however obscured) is that age stereotypes and sex stereotypes work together in constructing the oppression of women. The oppression has, up to now, been perceived simply as sexism. The age factor in sexism—the combined effect of ageism and sexism—has not been as obvious as it deserves to be, or needs to be if one is to understand the nature of the oppression of women.

Because of the extent to which we have internalized age-sex stereotypes we lead double lives. We live both our 'reality' and the 'reality' of the oppression. That is to say, we live what we know is true and we live the lie about us. We submit to the stereotypes and resist them simultaneously. Condor (Chapter 6) refers to this 'double consciousness' and this reflects the experience of the 45 women I have interviewed for my doctoral thesis (Itzin, in preparation). Their experience may, perhaps, be typified by the woman who wrote:

> What, fat, forty-three and I dare to think I'm still a person? No. I am an invisible lump. I belong in a category labelled *a priori* without interest to anyone. I am not even expected to interest myself. A middle-aged woman is comic by definition. The mass media tell us all day and all evening long that we are inadequate, mindless, ugly, disgusting in ourselves. Everything she reads, every comic strip, every song, every cartoon, every advertisement, every book and movie tells her that a woman over thirty is ugly and disgusting. She is a bag. She is to be escaped from. To be old when you have half your years still to wade through and when you don't feel inside much different than you did at 20 (you are still you!—you know that!), to be told then that you are cut off from expressing yourself sexually and often even in friendship, drives many women crazy—often literally so. I have insisted on using a pseudonym in writing this article because the cost of insisting I am not a cipher would be fatal. If I lost my job I would have an incredible time finding another. Listen to me! Think what it is like to have most of your life ahead and be told you are obsolete. Think what it is like to feel attraction, desire, affection toward others, to want to tell them about yourself, to feel that assumption on which self-respect is based, that you are worth something, surely he will be pleased to know that. To be, in other words, still a living woman, and to be told every day that you are not a woman but a tired object that should disappear. I am bitter and frustrated and wasted, but don't you pretend for a minute as you look at me, forty-three, fat and looking exactly my age, that I am not as alive as you are, and that I do not suffer from the category into which you are forcing me. (Moss, 1970)

This woman—like all the others in their different ways—testifies to the negative attitudes that have influenced her life, and how the attitudes are internalized—through fear in the oppressor and the oppressed. Stereotypes function to create fear and division between people. Images of older women are so overwhelmingly negative in their presentation of attitudes to wrinkles and greying hair that from an early age women fear what happens to their bodies. Younger women look at older women, and recoil. In that revulsion is their fear of what is going to happen to them. This negative fear of ageing is reinforced by the advertising put out by companies whose products are supposed to retard, diminish or disguise the effects of ageing.

The combined message of ageism and sexism is simple and devastating. Women have two functions: sexual and domestic. Each involves children: the first child-bearing and the second child-rearing. Each involves availability and services to men: sexual and domestic. Both functions begin for women from the 'age of marriage'. Both functions finish for women in their mid-forties: in *retirement* from reproduction and *retirement* from child rearing. Neither of these rites of passage is marked by celebration. They are characterized by gloom and misery (the stereotype of the menopause) and categorized by loss (the 'empty nest' syndrome of sociology). From the age of about 40 when men are in the prime of life, women embark on the second half of their life with little status and almost no value. This valuelessness is not inherent, but created; not biologically determined, but socially constructed—with the assistance of the media.

WHERE PATRIARCHY AND CAPITALISM COLLUDE

'That women's magazines are in the business of selling themselves and a variety of other commodities has become abundantly clear' (Winship, 1983). Cynthia White, in her study of women's magazines from 1693 to 1968, noted that 'the boom in women's periodicals has in fact paralleled the boom in domestic consumption and the vast expansion in advertising which has accompanied it', and that 'features which cannot be used to sell goods are wasted space as far as advertisers are concerned, and Editors are forced to keep them to a minimum' (White, 1970). Mary Grieve, editor of *Woman* from the 1940s to the 1960s, has written: 'It is because women of all ages hold in common this consumer-concern that a vast profitable press has grown up to service them' (Grieve, 1964). It is clear that the selling to women of a stereotyped image of themselves serves the interests of maintaining the system of patriarchy (or male power). It must be equally clear that it also serves the interests of capitalism.

Given the relationship, it is not surprising, then, to find a close connection between the advertising and editorial content in women's magazines. For example, in my 1983 content analysis of *Woman* magazine, I found a feature described as a 'Health Exclusive' and headlined in what sounded like a positive tone, 'The Good News about Growing Old'. On the credit side it provided some information that contradicted the myths—the stereotypes—of ageing:

> Society expects us all to behave in a certain way, and this is especially true
> when it comes to old age. We expect old people to be less creative, less capable
> of learning, less flexible. Physically we expect them to be bent, wrinkled and
> prone to illness. But it doesn't have to be so, and in reality often is not.

The stereotypes of bad memory and slow learning were shown to be false. The
article made it clear that food, friends and exercise would prolong good health
and active life. All well and good, but the beginning of the article cunningly
conjured up just the stereotypes it sought to banish:

> You thought growing old meant getting wrinkled, waving goodbye to your
> bikini, watching your body—and maybe your mind—go slowly, sadly out
> of control? Well, now for the good news: the latest research reveals that this
> picture of ageing is totally wrong—if you really want it to be. Now none
> of us have to give in gracefully to growing older—and we can all cheat the
> ageing trap.

We recognize it all immediately, and we identify with it too. The article is
premised on precisely that identification and the fear that stereotypes always
stimulate: if we were not terrified of the 'trap' we would not really 'want to cheat
it'. We would not need the exhortation to 'stay young and beautiful' which is
implied in the text.

The chronological checklist that accompanied the text (what to expect at ages
20–30, 30–40, 40–50), visually and textually reinforced the age categories (the
'trap') and the age stereotypes, assuming that at one end of the scale a woman
would be young and beautiful, and at the other old and unattractive (unless you
were lucky or like the elderly celebrities interviewed and 'boxed' along the bottom
of the page, with fame and fortune on your side). The illustration was of three
women silhouetted, one young and beautiful (foreground), the second thickening
and sagging (middle distance) and the third thickened and sagged (background).
There was a quiz to test how well we 'adapt' to old age, implying that it is 'a
slot that one has to fit into, adapt to'. But old age does not exist outside the person,
it is a feature of the person. The concept of 'losing one's figure', seeing old age
as somehow 'out there' contributes to 'our alienation from ourselves' (WMAG,
Report No. 5).

What was striking was the similarity of this editorial feature to an advertisement
headed 'How to Look Younger Longer', selling skin care advice and products for
a 'youthful looking face and a youthful looking body'; or even cruder advertisements
exhorting us to buy something to 'free ourselves of ugly stretch marks', or some
other product for lines and wrinkles around the mouth that mar the appearance
and make us look older, or something else to 'prevent the grey from reappearing'.
It all communicates the message that ageing is something to be feared; in short, it
is a disadvantage to grow old. This plays on the negative feelings women all have
after years of being conditioned to believe that no part of us is acceptable

or right. All of this conspires to create a context of acceptability and indeed necessity even for advertisements for cosmetic surgery. The editorial feature in the July 1983 issue of *Woman*, headlined 'Skin Shock' and subheaded 'Latest and most extreme ways to uplift and deep cleanse your face include being skinned alive, pierced with needles and painted in paraffin wax', was illustrated with a truly shocking picture of a woman being treated with needles on her face and looking more like a hedgehog than a human being. She, obviously, like 'Fat and Forty-three', had got the message of the media and internalized it sufficiently to suffer considerable pain.

Over 50 million women purchase a woman's magazine every month in the USA (1970 statistics). That constitutes practically three-quarters of the entire adult female population (Embree, 1970). The money spent on advertising to this audience and to that of the soap operas (whose purpose is to sell soap!) was $16.5 billion (in 1966). In one year (between July 1978 and June 1979) in the UK £121.5 million were spent on perfume, £58 million on make-up, £71 million on skin care, £96 million on hair preparations, £42 million on shampoos, and £37 million on other toiletries (Hogstan, 1980). The Magazine Publishers' Association in the USA advertised its products to the potential advertisers in a way that leaves no doubt about the connection between ageism, sexism and capitalism:

> Magazines turned legs into a rainbow. Magazines convinced a gal she needed a flutter of fur where plain little eyelashes used to work. Magazines have the power to make a girl forget her waist exists. And the very next year, make her buy a belt for every dress she owns. They can move a fashion trend from Paris to the Papa-Mama store as fast as somebody can sew it up. Magazines help distressed damsels remake their wardrobes, faces, hair, body. And sometimes their whole way of being. And the ladies love it. And beg for more. When she gets involved with herself and fashion in any magazine, she's a captive from cover to cover. (Embree, 1970, p. 207)

The 1982 EOC survey of advertising compared the effectiveness of using traditional stereotypes with using more modern and realistic images. They found that 'the treatment which incorporated a less restricted, modern female role-portrayal was consistently found to enhance the marketing-effectiveness of the brands' advertising'. This might suggest that advertisers and the media could cease to use stereotyped images to sell to women, that we might expect to see, for example, healthy, active, attractive older women in positions of occupational power in the pages of women's magazines and television. At first sight this would seem to make sense, but only if we (naively) take the advertisements at face value, and assume that they are *only* selling us products and not oppressive images of ourselves.

In the long run, if the stereotypes function as transmitters of oppressive attitudes on behalf of the oppressive society, then they are as essential to the ends of the advertisers as to the oppressive system. 'Real' women—women untainted by the ideology of patriarchy—would not have their faces cut and stitched or stuck with pins, or their breasts, bellies and buttocks butchered. They would not need make-up or high heels or restrictive clothing. The stereotypes function to keep the oppression operating by contributing to the 'construction of an identity' which is doubly jeopardizing to women — in terms of both age and gender.

REFERENCES

Adams, C. and Laurikietis, R. (eds) (1980). *The Gender Trap, A Closer Look at Sex Roles 3: Messages and Images.* London, Virago.

Against Ageism. (1983). Available from Search Project, 74 Adelaide Terrace, Newcastle upon Tyne.

Arnoff (1974). In: P. Webb, op. cit.

Bradly (1974). In P. Webb, op. cit.

Butler, R. (1975). *Why Survive: Being Old in America.* New York, Harper and Row.

Comfort, A. (1977). *A Good Age.* London, Mitchell Beazley.

Courtney, A. and Lockeretz, S. W. (1971). A woman's place: an analysis of the roles portrayed by women in magazine advertisements. *Journal of Marketing Research* (8 February).

Embree, A. (1970). Media images 1: Madison Avenue brainwashing — the facts. In: R. Morgan (ed.), op. cit.

Equal Opportunities Commission. (1982). *Adman and Eve: A Study of the Portrayal of Women in Advertising.* Carried out for the Equal Opportunities Commission by the Marketing Research Consultancy and Research Services, Department of Marketing, University of Lancaster.

Ferguson, M. (1983). *Forever Feminine, Women's Magazines and the Cult of Femininity.* London, Heinemann.

Francer (1973). In: P. Webb, op. cit.

Goffman, E. (1979). *Gender Advertisements.* London, The Macmillan Press.

Grieve, M. (1964). *Millions Made My Story:* London, Gollancz.

Hogstan, J. (1980). Cosmetic and toiletry preparations review, June, 1979. In: C. Adams and R. Laurikietis (eds), *The Gender Trap.* London, Virago.

Itzin, C. (In preparation): *Sexual and Age Divisions: A Study of Identity and Opportunity in Women.* Unpublished Ph.D. thesis. University of Kent, Canterbury.

Kenny, M. (1983). *She* (August), 6.

Millum, T. (1975). *Images of Women: Advertising in Women's Magazines.* New York, Rowman & Littlefield.

Morgan, R. (ed.) (1970). *Sisterhood is Powerful, An Anthology of Writings from Women's Liberation Movement.* New York, Vintage.

Moss, Z. (1970). It hurts to be alive and obsolete; the ageing woman. In: R. Morgan (ed.), op. cit.

National Council for One Parent Families. (1983). *Annual Report.* London.

Petersen (1973). In: P. Webb, op. cit.

Scheibe, C. (1979). Sex roles in TV commercials. *Journal of Advertising Research* 19 (February).

Segal, L. (1982). Unhappy families. *New Socialist* 16 (July/August). (Figures from L. Rimmer, *Families in Focus.* Study Commission on the Family and Department of Employment, Manpower Paper No. 11.)

TUC (1984). *Images of Inequality: The Portrayal of Women in the Media and Advertising.* Available from TUC, Congress House, Great Russell Street, London WC1B 3LS.

Tuchman, G., Daniels, A. D. and Benet, J. (1978). *Hearth and Home: Images of Women in the Mass Media*. New York, Oxford University Press.

Ward, T. (1983). In: *Against Ageism*, op. cit.

Wasner, L. C. and Banos, J. B. (1973). A woman's place: follow-up analysis of the roles portrayed by women in magazine advertisements. *Journal of Marketing Research* (May).

Webb, P. (1984). Images of old age. Paper delivered to British Society of Gerontology annual conference. Available from Medicus Productions Ltd., 9–13 Grape Street, London WC2H 8DF.

White, C. (1970). *Women's Magazines, A Sociological Inquiry*. London, Michael Joseph.

Winship, J. (1983). *Femininity and Women's Magazines*. Open University Course, 'The Changing Experience of Women', Unit 6. Milton Keynes, Open University Press.

Women's Media Action Group (WMAG). (1981–83). *Sexism in the Media*. Report No. 1: Women as sex objects; Report No. 2: Violence against women; Report No. 3: Stereotypes of women; Report No. 4: Sugar and spice; Report No. 5: Women and ageism. Available from WMAG, Hungerford House, Victoria Embankment, London WC2.

Chapter 8

Developing a Feminist Approach to Depression Following Childbirth

Paula Nicolson

INTRODUCTION

This chapter is particularly concerned with the development of a feminist methodology and a woman-centred perspective on women as 'new' mothers. The intention is to contrast findings and interpretations of data collected from an 'objective' standpoint with one which attempts to examine the way women perceive the world.

Depression following childbirth is exclusive to women, although the research findings and theoretical perspectives underpinning knowledge of this problem (which affects between 13 and 40% of women: Oakley, 1980) increasingly reflect male values. They do so, firstly, in the sense that research designs are relying more and more on standardized measures and 'objective' data, which mainly deny individual differences of experience (e.g. Kumar and Robson, 1978).

Secondly, such research designs include perspectives which firmly place women in the category of 'faulty machines'—whether this refers to their physiological or their psychological mechanisms (e.g. Dalton, 1980). Thirdly the term 'post natal depression'[1] has virtually transcended the state at which it needs to be defined or explained—and thus, despite lack of evidence, has become an accepted 'fact' of female life. In other words the use of this label has enabled men to account for women's behaviour without having to understand its complexities. As Oakley says:

> Post natal depression is not a 'scientific' term but an ideological one. It mystifies the real social and medical factors that lead to mothers' unhappiness. (Oakley, 1979)

For this reason I use the description 'depression following childbirth' to emphasize temporal rather than intrinsic qualities.

135

This is the starting point for my research, which is an attempt to unravel inconsistencies in contemporary thinking about depression following childbirth, and avoid the trap of social scientists who:

> . . . fail to report or discuss the contradictions between experience, consciousness and theory because the paradigm (they) work within tells (them) that these are unimportant or non-existent. (Stanley and Wise, 1983, p. 154)

To avoid this, my research relates women's accounts of childbirth and the early post natal months to a 'standardized' measure of depression. In particular, it contrasts the ways women evaluate their lives at this stage, with the 'insensitivity' of the 'objective' data, and with the popular theoretical position. Implicit in the findings are the *inadequacies* of assumptions made about women, motherhood and childbirth—which amplify women's oppression within an essentially male-oriented society, specifically in terms of pursuing 'objective' knowledge.

In addition, arguments surrounding the practice of feminist research within social psychology and related disciplines will be followed up in the context of developing a woman-centred and feminist perspective on depression following childbirth.

DEFICITS IN DESIGN AND THEORY

Before discussing the details of my own findings it is useful to illustrate the existing state of knowledge with some pertinent examples. These must be seen in the context of the dominance of a medically-oriented perspective, although sociologists, psychoanalysts and psychologists also claim access to this work. Even so, there is little evidence of effective interdisciplinary dialogue—a state of affairs which is reflected in the absence of a coherent paradigm. Thus it is no surprise that a recent review of the literature concludes:

> Methodological and conceptual shortcomings of existing studies have resulted in inconsistent findings, which in turn have prevented the development of a coherent theoretical framework for understanding the aetiology, course and treatment of the disorder. (Hopkins *et al.*, 1984)

The trend over the past 15 years has been an increase in medium scale longitudinal studies of cohorts of around 150 women through pregnancy and the early years of motherhood. They have attempted to be all-embracing, and have gained their credibility from voluminous data collection using standardized psychiatric measures.

Problems arise out of collecting such data at the expense of adequate conceptualization and from the failure to address the original problem within a well considered theoretical framework. Also designs suffer from 'overload' by aiming to establish criteria for identification, prediction and treatment of 'post natal depression', as well as to investigate a series of correlations between depression and a range of psychosocial factors. Thus debates concerned with the incidence of depression in pregnancy and after delivery (Kumar and Robson, 1978); the relationship between 'the blues' and later depression (Cox *et al.*, 1982); social class and social contacts and incidence of depression (Pollock *et al.*, 1980); and so on, characterize the disparate knowledge base of what may be described as 'the psychology of post natal depression'. Few of these studies report any qualitative data—even by way of illustration.

Some qualitative data are available from psychoanalytic case studies (e.g. Blum, 1978) and sociological and psychological accounts of childbirth and the transition to motherhood (e.g. Boulton, 1983; Breen, 1975; Oakley, 1980; Wearing, 1984). These do not appear to be highly valued by the majority of research workers publishing in 'mainstream' psychology and psychiatry journals and are rarely referred to in these. The only such reference I found was in Elliot *et al.* (1984), who incidentally mention Oakley's (1980) finding that 'post natal depression' was related to the amount of obstetric technology used in delivery.

It is difficult to discuss methodology and the nature of research findings in isolation from theory. A major inconsistency in research design has resulted from the underlying assumptions that, firstly, the concept of 'post natal depression' is inviolable, and secondly, that it is a product of hormone imbalances. Steiner (1979) has reviewed the literature relating to the psychobiology of mental disorders associated with childbearing, and like Hopkins *et al.* (1984), has drawn attention to the inconclusive nature of most of the data, in noting that 'postpartum mental distress is *not* a unitary phenomenon'—a suggestion which has remained largely ignored.

Despite the lack of systematic evidence, there is an overriding popular view that depression following childbirth can be treated by 'tinkering' with women's hormone levels. There are several reasons for this, not the least being the '. . . enormous re-assurance . . . (that) . . . makes those of us who suffer from it feel less ashamed to admit it . . .' (Rantzen in Dalton, 1980).

Dalton typifies the attitude of many medical practitioners in asserting that:

> The majority of women suffering from post natal depression do not even recognise that they are ill. They believe that they are . . . bogged down by utter exhaustion and irritability. . . . It is all too easy to blame their condition on to the extra work that the baby brings into their new life. . . . Once the condition has been recognised and treated the husband will be able to declare 'She's once more the woman I married'. (1980, p. 4)

Thus it may be that for those who suffer from depression, and for those who make their living from treating it, it is convenient to disregard evidence which suggests that there is no such entity as a specific illness 'post natal depression'.

It is the combination of the assumption that motherhood has a prescribed pattern from which variations represent 'illnesses', and the assumption that childbirth is a crisis point for hormonal fluctuations, that underlies the conceptual problems in the literature. These problems typify a male-oriented perspective on women — as objects without 'human' variation. In contrast woman-centred research would present a more *truly* 'value-free' picture of women: as multidimensional individuals whose psychological and social lives and experiences are as potentially variable as those of men.

THE WOMEN IN THIS STUDY

The aim of my research was to develop an analysis of women's accounts of early motherhood and relate these to scores on a standardized measure of 'post natal depression' (Pitt, 1968): see Table 1. The sample was to include women gaining low ('non-depressed') scores. The report on this research may be divided into three main areas:

(1)   How far do 'objective' measures of depression coincide with subjective accounts, and what does an objective measure contribute to knowledge of the *nature* of the depression? Do similar overall scores and similar scores on particular items really measure the same kind of emotion in different women?

(2)   How may analysing women's accounts of their experiences be more relevant to reactions following childbirth than 'objective' measures?

(3)   What is meant by a woman-centred perspective and a feminist methodology?

For the immediate purposes of this chapter I am not going to develop theoretical arguments relating to the causation of depression following childbirth, other than incidentally. The focus is upon the practice and development of a feminist methodology which enables women to define the nature of their experience.

The data discussed below are derived from 40 women's accounts of their experience of delivery and their feelings about childbirth and hospitalization. These accounts were obtained while the women were still in hospital, and at home three months later.

On both occasions they were given a depression measure as well as being asked to describe their feelings and experiences. All but one of the women lived with the baby's father, and their ages ranged from 16 to 35 years (mean age 26.5 years) with 21 having their first baby, 11 their second and 8 their third to sixth.

Ten of the sample were middle-class British women — an academic, a junior school teacher (both of whom were on maternity leave), a bank clerk, and four secretaries — none of whom intended returning to work for some time. The majority were working class, many of these had been machinists in the clothing

Table 1
Questionnaire to Measure Atypical Depression Following Childbirth[a]

Scoring
The answers underlined score 2 points; 'don't know' answers score 1; other answers score 0. Scores represent morbid answers; the maximum score is 48 points.

Instructions
I am asking you these questions in order to find out how you feel about things during this time of having your baby/now you are at home with your baby.[b] I want to know how you feel *at the present time,* that is today and over the past few days. Please listen to the questions carefully and then answer as frankly and as honestly as you can. Just answer 'yes', 'no', or 'don't know' if you really cannot make up your mind, but please try to avoid this.

At the present time:

(1)	Do you sleep well?	Yes	<u>No</u>
(2)	Do you easily lose your temper?	<u>Yes</u>	No
(3)	Are you worried about your looks?	<u>Yes</u>	No
(4)	Have you a good appetite?	Yes	<u>No</u>
(5)	Are you as happy as you ought to be?	Yes	<u>No</u>
(6)	Do you easily forget things?	<u>Yes</u>	No

At the present time:

(7)	Do you have as much interest in sex as ever?	Yes	<u>No</u>
(8)	Is everything a great effort?	<u>Yes</u>	No
(9)	Do you feel ashamed for any reason?	<u>Yes</u>	No
(10)	Can you relax easily?	Yes	<u>No</u>
(11)	Can you feel the baby is really yours?	Yes	<u>No</u>
(12)	Do you want someone with you all the time?	<u>Yes</u>	No

At the present time:

(13)	Are you easily woken up?	<u>Yes</u>	No
(14)	Do you feel calm most of the time?	Yes	<u>No</u>
(15)	Do you feel you are in good health?	Yes	<u>No</u>
(16)	Does food interest you less than it did?	<u>Yes</u>	No
(17)	Do you cry easily	<u>Yes</u>	No
(18)	Is your memory as good as it ever was?	Yes	<u>No</u>

At the present time:

(19)	Have you less desire for sex than usual?	<u>Yes</u>	No
(20)	Have you enough energy?	Yes	<u>No</u>
(21)	Are you satisfied with the way you're coping with things?	Yes	<u>No</u>
(22)	Do you worry a lot about the baby?	<u>Yes</u>	No
(23)	Do you feel unlike your normal self?	<u>Yes</u>	No
(24)	Do you have confidence in yourself?	Yes	<u>No</u>

Is there anything else you would like to add about your feelings at the moment?

[a]From Pitt (1968).
[b]This line of the instructions was adapted to my study.

industry, but others had only experienced casual employment. Three were Nigerians married to students, and intended returning home when their husbands graduated. Five were of West Indian origin, one Cypriot, three of mixed race and the remainder British or Irish. The majority lived in council or privately rented accommodation in the East End of London, although three had bought their own houses in a less central location.

The sample was selected from two different maternity units which were recognized as having opposing approaches to intervention and natural delivery. This was in order to gain some sense of the effect of high technology birth upon women. Evidence relating to this issue, although inconclusive, suggests that medicalized childbirth might have a depressing effect upon women (see Oakley, 1980; Day, 1982; Elliot *et al.*, 1984). The women were approached in the ward and asked whether they would talk to me about their experience of birth and complete a questionnaire for research purposes. The only refusals were from two Asian women who did not speak English.

As both Finch (1984) and Oakley (1982) point out, there are practical and ethical considerations for a feminist interviewing women. Women expect, and are used to being asked, detailed and personal questions, particularly at this stage of their lives (see also Oakley, 1980), and thus are vulnerable to 'exploitation' by researchers. Here it was important to avoid appearing to represent the authority of the hospital—in particular, because the midwives were supportive of me, they frequently 'introduced' me into the wards. However, I did stress to each woman that I was an independent researcher and they were not obliged to answer questions.

The interview was semi-structured, with the initial request to the women to talk about their experience of delivery. At appropriate points they were asked to clarify or to say more, particularly if there were specific difficulties. The questionnaire, which required responses about the way they were feeling at the present time, was then administered verbally. After that, they were asked biographical details: their address, marital status, educational level, employment details, number of previous children, whether the pregnancy had been planned, and whether they would agree to be re-interviewed after three months. All did agree at this time, although after three months some had moved and some 'forgot' appointments, so that only 22 were re-interviewed. Clearly, some of the women not seen again may well have avoided seeing me because they were depressed, but it was not possible to determine this. Also, I felt it was ethically unsound to pursue or press women into being interviewed again.

In some ways this contrasts with Oakley's reports of women who were eager to keep in touch (1982, p. 51). However, as Finch observed in her study of play group mothers, there was a contrast between 'frank' and 'enthusiastic' responses to relaxed discussions, and the 'grudging' answers to a structured interview schedule (1984, p. 73). Indeed, my relationship with the women *may* have been confounded by my use of 'formal' data collection technique. However, the women

I did follow up were generally willing to talk about their personal feelings in a way which seemed to be helpful to them, providing a chance to explore and articulate their perceptions of their worlds. Interviews on both occasions lasted between 6 and 80 minutes with all but three being 20 to 35 minutes long.

CONTRADICTIONS

The broad aim of social science within a clinical setting is to establish patterns of 'incidence', 'onset' and 'duration'. Pitt's (1968) questionnaire is claimed to be a valid and reliable instrument for measuring 'atypical depression' after childbirth, and is widely used in this context. However, the questions I wanted to raise concerned whether this questionnaire measures the *same* thing in different women (necessary to justify an identifiable pattern of a specific 'post natal depression').

The most striking feature of the questionnaire scores was the lack of any consistent pattern from interview one to interview two. Thus women who had high scores on the questionnaire (i.e. 20 and above) at first interview (ten women, 25% of the sample) might have high, medium or low scores at second interview. The same variability was true of women with medium or low scores at first interview. The only exception to this was that among the very high scorers at first interview, (i.e. 'the blues' stage[1]), there were six women whose delivery had been accompanied by medical complications; this must be seen as an experience of 'ill health' with its contingent stress (see Oakley, 1980). All of these women had extremely low scores three months later.

One said at the second interview:

> It is such a relief to have him (the baby) and to be in one piece myself . . .
> and be home with my husband . . . I can't imagine not being happy, everything
> before was so awful.

In her case there were anxieties about the baby's health before and shortly after birth, and depression following this was not 'atypical' in the sense that it was an unusual reaction; in fact one might say that it would have been unusual *not* to have been depressed.

Another woman with a high first score, and an even higher second score, once again had well founded reasons. She had had a previous still birth, and several miscarriages, and following this delivery was very anxious about her baby's health. No-one in the unit would listen to her anxieties about the baby's breathing, and it was not until four days later when the paediatrician rushed the baby (who *had* had respiratory problems) into intensive care, that she was taken seriously. Her first interview was on the fifth day and she was very depressed; by the time of her second interview (at home), the baby had been diagnosed as suffering from brain damage and she felt:

> My life is over, I have to care for this baby — it could have been prevented,
> but what can *I* do . . . they don't care . . .

Three of the other high scorers at the first interview felt that they were depressed because of the hospital. Two were Nigerian, and told me, without my probing, that the (mainly West Indian) staff did not like them because of their race. Both of these women had reduced scores later. A third was anxious that her husband would be angry because he wanted a son and she had had a second daughter.

It would appear to be the case that the questionnaire does reveal some form of depression — feelings of being down in the dumps, inability to cope, anxiety, stress and distress. What does not seem to be the case is that it has the ability to identify a specific *type* of depression triggered by childbirth. Further, there was some evidence that it does not reveal *all* cases of depression.

A dramatic example was provided by a 33 year old working class woman who lived on a large, bleak East London housing estate. She was interviewed after the birth of her sixth baby. Her score whilst in hospital was above average, but not significantly high. She said: 'It was not an easy birth . . . but I always feel better when I'm pregnant.'

This child was born six years after the previous one, and although a 'surprise', she said that she was glad she had had him. There were some problems with his thigh socket which kept springing out of place, but by the time I visited her three months later, he had been discharged from treatment. Her score at the second interview was low, and she declared herself to be happy. However, she looked very ill (and older than her 33 years). Her clothes and hair were unkempt; her flat, and two of her older children who were off school, smelt of urine and appeared rather grubby. She talked in a monotone without facial expression. It seemed that she was indeed depressed, but her experience of this was so persistent as not to 'register' on questionnaire items such as the following:

> Are you as happy as you ought to be?
> Are you worried about your looks?
> Do you feel unlike your normal self?

She was in fact, chronically *oppressed* [2].

It could be argued, of course, that the measure was not at fault because 'post natal depression' is specific to a time and an event and this woman's condition was more enduring. However, given the disparate accounts of the high scorers, the suffering of this woman probably only differs from the others' in duration. It may be that some of the women in this sample would remain depressed, but little attention has been paid to depression beyond the first year after delivery. Increasing oppression arguably goes hand in hand with motherhood, and may increase with each child, but there is no systematic research available on women with several children.

There are indications from the earlier work of Gavron (1977), Oakley (1976) and also more radical accounts (such as de Beauvoir, 1968; Friedan, 1979) that women at home with children often report unhappiness and dissatisfaction; these findings are also supported by the early work of Young and Willmott (1962). Other sociologists considering questions of stratification in relation to gender, have proposed ways in which this is also indicative of the subordination of women within heterosexual relationships (see Bell and Newby, 1976).

This woman was the only one in my sample for whom I would argue strongly against the evidence of both the objective measure *and* her own account on the grounds that she was *unaware* of her depression. Other women probably demonstrated the phenomenon of 'faking' (Beere, 1979), i.e. giving a socially desirable response.

One 29 year old at home in her neat, small East End flat after the birth of her second daughter, described her life as being ' . . . very happy — what you would expect with duties towards a man and a family'. Her depression score was low, her description of her life was positive, but throughout her account she used words such as 'obligation', 'what you have to do', and never referred to *pleasure* in her tasks.

Klein suggests that faking is quite common and further:

> It may well be that faking is necessary for the psychological survival of many women because without faking, reality would seem unbearable.

She goes on to suggest:

> Feminists should consider acknowledging and incorporating faking into our research methods . . . by accepting and taking it seriously, we accept and take ourselves seriously. (1983, p. 91)

So, this phenomenon is worth identifying — not in order to 'catch someone out' or find any kind of 'truth', but as another way of understanding how women experience and *interpret* their lives. It is this subjective interpretation of material which is absent from standardized measuring instruments.

THE NATURE OF DEPRESSION FOLLOWING CHILDBIRTH

Paykel *et al.* (1980) state in relation to 'the blues' that it 'is reasonable to regard so common and time-distinctive a phenomenon as related to massive hormonal changes'. However, if individual women are asked about their feelings and experiences there is a wide variety in their accounts, and the women tend to evaluate the way they behaved in childbirth and the 'outcome' within the context of their life history. Most frequently women expressed disappointment either with their inability to deal with the birth without making a 'fuss', or with the midwives' or obstetricians' desire that they accept medication.

Similarly, Graham and Oakley (1981) found that obstetricians and mothers have strongly contrasting frames of reference for 'success' in pregnancy and birth. The obstetrician only appears concerned that mother and baby are physically healthy, but the mother evaluates her experience in terms of her social circumstances and personal life goals. Morgan (1983) provides an account of mothers preferring a painful birth where they felt they were in control, to a pain—free one where they felt robbed of autonomy. These findings surprised the obstetricians involved in the research!

Furthermore, accounts from women depressed three months after delivery also suggest that they evaluate their individual experiences in different ways. It is these accounts which provide clues to the nature of their depression. Merely asserting that they are depressed after having babies, and that this is an 'atypical' and distinctive form of depression, is tautologous. Depression after childbirth is not something that happens to all women. However, for *some* women this period of their lives exposes them to the need to re-evaluate and change their social relationships (particularly, but not exclusively, in the case of a first baby), and possibly makes some women aware of their oppression for the first time.

One first time mother in her early thirties, who was a postdoctoral research fellow in science, had had a baby '. . . because I felt it was about time, and my boyfriend particularly wanted him'. She went on to say: 'I like the baby, and we (her boyfriend and herself) share all the tasks, but I miss my work, I miss my friends'—none of whom were parents themselves. She declared: *'My life seems to have jolted into change'*. It is this change that typifies childbirth and early motherhood, especially for the first time mother. It is not necessarily psychological change as such, but change in social interactions which gradually affect women's perceptions of who they are, and their ability to cope.

A 22 year old, three months after her second baby, felt 'trapped'. She said she had never had any confidence in herself and after her first baby arrived her parents-in-law seemed to spend more and more time telling her how to bring it up. Her husband, she felt, sided with them against her, and now she had a second child, he was even more keen that the in-laws should take charge, and she was left isolated, excluded and feeling useless. Her feelings of uselessness did not arise from inability, but from increasing oppression experienced as her once tolerable marital relationship disintegrated.

One middle-class woman in her late twenties, having her first baby, said:

> . . . I'm not completely happy . . . I cry a lot, almost every day. My husband
> is confused and probably 'fed up', and a barrier is coming up between us.
> I can see it, but I can't stop it . . .

She went on to say that she did not consider herself a career woman and had been relieved to stop work and have the baby. The birth had been difficult, and in the end, she had had an emergency Caesarian section. She had no clue as to why she felt as she did, but she did feel she was on a downward spiral—as she became depressed, this made her more so. In particular, she noted that as this happened she and her husband grew further apart in their needs and understanding of each other.

All of these women saw the arrival of their babies differently *because their lives were different*; but for each woman, the baby had provided an amplification, or realization of a set of oppressive circumstances and relationships.

Bell and Newby (1976) express this as a 'deferential relationship', which is a set of power relations that have become 'moral' through the process of legitimization, but with no *prima facie* reason. Stability is the keynote of this deference, and for the women in my study the stability or maintenance of the power structure in their relationship with a male partner was cemented by the arrival of the first, or another, baby—although the quality of the relationship itself often deteriorated. The existing form of social interaction remains deferential for most couples, despite Young and Willmott's (1973) visions of the 'symmetrical family'.

From another perspective, Chodorow and Contratto (1982) argue that the fantasy of the perfect mother '. . . has led to the cultural oppression of women in the interests of a child whose needs are also fantasized'. Further, they say that it is feminists who are constrained by models of child development, and need to make sense of it in an interactive rather than a prescribed way, in which the child is seen as a passive recipient of environmental influences, particularly those provided by the mother. Almost all the women interviewed were constrained by their notions of 'what is best for the child', which normally required physical and emotional sacrifice for them.

Relying on 'objective' measures, correlations, and the label 'post natal depression', effectively removes any awareness of this oppression. The evidence collected here led to speculation on the value of qualitative data of this kind for enabling women to explore the nature and causes of their oppression. Thus, it is an example of feminist research: i.e. research which, as Klein (1983) asserts, may 'contribute to ending the oppression of women'.

FEMINIST METHODOLOGY AND A WOMAN-CENTRED APPROACH

So far I have provided qualitative data in support of a critique of one standardized measure of 'post natal depression', and have presented some speculations on the limitations of other similar measures. The case still needs to be made for the contribution of personal accounts of childbirth and the subsequent period, and the ways in which this approach might be considered both woman-centred and feminist.

Although 'woman-centred' and 'feminist' research do not represent *competing* interests, they need to be defined separately. 'Woman-centred' refers to a perspective which takes women's accounts as *central* and does *not* consider women to be at the 'mercy of their hormones' or in any other way intrinsically pathological. It relies on the assumption that whatever individuals report about their experience should be taken as *their interpretation of reality*. 'Feminist' research includes this perspective, but in addition recognizes the importance of research *for* women, which is in part an *analysis of women's oppression* and so:

> The product . . . should be directly used by women in order to formulate policies and provisions necessary for feminist activities. (Stanley and Wise, 1983, p. 19)

Similarly, Klein (1983, p. 95) distinguishes between the psychology *of* women and a psychology *for* women where 'women are the centre of the study and neither compared to nor measured against normative (male) standards'. In order to achieve this, feminist methodology also concerns itself with the part played by the 'researcher', and with the breaking down of power differentials that exist between researcher and researched in the research process.

Most psychological research on childbirth and motherhood does not reflect this. Breen (1975) is an exception (in part), in that she concerns herself with changes in women's self-concepts with the birth of a first child although (following the psychoanalytic model), she sees motherhood as an inevitable evolutionary stage and does not confront assumptions about women's role and status. Even so her study is worth serious consideration as it demonstrates the contradictions between a 'woman-centred' perspective, where the concern is '. . . towards an *understanding* of femininity', and an analysis of women's oppression implicit in gender based concepts. Breen does, however, make some use of non-positivist methods in order to avoid the trap of being:

> . . . carried away by the desire to be 'scientific' to the extent that 'subjects' are more like 'objects' and treated as if they had no individuality. (1975, p. 65)

Wilkinson (Chapter 1, this volume) draws together feminist critiques of positivist social science and their suggested alternatives and comments on the parallels between these and the 'new' social psychology (e.g. Ethogenics and Personal Construct Theory) with its renewed interest in 'person-centred' investigation. Similarly, sociological theories such as Symbolic Interactionism (Becker, 1966) and methods such as life history taking (Faraday and Plummer, 1978), which are specifically criticized by positivists for their lack of *typicality*, are valuable in terms of developing a psychology for women, particularly in the context of understanding motherhood as a social process rather than a 'feminine' one. As Becker says:

To observe social process . . . takes a great deal of time. It poses knotty problems of comparability and objectivity in data gathering. It requires an intimate understanding of the lives of others. So social scientists have, most often, settled for less demanding techniques such as the interview or the questionnaire. (1966, p. xiii)

This is especially true when considering the process of becoming a mother, particularly as there are contradictions between 'expectations' and 'reactions' apparent in manifestations of depression. The difference between feminist methodology and interpretive methods in psychology and sociology lies in the *approach* of the researcher to the conceptualization of the problem; relationship with the respondents; and the collection, analysis and dissemination of the data.

CONCLUSIONS

This chapter, firstly, has set out to demonstrate the contradictions between women's accounts of the early days and months following childbirth, and the 'scientific' literature on 'post natal depression'. The latter assumes some ability to identify so-called 'atypical' depression from various 'objective' tests — the one used here serving as an example.

Underlying these contradictions are a set of assumptions which reflect women's role and status under patriarchy. Analysis of the interviews of women in this study suggests that women both reflect and are confused by this 'man-made' view of their bodies and their minds. Such a view is represented by the popular image of women: naturally adapted to motherhood (rather than child bearing), and also strongly influenced by uncontrollable hormones: a situation which requires that they seek 'treatment' from men. These interviews reveal that many women depressed after childbirth are reacting quite 'naturally' to anxieties and problems surrounding this particular crisis in their life. Further, there is evidence that some women who are chronically oppressed accept the domestic and social arrangements which perpetuate this, and do not overtly show signs of depression — at least on the 'objective' measure used.

The second, and more important, aim of the chapter has been to explore the consequences of a shift towards collecting data which explores subjective interpretations of reality, providing a perspective on how women see their lives. In this sense the research is woman-centred. However, it is also important that the women in the study benefit from the consequences of this research, and in this aim the research may be considered feminist.

In the case of depression following childbirth, enabling women to recognize the source of their anxieties, and to offer support as they operate changes — either interpersonally or intrapersonally — would be an important development. This requires debates to be opened up with helping professionals so that knowledge about women's perspectives informs their practice.

A further facet of feminist research is that of learning and changing on the part of the researcher. Not only does feminist research have to break out from the constraints of positivism, but so do the researchers. It is more difficult (although also more rewarding) to try to take account of the social processes which are part of the research dynamics, than it is to develop standardized measures from within a 'value-free' stance—if such a stance is possible. It is therefore appropriate to suggest the need to develop a debate within the feminist social psychology forum, and not simply to operate in terms of producing unassailable prescriptions along with each paper presented and each article in print.

NOTES TO CHAPTER 8

1. Oakley (1979) usefully subdivides categories of 'post natal depression' into:
   (a) 'The blues': weepiness and anxiety two to ten days after delivery which is usually transitory;
   (b) Depression and anxiety on arriving home with the baby which lasts a week or two;
   (c) Depressed 'moods' with good and bad days around three months after delivery;
   (d) Clinical depression which is enduring and includes other symptoms such as loss of appetite and sleep disturbance.

2. By 'oppression' I mean 'overwhelmed by irresistible power' or 'kept under by co-ercion' (OED).

REFERENCES

Becker, H. S. (1966). Introduction. In: C. R. Shaw (ed.), *The Jack Roller*. Chicago, University of Chicago Press.

Beere, C. (1979). *Women and Women's Issues: A Handbook of Tests and Measures*. San Francisco, Jossey-Bass.

Bell, C. and Newby, H. (1976). Husbands and wives: the dynamics of the deferential dialectic. In: D. L. Barker and S. Allen (eds), *Dependence and Exploitation in Work and Marriage*. Harlow, Longman.

Boulton, M. G. (1983). *On Becoming a Mother*. London, Tavistock.

Blum, H. P. (1978). Reconstruction in a case of postpartum depression. *Psychoanalytic Study of the Child* **33**, 335-362.

Breen, D. (1975). *The Birth of a First Child*. London, Tavistock.

Cox, J. L., Connor, Y. and Kendall, R. E. (1982). Prospective study of the psychiatric disorders of childbirth. *British Journal of Psychiatry* **140**, 111-117.

Chodorow, N. and Contratto, S. (1982). The fantasy of the perfect mother. In: B. Thorne and M. Yalom (eds), *Rethinking the Family: Some Feminist Questions*. New York, Longman.

Dalton, K. (1980). *Depression After Childbirth*. Oxford, Oxford University Press.

Day, S. (1982). Is obstetric technology depressing? *Radical Science Journal* **12**, 17-46.

de Beauvoir, S. (1968). *The Second Sex*. London, Jonathan Cape.

Elliot, S. A., Anderson, M., Brough, D. I., Watson, J. P. and Rugg, A. J. (1984). Relationship between obstetric outcome and psychological measures in pregnancy and the postnatal year. *Journal of Society for Reproductive and Infant Psychology* **1**, 20-31.

Faraday, A. and Plummer, K. (1978). Doing life histories. Published by the Department of Sociology, Essex University.

Finch, J. (1984). It's great to have someone to talk to: the ethics and politics of interviewing women. In: C. Bell and H. Roberts (eds), *Social Researching*. London, Routledge & Kegan Paul.

Friedan, B. (1979). *The Feminine Mystique*. Harmondsworth, Penguin.

Gavron, H. (1977). *The Captive Wife*. Harmondsworth, Pelican.

Graham, H. and Oakley, A. (1981). Competing ideologies of reproduction: medical and maternal perspectives on pregnancy. In: H. Roberts (ed.), *Women, Health and Reproduction*. London, Routledge & Kegan Paul.

Hopkins, J., Marcus, M. and Campbell, S. B. (1984). Postpartum depression: a critical review. *Psychological Bulletin* **95**(3), 496-515.

Klein, R. D. (1983). Thoughts about feminist methodology. In: G. Bowles and R. D. Klein (eds), *Theories of Women's Studies*. London, Routledge & Kegan Paul.

Kumar, R. and Robson, K. (1978). Neurotic disturbance during pregnancy and the puerperium: preliminary report of a survey of 119 primiparae. In: M. Sandler (ed.), *Mental Illness in Pregnancy and the Puerperium*. Oxford, Oxford University Press.

Morgan, B. (1983). Maternal attitudes to analgesia in labour. Paper presented at the Annual Conference of the Society for Reproductive and Infant Psychology, York.

Oakley, A. (1976). *Housewife: High Value-Low Cost*. Harmondsworth, Pelican.

Oakley, A. (1979). The baby blues. *New Society* (April).

Oakley, A. (1980). *Women Confined*. Oxford, Martin Robertson.

Oakley, A. (1982). Interviewing women: a contradiction in terms. In: H. Roberts (ed.), *Doing Feminist Research*. London, Routledge & Kegan Paul.

Paykel, E. S., Emms, E. M. and Fletcher, J. 1980. Life events and social support in puerperal depression. *British Journal of Psychiatry* **136**, 339-346.

Pitt, B. (1968). Atypical depression following childbirth. *British Journal of Psychiatry* **114**, 1325-1335.

Pollock, S., Blurton Jones, N., Evans, M., Da Costa Woodson, E. and Woodson, R. (1980). Continuities in post natal depression. Paper presented at the British Psychological Society Conference, Leicester, September.

Stanley, L. and Wise, S. (1983). *Breaking Out: Feminist Consciousness and Feminist Research*. London, Routledge & Kegan Paul.

Steiner, M. (1979). Psychobiology of mental disorders associated with childbearing: an overview. *Acta Psychiatrica Scandinavia* **60**, 449-464.

Wearing, B. (1984). *The Ideology of Motherhood*. Sydney, Allen & Unwin.

Young, M. and Willmott, P. (1962). *Family and Kinship in East London*. Harmondsworth, Penguin.

Young, M. and Willmott, P. (1973). *The Symmetrical Family*. London, Routledge & Kegan Paul.

Chapter 9

Introducing and Developing Q as a Feminist Methodology: A Study of Accounts of Lesbianism

Celia Kitzinger

INTRODUCTION

The pervert and the sinner, the guilt-ridden androgyne and the undiscriminating sexual opportunist, the man-hating castrating feminist and the victim of male lust seeking solace in another woman's arms—all are images of the lesbian familiar to most of us today. Promulgated by instant TV experts and agony columnists, perpetrated in classic novels and pornography alike, these images create a context within which we construct our own accounts of lesbianism. The research reported here elicits accounts of lesbianism from lesbians and explores the meanings of these accounts in relation to their social, ideological and political contexts. How are accounts of lesbianism constructed? Upon what theories of gender and sexuality do they draw? For what purposes can different accounts be used?

This approach makes my research very different from the vast bulk of previous work on lesbianism which has, overwhelmingly, attempted to provide objective, scientific evidence in support of one or other of these accounts, while discrediting rival accounts as 'unscientific'. Many psychoanalysts and psychiatrists, for example, present lesbians as 'sick'; in their accounts lesbianism features as a 'psychosexual disorder' (Allen, 1969), 'a serious psychiatric and social problem' (Bieber, 1971), 'a massive adaptational response to a crippling inhibition of hetero-sexual development' (Kaye *et al.*, 1967), or 'a symptom of neurosis and a grievous personality disorder' (Kronemeyer, 1980). Such authors offer a variety of evidence (usually derived from their own clinical work) in support of this account, and point out the various methodological, theoretical and/or ideological errors of those presenting alternative accounts—for example, the logical mistake of supposing that because lesbianism is common it must therefore be healthy (cf. Moberly, 1983) or that because it is 'natural' it should therefore be acceptable (cf. West, 1968).

Similarly, some psychologists present an account of the lesbian as a normal, healthy, well adjusted woman, providing evidence, in the form of statistical data culled from psychological tests and scales, which demonstrates lesbians to be significantly less neurotic than heterosexual women (Wilson and Greene, 1971) and more independent, resilient, self-sufficient and spontaneous (Hopkins, 1969; Freedman, 1971; Siegelman, 1972): these 'liberal' authors typically accuse their rivals of using biased theoretical models, inadequate control groups, problematic sampling procedures and of failing to control their variables.

Both sides in this debate claim to have discovered 'the truth' about lesbians, and both accuse their opponents of ideological contamination — of being influenced by religious fervour and moral evangelism on one hand, and of being swayed by the political arguments of 'gay lib' and 'women's lib' on the other. Each accuses the other of proselytizing for a particular ideological cause, while claiming that they alone are truly objective and scientific in their approach. In this ritualistic combat, the underlying assumptions comprising the notion of scientific objectivity are implicitly accepted and, therefore, reinforced.

For me, part of the process of carrying out research as a feminist has meant questioning this whole notion of scientific objectivity. I no longer believe that there is a single 'correct' account of lesbianism (or any other social phenomenon) that will stand revealed once we have peeled away the layers of prejudice, special pleading and personal bias that form a veil between us and 'the facts'. In place of the dominant positivistic or essentialist science exemplified by the studies cited above, many feminists are advancing versions of social constructionist theory in which knowledge is seen as a historically and culturally specific social construction, the dominant forms of which are used to legitimate the ruling male version of reality (Smith, 1974; Jackson, 1978; Rich, 1979; Spender, 1981; Westcott, 1981). Within the constructionist framework (which includes variants of sociology of science, ethnomethodology, phenomenology and symbolic interactionism) the researcher is not credited with any special access to 'the truth', and her role is not to unveil objective facts about the nature of reality, but only to describe the different ways in which people construct their realities: to be 'a listener to the many stories of human meanings and to retell those stories as faithfully as one is able' (Berger and Kellner, 1982, p. 77).

Conscious of the extent to which the meanings and constructions of women and lesbians have been silenced or distorted (cf. Faderman, 1980; Spender, 1980), many feminists are attracted by constructionism's claims to take other people's versions of reality seriously. But if we approach our research in this way, one of the problems we confront is the prospect of a nihilistic relativism in which all views are equally valid. If we eschew the essentialist techniques of dismissing what are to us ethically offensive or politically unacceptable opinions on the grounds that they are 'wrong', 'falsely conscious' or 'pathological', if we forgo the temptation to assign them to the negative ends of theoretical continua ('homophobia', 'sexism') or to the lower levels in hierarchal models of consciousness, is there then anything more politically useful we can say in presenting a set of accounts than merely, 'some people think X', 'some people think Y', 'some people think Z'? The argument that accounts can (and should) be assessed not in terms of their 'truth value' but in terms of their utility in achieving certain goals (these being, of necessity, defined within specific political frameworks) represents my current resolution of this issue, and the one on which I rely in this chapter.

It involves first presenting women's accounts, as far as possible, in their own words and in a form with which they would agree (and one or more representatives of all the accounts described here have read my report of their account and found it acceptable), and then discussing the accounts in a social context in terms of their utility or otherwise in achieving feminist goals, i.e. writing from 'within' a feminist account. My approach in this research, then, is not to offer an alternative ('feminist') version of 'the Truth about Lesbians', but to recognize the existence of numerous 'truths', multiple versions of reality, and then to explore the meanings and implications of each.

Many feminists working on similar premises have used a variety of purely 'qualitative' methodologies (e.g. Reinharz, 1981; Wetherell, 1982), and, as Wilkinson (1984; see also Chapter 1, this volume) points out, aspects of this approach are embodied in Personal Construct Theory (cf. Bannister and Fransella, 1971). An alternative method, suitable for use within this framework, is Q methodology—a technique which I used after interviewing lesbians (120 women, each for, on average, one and a half hours) as a way of dealing with the wealth of qualitative material thus obtained. Invented by William Stephenson in the 1930s (e.g. Stephenson, 1935; 1936a; 1936b; 1939), Q quickly fell into disrepute following attacks on it by psychometricians, Cyril Burt perhaps not surprisingly being the foremost among them, who were incensed that anyone should be interested in people's subjective understandings of themselves at a time when the new science of psychology was just beginning to devise objective tests for measuring what people were 'really' like. Following Burt (1937; 1940), but using rather more colourful language, Cattell (1951) claimed that Q was 'totally disabling by any truly scientific standard', and described its users as suffering from 'mental debility' in their attempt to '(retreat) from the scientific standards of behavioral psychology back to the era of introspection into private worlds'.

The theoretical basis on which Q methodology is founded relies on the axiom that researchers should acknowledge and present the reality constructions of different women and men without prejudging or discrediting them, and without insisting on the superior (more 'objective') status of the researcher's own construction of reality. The vast majority of traditional social science has, as Brown, a leading Q methodologist—and editor of the Q methodology newsletter, *Operant Subjectivity*—points out, 'begun with (the researcher's) vision of the world according to which all else has been measured' (1980, p. 1). And, like many other Q methodologists, Brown argues that:

> . . . our subjects have their own operational definitions and models of the
> world, and the social scientist must avoid becoming so intrigued with his
> [*sic*] own constructions that he becomes insensitive to those of others. (1980,
> p. 30)

A detailed guide to carrying out a Q methodological study can be found in
Brown (1980). Briefly, the designation Q was coined to distinguish the statistical
procedures of Q methodology, which rely on the correlation of persons, from
that of the vast bulk of quantitative psychology (95% according to Cattell, 1951),
which is referred to as R methodology: R being a generalized reference to Pearson's
product-moment correlation, 'r', generally employed in the study of trait
relationships. Where R methodology analyses a correlation matrix down its
columns (i.e. the scores of persons A, B, C over a single test, so that person A
is said to score higher on, for example, IQ, than person B, who scores higher
than C, etc. (see Fig. 1)), Q methodology analyses a correlation matrix along
its rows (i.e. the scores of person A over a variety of tests).

Except by resorting to the questionable procedure of double standardization
of test scores, Q methodological analysis is not possible using normative
psychometric tests and scales (for example, is a score of 120 on an IQ test higher
or lower than a score of 37 on an anxiety scale?). So it was at this point in the
development of Q that Stephenson made the radical theoretical switch of replacing
traditional tests with subjective assessments from the participants. Instead of
receiving 'objective' scores over a selection of different tests (IQ, anxiety,
machiavellianism, extraversion etc.), each participant is asked to rank such
attributes relative to each other in terms of her own construction of her personality.
The usual procedure is to offer the participant a pack of cards (anywhere between
15 and 100 or so) and ask her to sort them (generally, though not necessarily,
according to a quasi-normal distribution) according to some criterion of relevance:
personality descriptors can be sorted from 'most like me' to 'least like me',
statements of opinion from 'most agree' to 'least agree', cartoons from 'funniest'
to 'least funny', even, in one study (Stephenson, 1936b), odourous liquids from

		Tests			
		x	y	z	....
	A	Ax	Ay	Az	....
People	B	Bx	By	Bz	....
	C	Cx	Cy	Cz	....
	.		.	.	
	.		.	.	
	.		.	.	

Figure 1. Sample data matrix.

most to least 'pleasant'. The items so arrayed comprise a Q sort, and Q sorts from different people (or many Q sorts from a single person) are then correlated and factor analysed. The resulting factors indicate groups of people who have ranked the statements in essentially the same fashion; people with highly correlating Q sorts tend to define a single factor and to be differentiated from others, with whom they have little or no correlation, who may define a separate factor. Interpretation of these factors relies on inspection of the original sorts completed by defining participants: where only one person defines a factor, that person's Q sort is used as the factor array; when several people define a factor, as is more usual, their Q sorts are averaged (using a weighting procedure to allow for differences in factor loading) to provide a factor array. Observation of the significant differences between item scores over the different factor arrays provides the basis for distinguishing and interpreting the various attitudes, perspectives, identities, or whatever, which lead to the different Q sorts and, hence, to the factors which emerge.

In presenting my research here, I will concentrate on discussing the results rather than detailing the method: a full account of the latter (as well as a more complete version of the former) can be found in my doctoral thesis (Kitzinger, 1984).

METHOD

Forty-one self-defined lesbians, who were aged between 17 and 58 and who had all, except two, been interviewed, completed a 61-item Q sort (items — derived from earlier interviews — are illustrated in presenting factor interpretations) according to a quasi-normal distribution running from −5 ('Strongly Disagree') to +5 ('Strongly Agree'), with a central neutral category (0). The 41 completed Q sorts were analysed using factor analysis (principal components) (Nie *et al.*, 1975), and resulted in seven factors which were rotated to simple structure (varimax criterion). The results indicated that the original 41 sets of rankings reduce to seven independent orderings. That is, there are seven accounts of lesbianism which can be differentiated. Table 1 shows the factor loadings for each participant. Examples for each factor were selected to define the account using the criterion of a high loading on that particular factor with no substantial loading on any other factor. For each factor the separate Q sorts of these women were merged, taking factor weight into account (Spearman, 1927), to obtain a single set of factor scores for the statements. Interpretation of the accounts relied upon an examination of relative factor scores, supplemented by the participants' interview accounts. The last of these factors (VI and VII) were each defined by one woman only, and I was not confident that I had fully understood their accounts. Therefore, the first five accounts only will be presented.

Table 1
Factor Loadings for the 'Accounts of Lesbianism' Q sort[a]

Q sorter no.	I	II	III	IV	V	VI	VII
49	61[b]	36	19	22	06	08	00
58	68	04	21	39	36	−01	17
63	65	36	18	23	08	−04	18
69	69	16	39	30	12	17	−04
79	75	20	16	35	00	12	10
72	26	64	24	−11	12	07	13
57	10	82	15	00	09	02	09
33	36	14	65	26	10	07	06
38	23	28	70	11	12	04	18
01	28	14	11	74	05	05	04
05	33	13	15	75	11	02	00
09	15	36	26	63	13	08	06
37	32	03	34	67	27	07	02
71	−05	05	14	−07	78	02	17
65	00	12	06	−18	58	12	03
12	16	26	14	18	01	75	12
10	34	00	09	05	15	24	62
02	65[c]	36	21	46	08	05	03
03	51	00	22	55	03	11	23
04	30	55	12	48	07	00	−04
22	48	13	43	05	13	−11	25
27	49	19	30	36	14	12	21
52	00	27	11	45	27	02	65
59	51	52	02	24	−17	16	−02
61	65	19	41	11	25	17	07
70	06	28	29	02	17	22	12
74	57	20	11	48	−22	−06	08
75	61	18	00	46	−01	35	14
19	14	20	53	36	41	10	09
25	18	51	03	05	39	24	21
26	18	46	25	11	06	07	57
28	65	33	04	44	−12	21	09
29	36	00	26	45	−01	23	34
31	36	−12	28	42	−05	28	22
54	43	13	15	63	−15	12	−02
50	31	58	45	32	22	13	15
51	49	18	61	20	07	14	05
64	64	03	39	43	−02	14	19
80	72	03	26	41	06	00	09
81	52	40	00	18	45	06	24
90	24	29	43	12	54	04	05

[a]Loadings rounded off to two significant figures and decimal points omitted.
[b]Boxed loadings indicate those defining factors.
[c]Underlined loadings indicate significant loadings for each factor.

RESULTS

Factor I

As shown in Table 1, the Q sorts completed by participants 49, 58, 63, 69, and 79 define this factor, and although 14 others (e.g. No. 3, my own sort) load significantly on this factor, they also have high loadings on other factors, so do not define it.

This account emphasizes lesbianism as a source of self-fulfilment, true happiness and inner peace. It typically incorporates 'before and after' stories in which the pre-lesbian past is characterized as a life of conformity, attention to duty and sexual unresponsiveness, while the lesbian present is depicted as fulfilling, rewarding and passionate.

> I'd been through all the other things; I'd done everything I was meant to do and so on. I had *tried*, you know. I had really *tried* to be heterosexual and to do all the correct things and I just knew then that it wasn't possible and the only way I could conceivably be happy was to be this way. Francesca (No. 58)

> I thought for years, you see, that I was frigid and I didn't love Richard and I was frigid and unresponsive and a non-sexual kind of being . . . It really didn't occur to me that maybe I was making the wrong kind of . . . or going in the wrong direction for me. I just thought, you know, that that was the nature I was. And it's been extraordinarily liberating for me to find that I'm not as I thought I was. I am actually much more passionate and much more of a sexual being than I'd thought. Pippa (49)

This account stresses the advantages of lesbianism in terms of personal growth, happiness and freedom. The Q sort items quoted below (with their randomly assigned reference numbers) are cited as having significantly different scores in the Factor I array (as determined following the procedure outlined in the 'Method' section) as compared with the other factor arrays. (Q sort items presented in discussing Factor II—in the next section—are those with distinctive Factor II scores; those presented in dealing with Factor III have significantly different scores in the Factor III array, and so on.)

	Factor I scores
1. Being a lesbian gives me a sense of freedom.	+ 5
48. Being a lesbian has enabled me to grow up.	+ 4
61. I think I would have a happier life if I were not a lesbian.	− 5

The personal fulfilment accorded by lesbianism is central to this account:

> I have never stopped feeling relief and happiness about discovering myself and, you know, accepting about myself and finding all these other women,

and it means that I'm happy almost every day of my life. . . . Well, I mean, obviously one's had unhappy moments, but I've never regretted being a lesbian, or becoming a lesbian, if you want to put it that way, or coming out, or whatever. I mean, at least one was alive, you know, and doing the things that one was meant to do, doing the things that were natural to one.
Francesca (58)

The account represented by Factor I, then, depicts lesbianism in very positive terms as a route through which happiness, personal growth and fulfilment can be attained.

The last decade has produced a large proportion of lesbian (and lesbian feminist) literature which draws on this theme, and stresses, in sharp contradiction to Radclyffe Hall's *The Well of Loneliness* (1928), the positive nature of lesbianism as a source of self-fulfilment. Coming out as lesbian, 'I am whole, a rediscovered self' (Faye, 1980, p. 178), and through lesbianism 'I am reclaiming my true womynhood, learning to truly know and love myself and other wimmin' (Toll, 1980, p. 29, her spelling).

This account can be characterized as a lay-woman's version of Self-theory and the pursuit of positive psychological health (cf. Jahoda, 1958; Rogers, 1959; Maslow, 1962) which became socially sedimented during the decade 1965–1975 and acquired considerable socially persuasive power as a justification for otherwise questionable behaviour (cf. Tedeschi and Reiss, 1981, p. 293). From the perspective of the lesbian, this account is important not only in explaining and justifying lesbianism to a potentially hostile audience, but also in presenting it as a positive and attractive option. It explicitly challenges the traditional image (reinforced by so many psychology textbooks) of the lesbian as a shadowy creature haunting a seedy twilight world and enduring a life of unmitigated misery — 'the very antithesis of fulfilment and happiness' (Kronemeyer, 1980, p. 7). In its feminist form, this account uses the 'inner peace and self-fulfilment' discourse as part of its recruitment campaign: lesbianism leads to 'liberation of self . . . inner peace . . . love of self and all women' (Radicalesbians, 1970). This approach is common enough for the lesbian feminist witch and sociologist, Susan Leigh Star (1980, p. 232) to have commented on the public relations policy that underlies the account, in an autobiographical vignette:

'Hey, they want me to give a talk at Foothill College next week. Does anybody want to talk next week to a women's studies class?'

'On what?'

'Lesbianism.'

We howl. 'Yes, before I was a Lesbian I had no natural rhythm, my acne was terrible, I was constipated. And now . . .'

'. . . you see before you . . .'

'. . . the natural wonder of the earth . . .'

'. . . the bliss of being queer . . .'

'. . . the glory of sisterhood fulfilled . . .'

However, in overselling lesbianism as the route to perfect bliss and inner harmony, this account leaves women with no language (except adaptations of traditional psychoanalysis) in which to articulate their actual experience as lesbians when it fails to conform to the advertised image: our confusions, problems and unhappiness are silenced and become 'open secrets' (Stanley, 1984).

Moreover, whether one argues *for* lesbianism on the grounds that it can supply true happiness and inner peace, as in this account, or *against* lesbianism on the grounds that 'despite propaganda to the contrary, there is no such thing as a happy, well-adjusted homosexual' (Kriegman, 1969), the debate remains firmly within the framework of the liberal-humanistic discourse prescribed by the dominant value system. The 'self-fulfilment and inner peace' account supports a fundamental aspect of the dominant ideology—the focus on personal change as a substitute for political change.

> Achieving inner peace . . . surrounded by this society as it is, is a conformist rather than a revolutionary goal. It is impossible, unless one resigns oneself to all the other horrors of society. Americans dearly love the notion of 'inner peace', and 'inner peace' salespeople abound. Young people of the late sixties and early seventies returned to the land for it, became vegetarians for it, took up with Jesus and the Mahara Ji for it . . . Suggesting that lesbianism was the only way to inner peace became an important propaganda tactic. Now heterosexual feminists were told that not only were they politically incorrect and that they had been dullards as children, but that they had missed out on finding 'peace of mind'! All the propaganda techniques were employed— everything but the real radical truth of the matter: that a massive turn to lesbianism *can* undermine the patriarchy and help to achieve the attainment of our rights. (Fritz, 1979, pp. 99–100; her emphasis)

In representing lesbianism predominantly as a route to self-fulfilment, inner peace and personal growth, we run the risk of reducing it to the status of a private solution to an individual malaise—of taking lesbianism out of the political arena.

Factor II

This factor is defined by participants 72 and 57, and six other women also have significant loadings. The theory on which this account of lesbianism depends is that women respond to 'the person not the gender' and 'it all depends who you fall in love with'.

> For me, it's so rare that I find someone with whom something magic happens. . . . I can't think of a way of saying it that doesn't sound one hundred per cent corny, but I suppose I might meet a man I'd feel that way about, and I might meet a woman. Alison (57)

I think that having reached my age and stage now, that if I got involved with somebody then that would be *it*. But I mean, it could be a male or a female. . . . So at the stage where I am at the moment, I have no sexual relationships, but I would just as happily have a relationship with a man as with a woman. Wendy (72)

	Factor II scores
18. I am/have been deeply in love with a woman.	**+5**
9. I have been deeply in love with a man.	**+3**

More than women defining any of the other first five factors, these women present an account of themselves as bisexual:

I definitely do think that I'm bisexual. Wendy (72)

Bisexual can sound like such a cop-out. I think it generally does apply to me probably. Not totally, but yes. . . . I certainly wouldn't emphasise 'heterosexual'. I think 'bisexual' is more accurate—but I usually just say I'm gay. Alison (57)

	Factor II score
38. My underlying sexual orientation is bisexual.	**+2**

According to this account, then, lesbianism is the result of 'falling in love' with a person who happens to be a woman; it is not an essential state of being, and the 'lesbian' can become 'heterosexual' if her next 'true love' is male.

Similar accounts are manifested in a number of autobiographical and fictional works by lesbians (e.g. Rule, 1975, p. 10; Schwartz, 1978; Baetz, 1980, p. 15); and Cartledge and Hemmings (1982) have described a process they call 'Cupid's Dart' (the romantic conversion), which largely parallels pair-bonding themes presented in the account of Factor II. Jill Johnston (1973, p. 92) describes 'the dark ages of our political consciousness' when 'the person you were involved with was first and foremost a person or special love object with no certain significance as to gender to that if it happened to be a woman it could as well be as man the next time if the right *person* came along' (her emphasis).

In terms of the dominant order of western culture, the rhetoric of romantic love offers a powerful source of justification and provides a legitimating context for sexual activity (cf. Gagnon, 1977, p. 180). The extent to which the romantic love discourse 'belongs' to the dominant culture is demonstrated in the frequency with which lesbianism is judged in these terms: 'true love' is depicted as a moral imperative, the overwhelming effects of which may excuse, but the incapacity for which must condemn, lesbians and our relationships. Those professionals who present lesbianism as a sickness are at pains to deny the homosexual's ability to form loving relationships: lesbian liaisons are 'inherently self-limiting' (Moberly, 1983) and 'do not contribute to the individual's need for stability and love' (Wilbur, 1965, p. 281). Liberal apologists draw on the *same* rhetoric of romantic love to argue the basic equality or isomorphism of heterosexual and homosexual relationships:

> The essence of a committed relationship is the same whether the union is between two men, two women, or a man and a woman. . . . Love and commitment transcend sexual orientation. (Mendola, 1980, p. 2)

This same rhetoric is, of course, used within a feminist framework to argue the advantages of lesbianism by asserting, for example, that because of social inequalities between men and women, 'the conditions for learning to love fully and without fear are at present met only in a homosexual setting' (Kelly, 1972).

However, whether one argues that lesbianism is *inferior* to heterosexuality because true love must for ever elude us; *superior* to heterosexuality because only for us is 'true love' possible; or that lesbianism and heterosexuality are equal in so far as either can yield deeply loving and committed relationships — whichever position you opt for, the debate is still conducted within the terms laid down by the dominant value system of western culture, and 'falling in love' is presented as a fundamentally personal experience, an expression of inner drives, needs and passions independent of social control.

Factor III

The women who define this factor (33 and 38) account for their lesbianism as a personal sexual orientation and express their dislike of being defined solely in terms of this small part of themselves. This account emphasizes the other facets of their personalities, their other interests and involvements.

	Factor III scores
13. Being a lesbian is *not* one of the most important things about me.	**+3**
40. I don't like my sexuality being labelled and categorized.	**+4**

> I don't like labels. I wouldn't say 'I'm a lesbian', because I'm a hell of a lot of other things besides. I'm interested in art; I'm a bit of a philosopher; I'm a bit of a poet, right? I wouldn't say 'I am a lesbian', because that seems to exclude everything else. Charlotte (33)

> I'm me — I'm Phyllis Jones [*pseudonym*]; I'm a social worker; I'm a mother; I've been married. I like Tchaikovsky; I like Bach; I like Beethoven; I like ballet. I enjoy doing a thousand and one things, and, oh yes, in amongst all that, I happen to be a lesbian; I love a woman very deeply. But that's just a *part* of me. So many other lesbians seem to have let it overtake them, and they are lesbians first and foremost. Phyllis (38)

At the same time, however, this account relies on a firmly essentialist conception of lesbianism:

26. You cannot choose to be a lesbian; if you are,
   you are.   **+2**

34. I believe I was born lesbian.   **+3**

> I think I was born this way. I just think some people are born this way and
> some people are born that way. Some things are shaped in the way of a tree
> and others become cabbages, and yet other things become birds; and I just
> happen to be a lesbian. Charlotte (33)

> It is part of me, as is the colour of my hair and the colour of my eyes. That
> is what I am. That is my sexual preference. It's what turns me on. So I believe
> that it's something genetic. Phyllis (38)

The account represented by this factor, then, explains lesbianism as a private
sexual preference or orientation, innately determined, and as natural and normal
as heterosexuality. Lesbianism is characterized as a personal matter which
describes only a small and relatively insignificant part of the 'whole person':
lesbians are *people* first and foremost.

This account is widely represented in lesbian writing, such as this letter in
Sappho (1978) in reply to an earlier more 'political' article:

> We, together with many others, consider ourselves people in the first instance.
> Our sexuality is incidental and does not set us apart from our fellow men
> and women. Therefore we do not find it necessary to put labels on ourselves
> setting us apart by saying 'we are lesbians' and then begging for acceptance.
> We agree with Myrtle . . . that a large section of the population are ignorant,
> fearful and lacking in understanding about us. For years we and others like
> us have quietly beavered away in society, just being ourselves with certainty
> and without fear. We have many friends and acquaintances who must know
> of our gayness though this is only discussed with close friends, not because
> we are afraid, but because we believe that such a personal matter as one's
> sexual preference should be private whether one be homo or heterosexual.
> So, dear Myrtle, you do your thing—wear your badges and labels, proclaim
> your sexuality to the Universe as childlike you shriek for acceptance and
> approval, (or is it martyrdom?)—but don't knock us well-adjusted gays by
> calling us cowards!

The emphasis is on the fundamental similarity of the lesbian and the heterosexual
woman, and the (ideally) minor or incidental nature of sexual preference in
everyday human interaction:

> I'm the same as thee,/Just differently orientated sexually. (Gill, 1977)

Compared with the traditional account of lesbians as sick (to be discussed in
the context of Factor V), this account is useful to lesbians in so far as it depicts
us as equal with rather than inferior to heterosexuals. Moreover, this account
is very successful in its elicitation and promotion of a form of social acceptance.

Women who behave in accordance with this account are the 'nice' or 'well-adjusted' lesbians: they are following exactly the guidelines laid down for them by representatives of the dominant moral order. Discussing the social management of stigmatized persons, Goffman (1963, p. 140) says:

> The individual is advised to see himself [*sic*] as a fully human being like anyone else, one who at worst happens to be excluded from what is, in the last analysis, merely one area of social life. He is not a type or a category, but a human being.

This advice is reflected in much of the literature prepared by heterosexuals for consumption by lesbians and homosexual men (e.g. Westall, 1978): it can be understood as instruction material designed to inform us how to construct our lesbianism so that it will be found acceptable on their terms.

Factor III, then, represents an account well adapted to the demands of the heterosexual social system. Drawing on socially sedimented themes concerning the privatization of sex, the concept of 'sexual orientation' as a fixed and given entity, and the liberal reluctance to identify ('label') 'people' as members of oppressed groups, this account justifies, for the lesbian, the need to think and act in accordance with the recommendations of the dominant culture.

Factor IV

The account of Factor IV (defined by Q sorts completed by participants 1, 5, 9 and 37) presents lesbianism within the political context of radical feminism, and two of the defining women are the only self-defined political lesbians to have participated in the study. Only Factor IV gives a positive score to the item:

	Factor IV score
10. I came to lesbianism through feminism.	**+ 4**

> It was only through feminism, through learning about the oppression of women by men and the part that the enforcement of heterosexuality, the conditioning of girls into heterosexuality, plays in that oppression, it was through that that I decided that whatever happens I will never go back to being fucked by men. My resolution to choose sexual partners from among women only, that decision was made because I'm a feminist, not because I'm a lesbian. I take the label 'lesbian' as part of the strategy of the feminist struggle. Alice (1)

This is a fundamentally constructionist account of sexuality: it is argued that heterosexuality is constructed in a patriarchal society for the benefit of men.

> I think I was brought up in a heterosexual society and took in male definitions of sexuality. You know, I was brought up as a heterosexual and I really sort of

soaked in the patriarchal values. It wasn't until I got into the Women's
Movement that I saw that there could exist a different value system, a different
way of looking at things which was better for me as an individual and for
womankind in general. You know, that the things I'd been brought up to
believe were very much for the benefit of men, and I realised that there was
another way of looking at things which was sort of a woman-centred,
woman-identified way. So no, I don't think I was a latent lesbian. I do think
every women can be a lesbian, but I . . . No I just don't believe in an essential
sexuality. I think sexuality is constructed in terms of ideas and consciousness.
Lesley (37)

For these women it is central to their identity that they are women and
lesbians:

	Factor IV scores
42. Being a lesbian is *not* one of the most important things about me.	**− 5**
36. Being a woman is very important to me.	**+ 5**

In this account, then, lesbianism is identified within a social and political context,
and the constructed nature of sexuality is emphasized. Where the preceding three
accounts have incorporated lesbianism into the normative order (as a source of
personal fulfilment, or 'true love', or as a sexual orientation), this account explicitly
presents lesbianism as a departure from, and challenge to, the dominant social
system. This account is familiar from a great deal of radical feminist writing and
it is within this account that many of the arguments surrounding political
lesbianism are constructed (e.g. in *Love Your Enemy?*, 1981): it is also the account
on which I have relied most heavily in constructing my own account of lesbianism
and as such constitutes the context from within which I assess and discuss the
other four accounts.

Factor V

This factor represents the traditional account of lesbianism as a 'sorry state'—a
personal inadequacy or failing. In this account, lesbianism is not something chosen
or welcomed, but 'a cross to bear' (Elizabeth (65)).

	Factor V scores
61. I think I would have a happier life if I were not a lesbian.	**+ 5**
8. If I had a choice I would never have chosen to be a lesbian.	**+ 5**
55. However hard I try not to, there are times when I am ashamed that I am a lesbian.	**+ 1**
20. I find my lesbianism difficult to come to terms with.	**+ 1**

Unlike the Factor I account, this account stresses the absence of any personal fulfilment derived from lesbianism.

	Factor V scores
48. Being a lesbian has enabled me to grow up.	**− 3**
53. Being a lesbian has enabled me to feel at home in my body.	**− 3**
1. Being a lesbian gives me a sense of freedom.	**− 4**

In the interviews, women presenting this account emphasized the limitations they feel their lesbianism imposes on them:

> My friends had been gay, you see, and they were trying to convey to me that the world had more to offer than just that. Why cut out half of humanity? They were right. It's just that gap I can never bridge. . . . I suspect we're in a slightly retarded state. Well, 'retarded' is perhaps not quite right. It's a fear, an inability to relate to the opposite sex. There's nothing you can do about it. Jane (71)

This account can be seen as reflecting traditional constructions of lesbianism in terms of sin and sickness, common in both academic and folk theorizing from the early twentieth century on, and clearly serves the purposes of the dominant social order. It nihilates lesbianism as a threat to the reified norm of heterosexuality: in assigning lesbianism an inferior ontological status, the institution of heterosexuality is validated and reinforced. While the utility of this account from the perspective of the dominant order is patent, it is less obvious why lesbians themselves should accept this version: clearly there must be powerful explicit and implicit social mechanisms leading some lesbians to construct their experience in this way, and a corresponding inaccessibility of alternative versions. One possibility is that lesbians employing this account can be characterized as the victims or dupes of a heterosexist social system — women so terrorized or indoctrinated that they passively accept, absorb and reflect back society's image of themselves. This is, in fact, a very common retrospective explanation offered by women charting their autobiographical progression from this to other accounts of lesbianism (cf. Cruikshank, 1980; Stanley and Wolfe, 1980). But instead of characterizing these women as just passive recipients and relayers of accounts foisted onto them by the oppressors, as mere puppets of the patriarchy, it can be useful to see them also as active participants in the process of account construction. Women who provide this account are involved in a good deal of interpretative effort in, for example, pathologizing their personal histories — selecting and applying a particular aetiological explanation, constructing an appropriate autobiography and, in the case of many lesbians today, simultaneously resisting, invalidating and denouncing alternative accounts (e.g. radical feminist) which compete with their own. Far from representing mere 'acquiescence' to the dominant version of lesbianism, then, this account can be seen as the product of energetic and ingenious efforts at account construction.

The advantage of such a construction for lesbians may lie primarily in its attenuation of personal responsibility or culpability for the alleged 'deviance', and in the attainment of certain limited social privileges as reward for confirming the dominant ideology. In employing this account, a woman herself undermines any suggestion that she is a threat to society or to the heterosexual hegemony: she depoliticizes her deviance in a bid for acceptance.

DISCUSSION

Obviously these five accounts are not the only possible ways of accounting for lesbianism, nor do I see them as static and unchanging monuments to human subjectivity. They represent only some of the possible accounts constructed by the 41 women who participated in this research, each of whom, on a different occasion or in a different context, might have offered a very different account. And they represent fairly gross distinctions on the sociopolitical spectrum: a different Q sort could enable a much more fine-grain analysis, perhaps dispersing women who now all define a single factor onto a number of different factors.

But the accounts presented here have, nevertheless, given me a way of perceiving and understanding some of the arguments I come up against as a lesbian feminist. Opposition to the radical feminist account of lesbianism is derived from, and can be understood in terms of, the ideologies underlying the other accounts of lesbianism presented here. For example, the suggestion I've frequently encountered that feminist ideology is a constraining dogma which inhibits personal growth can be seen as rooted in the 'true happiness and personal fulfilment' account of Factor I. One male gay author writes of his 'discovery' that:

> There was as much danger in losing the integrity of my individual identity in conforming to the radical gay partyline as in comforming to establishment values. The real enemy was unmasked as *orthodoxy of any kind*. Liberation does not lie in the direction of seeking the right set of rules to govern one's life. On the contrary, individual identity and freedom require the relinquishment of all dogmas. (Rochlin, 1979, p. 166, his emphasis)

Such critics rarely consider it necessary to explain why radical ideologies should be more constraining and limiting than their own (unrecognized) liberal-humanistic ideology of 'personal growth'. Instead they insist that, for example, 'a personality which needs polemics and provocation cannot develop to a higher level than the world it chooses to defy' (Rosenfels, 1971, pp. 137–138) and describe political involvement as a kind of escape from the struggle of self-actualization:

> It is relatively easy to escape from the burdens of the growth process by remaining in the rebellious and heretical stage, accepting a life pattern which rests on hatred and anger at the conventional world. (Rosenfels, 1971, p. 36)

Similarly, the argument that radical feminist lesbians are not 'real' lesbians is based on the concept of sexual orientation fundamental to the account of Factor III:

> When the straight women became lesbians, I was sure it was for 'political reasons'. I was repelled by them. They could not possibly understand a 'real lesbian' like me. They hadn't suffered like me. They had been accepted and acceptable all their lives. They didn't live a lie, with the fear and self-loathing I had. Their lesbianism must be a gimmick. (Shea, 1979, p. 23)

Sex, for women constructing this account, is described as being merely an obligatory political act: Chrystos (1982) is typical in asserting, 'I wouldn't want to make love with a woman who felt that she was doing her political duty'.

Finally, the radical feminist account is also assessed in terms of the ideology of romantic love:

> I cannot understand the lesbian liberation movement except as an assertion that ardent love, fervent love, is essential to healthy functioning; we have a right to love because we have a right to be healthy. Liberation will save the original purity and joy of this love and let our inner child go on generating it as birds go on singing. . . . I am bewildered by lesbians who will shout in the streets for liberation and then reject ardour in favour of something more bland that won't interfere with other parts of their lives. Why be an outcast except for something essential? Why not marry a man and have a house in Westchester if you don't know that ardent love is essential? (Routsong, 1978, pp. 50–51)

Some adherents of this 'true love' ideology explicitly attack their more politically engaged sisters:

> You're worse than the blacks. Don't you ever get tired of telling others and reminding yourselves that you're being oppressed and insulted? . . . I still say: 'Stick oppression down the loo-hole, and up with good old love!' (Breinburg, 1977, p. 24)

My understanding of the arguments in these terms has had implications for the way in which I present myself as a lesbian in everyday life: it has meant that, in an effort to resist assimilation, I have become increasingly less willing to account for my lesbianism in ways which, while they may be experienced as subjectively 'true' expressions of my 'inner self' (e.g. being 'happy' to be lesbian, being 'in love') are too readily absorbed by participants into prior belief structures which legitimate *status quo* ideologies.

By way of conclusion, I would like to consider some of the ways in which Q could be developed within a feminist framework. In this research, as in all other Q studies I know of, the selection of Q sort items and the burden of factor interpretation rest with the researcher. I would like to explore the possibility of 'democratizing' Q by, for example, using collective Q sort construction from a group (such as a self-help group or political campaigning group). Debate within the group could be represented in the form of a collective Q sort composed by the group, and the group, as a group, could interpret the factors that emerged. This would be a starting point for attempting to find a way in which control over the research process could ultimately be handed over completely to the participants themselves—though this would probably necessitate the development of more accessible technology and sophisticated software that could make the computerized factor analysis of Q sort data available to the non-specialist. The value of Q to such groups would be in identifying and clarifying potentially divisive differences of opinion between members, and Q has already been used to facilitate group discussion in undergraduate classes and (informally) in a Women's Group in this way.

An alternative way of attempting to get at the processes underlying the 'doing' of Q methodological research, might be to organize a group discussion as suggested above, but to have each individual member separately develop a Q sort based on her or his perception of the salient differences. Each group member would complete the separate Q sorts compiled by each other member, and each Q sort factor analysis would then be individually interpreted by the researcher responsible for developing the sort. The result would be as many different Q sort studies of the original group discussion as there were people in the group: the same data would be analysed using the same methodology by different people. My interest would be in looking at the question: How different are the resulting Q sort studies in terms of the items used and the factor interpretations derived, and how can we (separately and collectively) account for these differences?

In my own subsequent research I have used Q for structuring group discussion, and have used literary accounts of lesbianism, in conjunction with Q, as a resource for tapping the dialectic between accounts. In a recent study, aiming both to give personal experience a central place in the research (as recommended by many other feminists, e.g. Stanley and Wise, 1983) and to dispel the notion that accounts and the people presenting them stand in one-to-one correspondence with each other, I used a Q sort to represent my own (and others') multiple perspectives, after six months unemployment, on my own apparent unemployability. Items such as:

Celia is wallowing in self-pity.

It would be lovely if Celia would just settle down and have a baby.

Celia should be more flexible in her career aspirations.

were sorted by myself, my thesis supervisor, friends and parents according to whatever criteria seemed appropriate (e.g. 'when I'm depressed', 'when I've just been offered an interview', 'when I'm trying to write a paper'). It is hoped that this research will demonstrate some of the flexibility of Q methodology, and its possible uses in the 'real world'.

In addition to my own research, recent work by feminists using Q to research the construction of gender in relation to the Greenham Common Women's Peace Camp (Kitzinger, J., 1985), attitudes to hysterectomy (Roaf, in prep.), the role conflicts of women lawyers (Marshall, 1984), incest (Pal, in prep.) and attributions of masculinity and femininity (Thomas, 1985) combine to suggest that the development of Q as a feminist methodology is an important and productive task.

NOTES TO CHAPTER 9

1. An earlier, shortened version of this chapter appeared in the *European Journal of Social Psychology* (Kitzinger and Stainton Rogers, 1985).

2. I wish to acknowledge the support of the Economic and Social Research Council, who provided three years' funding for research on lesbianism, of which the work reported here formed a part.

REFERENCES

Allen, C. (1969). *A Textbook of Psychosexual Disorders.* Oxford, Oxford University Press.

Baetz, R. (1980). I see my first lesbian. In: M. Cruikshank (ed.), *The Lesbian Path.* Monterrey, California, Angel Press.

Bannister, D. and Fransella, F. (1971). *Inquiring Man: The Psychology of Personal Constructs.* Harmondsworth, Penguin.

Berger, P. and Kellner, H. (1982). *Sociology Reinterpreted: An Essay on Method and Vocation.* Harmondsworth, Penguin.

Bieber, I. (1971). Speaking frankly on a once taboo subject. In: R. V. Guthrie (ed.), *Psychology in the World Today: An Inter-Disciplinary Approach.* (2nd ed.) Reading, Massachusetts, Addison-Wesley.

Breinburg, P. (1977). Review of *A Woman's Right to Cruise. Sappho* **5**(9), 24–25.

Brown, S. R. (1980). *Political Subjectivity: Applications of Q Methodology in Political Science.* New Haven and London, Yale University Press.

Burt, C. (1937). Correlations between persons. *British Journal of Psychology* **28**, 59–96.

Burt, C. (1940). *The Factors of the Mind.* London, University of London Press.

Cartledge, S. and Hemmings, S. (1982). How did we get this way? In: M. Rowe (ed.), *Spare Rib Reader.* Harmondsworth, Penguin.

Cattell, R. B. (1951). On the disuse and misuse of P, Q, Qs and O techniques in clinical psychology. *Journal of Clinical Psychology* **7**, 203–214.

Chrystos (1982). Nidishenok (sisters). *Maenad: A Women's Literary Journal* **2**(2), 23–32.

Cruikshank, M. (ed.) (1980). *The Lesbian Path.* Monterrey, California, Angel Press.

Faderman, L. (1980). *Surpassing the Love of Men.* London, Junction Books.

Faye, C. (1980). Come again. In: S. J. Wolfe and J. P. Stanley (eds), *The Coming Out Stories.* Watertown, Massachusetts, Persephone Press.

Freedman, M. (1971). *Homosexuality and Psychological Functioning*. Belmont, California, Brooks/Cole.

Fritz, L. (1979). *Dreamers and Dealers: An Intimate Appraisal of the Women's Movement*. Boston, Beacon Press.

Gagnon, J. H. (1977). *Human Sexualities*. Glenview, Illinois, Scott, Foresman and Co.

Gill (1977). Untitled poem. In: *Close Encounters of the Lesbian Kind: Journal of the Aberdeen Lesbian Group* (unnumbered).

Goffman, E. (1963). *Stigma: Notes on the Management of Spoiled Identity*. Harmondsworth, Penguin.

Hall, Radclyffe (1928). *The Well of Loneliness*. (Reprinted 1981.) New York, Bard Avon Books.

Hopkins, J. (1969). The lesbian personality. *British Journal of Psychiatry* **115**, 1433–1436.

Jackson, S. (1978). *On the Social Construction of Female Sexuality*. London, Women's Research and Resources Centre.

Jahoda, M. (1958). *Current Concepts of Positive Health*. New York, Basic.

Johnston, J. (1973). *Lesbian Nation: The Feminist Solution*. New York, Simon and Schuster.

Kaye, H. E. *et al.* (1967). Homosexuality in women. *Archives of General Psychiatry* **17**, 626–641.

Kelly, J. (1972). Sister Love: An exploration of the need for homosexual experience. *The Family Coordinator* (October), 473–475.

Kitzinger, C. (1984). *The Constructing of Lesbian Identities*. Unpublished Ph.D. thesis, University of Reading.

Kitzinger, C. and Stainton Rogers, R. (1985). A Q-methodological study of lesbian identities. *European Journal of Social Psychology* **15**, 291–312.

Kitzinger, J. (1985). Take the toys from the boys: The social construction of gender in relation to the Greenham Common women's peace camp. Paper presented at the Annual British Psychological Society Conference, Swansea.

Kriegman, G. (1969). Homosexuality and the educator. *Journal of School Health* (May), 305–311.

Kronemeyer, R. (1980). *Overcoming Homosexuality*. New York, Macmillan.

Love Your Enemy? The Debate Between Heterosexual Feminism and Political Lesbianism. London, Onlywomen Press.

Marshall, H. (1984). Paper presented at the Cambridge University Women's Studies Group, based on work in progress at University of Edinburgh.

Maslow, A. (1962). *Toward a Psychology of Being*. Princeton, New Jersey, Van Nostrand.

Mendola, M. (1980). *The Mendola Report: A New Look at Gay Couples*. New York, Crown Publishers Inc.

Moberly, E. R. (1983). *Psychogenesis: The Early Development of Gender Identity*. London, Routledge & Kegan Paul.

Nie, N. *et al.* (1975). *SPSS: Statistical Package for the Social Sciences*. Second Edition. Reading, Massachusetts, Addison-Wesley.

Pal, J. Research in progress, Department of Psychology, University of Leicester.

Radicalesbians (1970). *Woman-Identified Woman*. Somerville, Masachusetts, New England Free Press.

Reinharz, S. (1981). Experiential analysis: A contribution to feminist research. In: G. Bowles and R. Duelli-Klein (eds), *Theories of Women's Studies II*. Berkeley, University of California Press.

Rich, A. (1979). *On Lies, Secrets and Silence*. New York, W. W. Norton.

Roaf, E. Research in progress, Department of Psychology, University of Edinburgh.

Rochlin, M. (1979). Becoming a gay professional. In: B. Burzon and R. Leighton (eds), *Positively Gay*. Milbrae, California, Celestial Arts.

Rogers, C. R. (1959). A theory of therapy, personality and interpersonal relationships as developed in the client-context framework. In: S. Koch (ed.), *Psychology: A Study of a Science*, Vol. 3. New York, McGraw Hill.

Rosenfels, P. (1971). *Homosexuality: The Psychology of the Creative Process*. New York, Libra Publishers, Inc.

Routsong, A. (1978). Love and courtship. In: G. Vida (ed.), *Our Right to Love: A Lesbian Resource Book*. Englewood Cliffs, New Jersey, Prentice-Hall.

Rule, J. (1975). *Lesbian Images*. London, Peter Davis.

Sappho. A Magazine for Gay Women. London, Sappho Publications Ltd.

Schwartz, J. (1978). Untitled short story. *Sinister Wisdom* **7**, 15–17.

Shea, P. (1979). Bloodroot: Four views of one woman's business. *Heresies* **7**(2), 23–25.

Siegelman, M. (1972). Adjustment of homosexual and heterosexual women. *British Journal of Psychiatry* **120**, 477–481.

Smith, D. (1974). Women's perspective as a radical critique of Sociology. *Sociological Inquiry* **44**, 7–13.

Spearman, C. (1927). *The Abilities of Man*. New York, Macmillan.

Spender, D. (1980). *Man Made Language*. London, Routledge & Kegan Paul.

Spender, D. (1981). Theorising about theorising. In: G. Bowles and R. Duelli-Klein (eds), *Theories of Women's Studies II*. Berkeley, University of California Press.

Stanley, J. P. and Wolfe, S. J. (eds) (1980). *The Coming Out Stories*. Watertown, Massachusetts, Persephone Press.

Stanley, L. (1984). Open secrets. Paper presented at British Sociological Association Sexual Divisions Study Day, Manchester.

Stanley, L. and Wise, S. (1983). *Breaking Out: Feminist Consciousness and Feminist Research*. London, Routledge & Kegan Paul.

Star, S. L. (1980). How I spent at least one summer vacation. In: J. P. Stanley and S. J. Wolfe (eds), *The Coming Out Stories*. Watertown, Massachusetts, Persephone Press.

Stephenson, W. (1935). Techniques of Factor Analysis. *Nature* **136**, 297.

Stephenson, W. (1936a). A new application of correlations to averages. *British Journal of Educational Psychology* **6**, 43–57.

Stephenson, W. (1936b). The inverted factor technique. *British Journal of Psychology* **22**, 344–461.

Stephenson, W. (1939). Two contributions to the theory of mental testing: I. A new performance test for measuring abilities as correlation coefficients. *Journal of Clinical Psychology* **30**, 19–35.

Tedeschi, J. T. and Reiss, M. (1981). Verbal strategies in impression management. In: C. Antaki (ed.), *The Psychology of Ordinary Explanations of Social Behaviour*. London, Academic Press.

Toll, B. J. (1980). Strong and free: The awakening. In: S. J. Wolfe and J. P. Stanley (eds), *The Coming Out Stories*. Watertown, Massachusetts, Persephone Press.

Thomas, A. (1985). The meaning of gender in women's self conceptions. Paper presented at the British Psychological Society Social Psychology Section Annual Conference, Cambridge.

West, D. J. (1968). *Homosexuality*. Harmondsworth, Penguin.

Westall, R. (1978). Hetero, homo, bi or nothing. In: M. Dickins and R. Sutcliff (eds), *Is Anyone There?* Harmondsworth, Penguin.

Westcott, M. (1981). Women's studies and a strategy for change: Between criticism and vision. In: G. Bowles and R. Duelli-Klein (eds), *Theories of Women's Studies II*. Berkeley, California, University of California Press.

Wetherell, M. (1982). Socio-psychological and literary accounts of femininity. In: P. Stringer (ed.), *Confronting Social Issues: Applications of Social Psychology*, Vol. 2. London, Academic Press.

Wilbur, C. B. (1965). Clinical aspects of female homosexuality. In: J. Marmor (ed.), *Sexual Inversion: The Multiple Roots of Homosexuality*. New York, Basic Books.

Wilkinson, S. (1984). Feminist research: Ethogeny revisited? Paper presented in symposium *Feminist Research in Social Psychology: Extending the Perspective*, BPS Social Psychology Section Annual Conference, University of Oxford, 14-16 September 1984.

Wilson, M. and Greene, R. (1971). Personality characteristics of female homosexuals. *Psychological Reports* **28**, 407-412.

Chapter 10

Qualitative Methods and Female Experience: Young Women from School to the Job Market

Christine Griffin

INTRODUCTION

Qualitative research methods have been regarded with considerable suspicion in mainstream social psychology. They have either been dismissed as 'subjective' and 'unrepresentative', or at best treated as a source of 'rich' anecdotal material which can only be subordinate to quantitative methods (see Campbell, 1978). Qualitative methods are less amenable to the research designs and statistical analyses of experimental social psychology, and they generate quite different information to the quantitative techniques used in most social science research.

This chapter looks at the potential advantages of qualitative research methods for social psychology in general, and for our understanding of gender relations and female experience in particular. It also examines the implications of focussing on female experience as a means of moving beyond gender-specific analyses in social science, and for the development of a feminist social psychology.

The chapter begins with an assessment of the male-as-norm principle which pervades most social psychological research. The majority of theories in the social sciences are developed from studies which either focus entirely on men's experiences, or treat women as marginal and deviant beings, who can only be defined in terms of their similarity to, or difference from, the male norm (cf. Broverman *et al.*, 1972).

I want to draw on my own experience in a specific research project to illustrate the pervasive influence of this male norm on analyses of young people's lives, and to look at ways of moving beyond the male norm. The use of qualitative methods and research which focusses on female experience can make valuable contributions to the development of a feminist social psychology.

THE MALE NORM IN RESEARCH ON YOUNG PEOPLE

Most studies of the so-called 'transition from school to work' have focussed on education and the labour market (e.g. Brannen, 1975; Watts, 1983), with some analysis of leisure activities (e.g. Corrigan, 1979; Roberts, 1984), but limited consideration of domestic work or family life. This is partly a result of their tendency to concentrate on the experiences of young white working class men. Young women have either been almost completely ignored (e.g. Halsey *et al.*, 1980; Corrigan, 1979), or young men have been taken as the norm against which young women's experiences must be judged (e.g. Jenkins, 1983; Robbins and Cohen, 1978).

This has had two unfortunate consequences: studies of men's experiences have developed gender-specific theories which have been presented as universally relevant, and researchers have struggled with difficulty to 'fit' young women's experiences into inappropriate and unsatisfactory models (e.g. McRobbie and Garber, 1975; Davies, 1979).

Conversely, research on men has seldom examined the influence of gender relations or masculinity (though see Connell, 1983; Willis, 1979; and Tolson, 1977 for exceptions to this tendency). We are left with a large body of theory and research which is gender-specific, whilst having relatively little to say about gender relations, and this limits our understanding of women's *and* men's lives.

The recent sharp rise in youth unemployment levels has precipitated a reassessment of existing theories on the school to work transition and on youth cultures. Most of the latter were developed in an era when the youth labour market was far more buoyant, often in situations of almost full employment. Many school leavers in the 1980s face an uncertain future, with few prospects apart from government training schemes or the dole (cf. Ashton and Field, 1976 and Bates *et al.*, 1984).

Current analyses of youth unemployment, and of unemployment in general, seem to be reproducing and reinforcing the deficiencies and the male focus of earlier research. John Hayes and Peter Nutman, for example, state in the introduction to their review of research on the psychological impact of unemployment:

> The place work occupies in the life of women has dramatically changed over the years. These changes are not reflected in many studies of unemployment reported in this book. In the majority of cases these studies examined *only the effects of unemployment on men*. Wherever possible we have included studies which embraced women, and we believe that the models and explanations that we have developed are *equally applicable to both men and women*. (1981, p. 3, my emphases)

A short article by Peter Warr, which reviews the work of Sheffield University's Social and Applied Psychology Unit, illustrates the continuing influence of the male norm on social psychological theory and research. This six-page article cites evidence on the psychological effects of unemployment on *men* for the first four pages. Professor Warr does acknowledge the male bias of his analysis, and he actually mentions gender differences at the end of his first section:

> Finally, what about sex differences in the effect of unemployment? Most of the results I have described have come from samples of men. However, we have also looked at aspects of women's unemployment, attempting to bring together a wide range of findings within an overall model. (1983, p. 308)

Warr then quotes in brief some research on differences in the psychological effects of paid work for women with children, which actually focusses on *class* rather than gender differences. He makes no mention of those SAPU studies which have looked at gender differences to some extent (e.g. Ullah and Banks, 1983; Fryer and Payne, 1983).

The examples quoted above illustrate that some social psychologists are willing to tolerate an extremely high level of academic imprecision and even sloppiness in their theoretical analyses. One wonders whether this same tolerance would have been so much in evidence had the topic at issue not been research on gender relations and women's experiences. It is worth noting here that social psychology is not alone in its continued focus on male experience. Sociological analyses of unemployment have also developed from studies of men's lives (e.g. Norris, 1978).

MOVING BEYOND THE MALE NORM: THE FOCUS ON FEMALE EXPERIENCE

The male-as-norm principle has dominated mainstream academic research to such an extent that Dale Spender (1980) renamed the latter 'men's studies', and Janet Siltanen and Michelle Stanworth (1984) have called it 'the academic male-stream'. Over the past two decades, feminist researchers have been challenging the male norm through a focus on women's experiences. Recent feminist critiques of social psychology and social science in general are not simply arguing for a more 'balanced' focus in research work along gender lines; an increased concern with women's experiences is only one part of their intentions. As Liz Stanley and Sue Wise have pointed out:

> If you take women seriously, if you make women's experience the central feature of what you're doing, then you just *can't* leave the rest undisturbed. (1983, p. 3, original emphasis)

Concentrating on women's experiences is only one stage in a long process, the starting point for an analysis which will enrich and extend our understanding of women's *and* men's lives. Some male academics have begun to take notice of feminist critiques and feminist theories and they are starting to examine the impact of gender relations on their areas of study (see Wood, 1984; and Willis, 1984, for two recent examples).

One of the main consequences of the male norm in social science research is the preponderance of gender-specific theories. Anyone wishing to develop an analysis of women's lives is faced with a range of theoretical frameworks and concepts which have been designed to explain specific male experiences.

I experienced the limitations of the male norm all too clearly during the research for a study of 'Young Women and Work', which was based at Birmingham University's Centre for Contemporary Cultural Studies (CCCS). One of the original aims of the study was to develop a sort of female equivalent to Paul Willis's work with young white working class 'lads'. I was therefore under considerable pressure to identify female versions of Willis's 'lads' and 'earoles': working class male anti- and pro-school cultures respectively (see Willis, 1977). I want to look at my attempt to apply Willis's analysis to the young women I interviewed in some detail, because it provides an example of the male-as-norm principle in operation, and demonstrates one means of moving beyond that norm via a focus on women's experiences.

THE YOUNG WOMEN AND WORK STUDY

This research was carried out in Birmingham during the early 1980s for a three-year project which was funded by the Social Science Research Council (now the Economic and Social Research Council) as part of their 'Young People in Society' initiative (for more details see Griffin, 1984; 1985b).

This project was relatively unusual for a number of reasons: it was designed to be innovative firstly in its reliance on qualitative methods, and secondly in the focus on female experience. The project fell into two main stages which were based in a range of schools and workplaces respectively. As the sole research worker, I visited six Birmingham schools, both single sex (girls) and co-educational; Catholic, Church of England and non-denominational; ranging in size from 500 to over 1500 students. I talked to 180 school students either individually or in small groups — including young middle- and working class women; Asian, Afro-Caribbean and white students; fourth, fifth and sixth formers; and some young men. I also talked to headteachers, careers officers, form and careers teachers. These interviews were informal and loosely structured, and I asked students about their experiences of education, leisure and family life, as well as their expectations about waged work and unemployment.

The second stage of the research involved following 25 fifth formers from five of these schools into their first two years in the full-time job market. Limitations on my time and energy meant that this stage focussed on the experiences of young, white, working class women whose academic qualifications ranged from four

'O' levels down to none at all. I visited these young women regularly—at home, in local coffee bars and pubs, and in their workplaces—wherever possible. This stage of the research was based on an extensive series of informal interviews with the young women, their families and friends, and on systematic observation in ten of the young women's workplaces. The latter were divided between those in traditionally 'female' office and factory jobs, and those who had moved into the male world of engineering. This phase also included interviews with those young women who experienced prolonged periods of unemployment.

Willis argued that the lads' counter-school culture acted as a bridge between school and the labour market, leading them to 'choose' hard, heavy manual jobs. I was unable to identify equivalent pro- and anti-school cultures for young working class women which prepared them for office and factory work along the lines of the cultural transition described by Paul Willis. The situation was more complex than Willis's analysis might lead one to expect, not because his arguments were incorrect, but because they could not be applied in any straightforward manner to young women's experiences.

There were several reasons for this. Firstly, the definition of conformity and deviance in school for young women was quite different to that for young men (Davies, 1979; Casburn, 1979). 'Deviance' for female students tended to be defined according to their sexuality, whilst for young men it centred around their perceived levels of verbal and physical aggression (Millman, 1975; Griffin, 1982b). Secondly, the social structure of male and female friendship groups was quite different. Young white working class men spent most of their time in those 'gangs of lads' which have provided the foundation for numerous studies of youth sub-cultures (Hall and Jefferson, 1975; Brake, 1980). Young women either had one extremely close 'best' girl friend, or a small group of two, three or four girl friends (cf. McRobbie, 1978). It was therefore more difficult to identify a specific group of young women as part of a pro- or anti-school culture, especially since the membership of these friendship groups could change if young women shifted their allegiances elsewhere.

Finally, there was no obvious connection between young women's status in school and their eventual positions in the labour market. Berni, for example, described herself with some pride as a 'trouble-maker', as did the rest of her main friendship group at school. Their form teacher referred to this group of four white working class fifth formers as 'a bit of a handful'. They distanced themselves from the 'swots' and 'pets' who wanted to stay on at school, and had an even lower opinion of the 'snobs' who hoped to get office jobs. Yet Berni went straight from the fifth form into an office job, so for her there was no clear link between school friendship groups, attitudes to school and academic work, conformist or deviant status, and her eventual destination in the labour market. Berni was not the only young woman I interviewed for whom the transition from school to work did not follow the pattern suggested by Willis's analysis (for a more detailed account see Griffin, 1985b).

I was not alone in my struggle to apply a 'male' theory to women's experiences. Several other researchers (all of them female) have tried to use Willis's theory with varying degrees of success (e.g. Davies, 1979; McRobbie, 1978; 1980; Thomas, 1980; Walkerdine, 1981). Moving beyond such gender-specific theories requires considerable confidence in oneself as a research worker, and in the experiences of the central participants in the study: the young women. I did eventually develop an analysis which reflects some of the complexity of these young women's lives (see Griffin, 1985b). The use of qualitative methods and cultural analysis were at least as valuable in this respect as was the focus on female experience.

QUALITATIVE RESEARCH TECHNIQUES

As already noted, most research designs in social psychology involve the use of quantitative research techniques. As the name suggests such techniques emphasize the importance of recording and analysing information in numerical form. In addition, quantitative techniques are frequently used in conjunction with a positivist approach developed from the natural sciences. This (to put it crudely) involves the construction of hypotheses which the research is designed to test; compiling representative samples of 'subjects'; and a ceaseless striving for a state of scientific objectivity. This combination of quantitative research techniques and a positivist approach is characteristic of experimental social psychology in Britain (see Armistead, 1974; Billig, 1978).

In discussing the positive aspects of qualitative techniques, I am not necessarily rejecting quantitative methods out of hand. Both methods have their own advantages and limitations, but the dominance of quantitative techniques when tied to a positivist approach has placed qualitative methods in a marginal position within social psychology. The two methods are best employed as different sets of research techniques which can *each* make valuable contributions to social psychology in their own right (Griffin, 1985a).

The research methods used in the Young Women and Work study were based on informal interviews and systematic observation of these young women over some two and a half years in a range of different sites: at school, during leisure time and in their workplaces. Most of the interviews were taped (with the respondents' permission), and supplemented with detailed fieldnotes. Where taping was difficult or impossible (e.g. in workplaces with loud background noise), I recorded the interviews in as much detail as possible in fieldnote form. I did carry out some limited quantitative analysis of the school interview material (see Griffin, 1984; 1985b) but the research fieldwork and analysis relied mainly on qualitative techniques.

Flexibility

The use of qualitative methods allowed for a considerable degree of flexibility within the research process (cf. Willis, 1980). I approached each interview with a number of pre-selected questions and issues which I intended to cover. If any additional (and perhaps unexpected) topic came up during the interview, I could follow this up 'on the spot' if there was sufficient time and further questions were appropriate.

The most notable example of this concerned the importance of leisure in young women's lives. Once I realized just how crucial a role leisure played, I was able to change the research design to accommodate a continuing focus on young women's leisure during the second stage of the project. As the research progressed, it became increasingly clear that leisure was an important site in which social and financial pressures to get a boy friend/husband/partner were played out.

Pressures to get a boy friend began to intensify once the young women reached 16 (if not before), and after they had left school. If one young women began to see a 'steady' boy friend, she often lost touch with her girl friend(s), sometimes at the young man's insistence. This process was known as 'deffing out', and young women developed a range of strategies designed to avoid this breakdown of female friendship groups. Although they promised to stay faithful to each other, the pressures to get a boy friend combined with different work experiences meant that over half of the young women had lost touch with their girl friends a year after leaving school.

Sandra and Mandy tried to continue as 'best friends' after they had left school. Unfortunately this did not work out according to plan, as Sandra explained to me in the summer of 1981:

> **Sandra:**
> Mandy's been out with a few boys, and whenever she does, she never bothers ringing me. Or she goes out with them and doesn't tell me, and I'm stuck in all the time. Whenever I go out with Mandy she's with her fella and she leaves me with all his friends. They're all going on about this girl and that, so I try to get up another conversation. It's no fun standing around listening to them go on about sex and girls. We always said at the beginning that we wouldn't deff each other out if we went out with fellas, but she always does in the end. If I do meet someone, it doesn't last, or I don't like them much [*laugh*].

There was no male equivalent to this 'deffing out' process which was anywhere near as pervasive as the breakdown of female friendship groups. 'The lads' still saw their male 'mates' in local pubs and at football matches if they had a steady girl friend, continuing to mix with those 'gangs of lads' which have played such a central role in studies of youth sub-cultures. Some young men did see less of their male friends if they were 'courting', but this usually led to considerable resentment from 'the lads'. The latter would put pressure on the young man to return to the male gang. There were variations in the patterns of 'deffing out', but overall it was the smaller, female friendship groups which tended to fragment as the heterosexual couple became an almost obligatory part of most young women's leisure time.

There is insufficient space here for more than a brief account of the repercussions of the 'deffing out' process on young women's leisure time, their position in the family, school and the workplace (see Griffin 1985b). The use of qualitative methods enabled me to examine this process in a detail which would have been difficult, if not impossible, with quantitative methods and a positivist approach.

Confidentiality and Contradictions

The informal, semi-structured nature of the group interviews in schools meant that young women sometimes began to discuss particular issues amongst themselves, without waiting for my next question. This usually occurred towards the end of the interviews, when the students had relaxed a little and developed a degree of trust in my promise of confidentiality. Once again, these discussions did not always fall within my list of pre-selected topics, and I was able to amend this list as the research progressed.

In one case, a group of Afro-Caribbean fifth formers began to discuss a series of confrontations between police and students outside the school. They interrupted this discussion soon after the start to check with me that the tape would not be played to teachers or other figures in authority. Another incident which occurred in several group interviews concerned young women's responses to my questions on whether they expected to marry and/or have children in the future, and how this might combine with waged work.

Young women's expectations about their future marriage, childcare and employment prospects were riddled with contradictions, although these varied depending on whether they were middle- or working class, Asian, Afro-Caribbean or white. Marriage was not such an economic necessity for young white middle-class women, who stood a better chance of getting a reasonably paid job than their black and working class peers. Yet some sixth formers did talk of planning, even choosing their 'careers' to fit in with domestic commitments, and the majority expected to marry, have children and leave paid work for between two and ten years to look after the children (cf. Prendergast and Prout, 1980).

Childcare was seen as essential work which could not easily be combined with a full-time job. Some young women felt that childcare was too important to be left to men, but there was no clear consensus on this issue. White middle-class sixth formers from two prestigious academic girls' schools discussing marriage, motherhood and employment:

CG:
So what puts you off combining family with a job — is it that your job would mean travelling a lot?
Ann:
No, not really. I just don't think it's fair on any child — if I did have children — to work. I just want to bring it up, live with it completely. I just couldn't do that with my job. [*Ann wanted to be an archaeologist.*]
Marie:
You have to give up work once you get married.

CG:
Do you think that women should give up work to look after children?
Marie:
Oh yes, you couldn't trust men to do it.
Sally:
Oh no, god, you'd think that was all women were made for.
Marie:
No I don't, but I think that if you had a child you shouldn't not commit yourself and put it in a nursery and not have any interest in it yourself.
Sally:
For a few years, but not for the rest of your life!

Marriage and motherhood were seen as distant events which might occur some ten years in the future, but they were also seen as inevitable for most young women. Few financially feasible or socially acceptable alternatives were available, particularly for young working class women. Asian and Afro-Caribbean students were more sceptical of the dream of romantic love than their white working class peers, since their cultural traditions and family structures did not place such a strong emphasis on the link between 'love and marriage' (see Wilson, 1978; Amos and Parmar, 1981; Westwood, 1984). Two Asian fifth formers from a mixed inner city comprehensive:

Jasbinder:
They [*teachers*] expect all us Asians to be having arranged marriages. Well it's not true that.
Dalbiro:
And anyway, what's the big problem with it? I know lots of white people that get into a mess with their marriages. Worse even. I do have trouble with my family sometimes, but nothing like what the teachers say.

Afro-Caribbean students from the same school:

Carol:
I don't believe in marriage me. Waste of time.
Sonia:
Nor me.
CG:
What about you? [*to Clare and Jane*] Do you think you might?
Clare and Jane [white students]:
Yeh.

Carol:
I knew *they* would [*laugh*].
CG:
In the future do you think you'll get married?
Marjory:
No no no. Definitely not. Not marriage. You just suffer man. You've got
to rush home from work and cook and tidy up and . . .
Babs:
You want a good time before you get married. You get tied down.
Marjory:
Enjoy yourself yeh. I'd live in sin really. And you have to do everything.
You're fighting, arguing. I'd live with my man, yeah, but not marry him,
I can chuck him out when I like.

Despite their different perceptions of marriage and motherhood, these young
women were all expected to put domestic life, childcare, and/or marriage before
waged work and their own financial independence. This was certainly not
welcomed as an attractive prospect by all of the young women I interviewed.
Although they looked at their futures from different class and race positions, these
discussions were all characterized by the complexity of the arguments and the
lack of any potential solutions to the dilemmas facing the 'working mother' (see
Sharpe, 1984). I have described these young women's position as caught at crucial
transition points in the sexual marketplace, the marriage market and the job market
(see Griffin, 1982a; 1985b).

'Touchy Subjects' and Longitudinal Research

Along with the ability to reflect the complexity and the contradictory nature of
people's experiences, qualitative methods have other advantages when used in
longitudinal studies such as the Young Women and Work project. The latter
allowed me to look at more sensitive issues such as sexuality and male domestic
violence. Dealing with male demands for sex, comments about their appearance,
thinking about romance, love and marriage were all central concerns for these
young women, but the more 'touchy' subjects were not covered in the initial
school interviews.

Here is one group of white working class fourth formers talking in a park after
school, which was a mixed Catholic comprehensive:

Treena:
But if a bloke asks you for sex, what do you do?
Brid:
I'd tell him to go off and have a wank!
Stella:
You dirty thing!
Kate:
It's wrong, you ought to get married in a white dress.

Stella:
But I don't think it is — if you like the bloke why not? Why wait until you're married?
Treena:
She's talking — I bet she's done it!
Kate:
You ought to sleep with a bloke if you loved him and he asked you to.
Stella:
But you just said that you have to get married in white!

Exchanges of this kind were by no means unusual, and they were characterized by an even greater degree of complexity and contradiction than the discussions on marriage and motherhood. There seemed to be no answer to the crucial question of 'what to do if a boy asks you for sex'. If a girl said 'yes', she was condemned as a 'slag', if she said 'no', she was likely to be branded as frigid, or a 'lezzie' (lesbian) (cf. Cowie and Lees, 1981; Griffin, 1982b; McRobbie, 1978).

Systematic Observation

The qualitative methods used in the project involved systematic non-participant observation as well as an extensive series of interviews. The former was particularly important in the workplace case studies, since it was often too noisy or too busy to record an interview, and relevant episodes could not always be captured on tape. Keeping detailed and accurate fieldnotes was vital, and I became obsessed with this task for fear of missing some important event or comment.

Much of the academic literature on social science methodologies is highly theoretical (e.g. Giddens, 1976; although see Miles and Oberman, 1984, for one recent exception). The considerable mental and physical effort involved in research work is seldom mentioned, but I certainly found the experience of actually doing qualitative fieldwork exhausting. The focus on other people's lives, combined with the strain of concentrating on every behavioural nuance and event, made days spent 'in the field' extremely tiring. I would pay frequent visits to the women's toilets to scribble notes on scraps of paper, and would write these up in full at the end of each day.

Most of the interviews were transcribed from the tapes by part-time secretarial workers, and I was extremely grateful for their painstaking and vital work. My field-notes were all dated, giving details of place, context and who was present, as well as dialogue, including my own contributions. A degree of selectivity was inevitable in the production of these fieldnotes, since neither qualitative nor quantitative methods can reflect every aspect of respondents' lives. When whole working days were spent 'in the field' in offices, schools or factories, I recorded those episodes which I judged to be relevant, surprising, or which seemed to illustrate commonly occurring themes. I also included my own initial interpretations of the events in a 'Theory' file, and reactions such as 'felt at ease' or 'terrified'.

This systematic observation did not include true participant observation (PO), which would have meant working alongside young women on typewriters, data processors, sewing machines or lathes for those in engineering. Apart from the disruption which this would have caused, I would have been doing unpaid work in a situation of rapidly rising youth unemployment. PO does allow researchers to share some of the experiences of their 'subjects', and to blend into their lives to a limited extent (cf. Willis, 1980; Westwood, 1984), but I preferred in this case to use the non-participant 'fly on the wall' technique.

During visits to young women's workplaces I would observe the pattern of the working day, either sitting in a corner or walking around the office or factory floor. My presence was explained as 'seeing what X's job involves' for a project on 'young women leaving school to start their first full-time jobs'. Once the initial novelty had worn off and everyone knew who I was, pressure of work usually meant that I was more or less ignored. Several managers and employees remarked that they had soon forgotten about my presence. As one office supervisor put it:

Ms Stewart:
I hope you haven't been bored. I forgot all about you. Mind you, I suppose that's a compliment to you, isn't it? [*laughs*]

I have summarized above some of the advantages of using qualitative methods for a study of women's experiences which aimed to overcome the male focus of most social science research. I want to turn now to an area which is seldom covered in the academic literature on social science methodologies: how to develop a reasonably coherent analysis from a pile of tape transcripts and volumes of fieldnotes.

CULTURAL ANALYSIS

Analysing and writing up research which is based on quantitative positivist methods is a well documented part of the academic tradition. Social psychology undergraduates, very much like their peers in physics and chemistry departments, learn the immutable laws and etiquette of the natural scientific method. Most articles in social psychological journals reflect this tradition, divided as they are into sections on method, results and conclusions. Analyses are interspersed with neat tables of figures and the results of various probability tests for statistical significance.

The 'results' of a piece of qualitative research look very different, full of quotations and apparently contradictory 'findings'. In an academic discipline in which qualitative methods occupy a secondary position, the experience of analysing such research material can seem chaotic, even frightening. Partly because the study relied so heavily on qualitative methods, and partly because of my focus on female experience in an area dominated by theories about 'lads', I frequently felt that I was working in an uncharted, academic no-man's land. This was a simultaneously terrifying and exhilarating experience.

I found few guidelines on how to analyse my 'data' or how to structure my theoretical analysis (though see the Ethnography section in Hall *et al.*, 1980). Fortunately, other researchers at CCCS, who were also using qualitative methods, provided invaluable advice and support. I kept a number of 'Fieldnotes' files throughout the study which included notes from visits to schools, workplaces, and a 'Family Life and Leisure' file based on interviews in young women's homes, and in coffee bars, pubs and parks. A 'Method' file contained my own developing ideas on research methodology, participants' views of my role and of the project. The 'Theory' file, referred to in the last section, consisted of notes towards a theoretical framework and points from relevant texts. I could not incorporate all of these notes into the full research analysis, but they have proved invaluable for the development of that analysis. These files are a record of what has been termed the 'reflexivity' of the research process, of the continual examination of my role as a researcher, and of the project's progress (cf. Willis, 1980).

Once all of this 'data' had been amassed and checked, I worked through the fieldnotes and tape transcripts categorizing the material under a series of topic headings. These were designed to cover the main research areas as recorded in my list of interview topics; to be exhaustive with the minimum of overlap; and to be fairly manageable without undue loss of detail. The topics were divided into two parts, following the first and second stages of the project, including young women's experiences of school, teachers, friendship groups, expectations and actual experiences of full- and part-time employment, of 'women's' and 'men's' jobs, of family life, domestic work, leisure and unemployment.

This categorization was recorded on a card index system which provided the structure for the analysis. Each general topic was broken down into subheadings, and these included any additional issues which had arisen from the fieldwork, such as the prevalence of male domestic violence, sexual harassment in and outside the workplace, and the incidence of racist attacks and abuse in young women's (and men's) leisure activities.

The theoretical analysis of this material was not a discrete event which occurred outside 'the field' when the time came to write up the 'results', but it formed an integral part of the research process. My 'Theory' file in particular was a clear example of what has been called 'theoretical sampling', in which theory is generated throughout the fieldwork via the continual interaction between research 'in the field' and a developing theoretical framework (see Glaser and Strauss, 1967; Willis, 1980). Such a process is not unknown in quantitative or positivist research, but qualitative studies are far more likely to acknowledge the potential value of theoretical sampling.

I used qualitative techniques to develop an ethnographic account of young women's lives which was based on a form of cultural analysis. The latter provided a potential means of understanding individual experience in a wider group context. Social psychology itself is devoted to just this aim, but I was unable to find any theoretical framework which could easily be used in conjunction with qualitative methods, and within which I could develop a comprehensive analysis of the young women's experiences.

Cultural studies in Britain has developed a form of ethnographic cultural analysis based on qualitative methods, which aims to identify specific cultural processes 'as they are lived'. In this context, 'culture' has been defined as:

> . . . shared principles of life, characteristic of particular classes, groups or social milieux. Cultures are produced as groups make sense of their social existence in the course of everyday experience. (Education Group, CCCS, 1981, p. 27)

Individuals are both determined by, and potential determinants of social forces. We are not simply passive reflections of stereotyped images and ideas, or acquiescent victims of oppressive social conditions. Conversely, we are not all active 'social agents', able to make 'free choices' and rise above the most harrowing social conditions through sheer effort of willpower and 'individual resourcefulness' (e.g. Rapoport and Rapoport, 1975; for critique see Griffin et al., 1982).

Qualitative cultural analysis tries to maintain that tension between the individual as an active social agent, the product of a given 'life history', who is capable of making positive choices and decisions, and the individual as shaped by specific social structures and ideologies. The role of particular cultures and cultural forms as they tie the individual to a range of different social groups is central to cultural analysis, and this seemed to provide the key to both sides of the relationship mentioned above (see the Introduction to Hall et al., 1980).

Cultural analysis acknowledges the importance of power differentials in social relations, an area about which social psychology has always been wary. This is particularly valuable for any analysis of gender relations which aims to develop beyond a descriptive account of sex role stereotypes to examine the power imbalances between women and men. Cultural analysis has a degree of theoretical sophistication and an affinity for qualitative methods which is seldom reflected in social psychological theory (see Billig, 1978). One of its main advantages from my point of view was the rejection of the positivist insistence on the apolitical and objective nature of research work.

THE MYTH OF THE APOLITICAL RESEARCHER

Numerous studies of the school to work transition for young men have passed without comment as normal and unremarkable (e.g. Halsey et al., 1980; Corrigan, 1979; Willis, 1977), yet I was frequently being asked 'Why are you only talking to girls?' by teachers, school students, employers, and even by other researchers. I *did* interview some young men, but the project was never intended to be fully comparative, and young women's experiences were the main focus of the research. Male-only studies have seldom been criticized for their gender-specific bias (at least not in mainstream academic circles, though see McRobbie, 1980; Stanley and Wise, 1983; Spender, 1980), whilst studies of women's experiences are often seen as 'sexist', biased, or at the very least unusual. More disturbing still, this gender imbalance is also reflected in the funding of social science research.

I was not only seen as unusual, but as unusual in a political sense. On his own admission, Paul Willis was never questioned about the gender-specific nature of his research with young men during the fieldwork period in school, yet several teachers, employers and young women assumed that I was a feminist (in some cases before they had even seen me), simply because I was a woman interested in young women's lives. For most women this carried a positive connotation, whilst for men it was more likely to be seen in negative terms. One headmaster took me into his office especially to tell me just why 'this equal opportunities thing is a waste of time' (see Griffin, 1985a).

Throughout the Young Women and Work study I aimed to balance the simultaneous pressures of 'making the strange familiar and the familiar strange' which is so important in qualitative research. I aimed to maintain a responsiveness to new insights, a capacity for 'being surprised', and a willingness to examine and 'see beyond' my own preconceptions about the study (cf. Willis, 1980; Hobson, 1978). All research workers, regardless of the techniques or theoretical analyses they employ, bring their own set of assumptions and expectations to a project. My main objection to the positivist tradition is that researchers are presented as objective and value-free, engaged in an apolitical and unbiased search for Universal Truths (cf. Stanley and Wise, 1983).

In practice, I had no chance to construct any such pretence of objectivity, nor to work out how I might best avoid 'contaminating the field' — even if I had wanted to do so. I visited one young woman in her job as an office junior in a small printing company. Jeanette introduced me by striding into the middle of the factory floor, raising a clenched fist and shouting: 'This is Chris, she's doing a project on me — women's lib!'. We had never discussed feminism as such, although in interviews Jeanette had made several comments which were very similar to feminist ideas, like most of the women to whom I spoke during the study. Any misguided hopes of passing as an apolitical and inconspicuous observer on my part vanished with every shake of Jeanette's clenched fist.

These assumptions about my political intentions, and of the feminist nature of the project, forced me to examine my status as a research worker, and the relationship between research and 'politics'. Why was I seen as political, biased, subjective and a feminist, whilst male researchers and/or those who focussed on men's experiences could pass as objective, unbiased, apolitical and rigorous? These phenomena provided one more clear example of the treatment of male experience as the norm against which women's experience is judged, and is then frequently defined as deviant or unusual (cf. Stanley and Wise, 1983). These questions eventually led me to consider the political nature of research in general, and the status of feminist research in particular.

'POLITICAL' RESEARCH AND FEMINIST SOCIAL PSYCHOLOGY

I would define politics, at its most general level, along the lines suggested by Janet Siltanen and Michelle Stanworth in their introduction to a book on women's involvement in politics and the public sphere:

> Politics is, then, an activity which may take individual or collective forms, centred around the struggle over power. Power is the capacity to shape or form social and political relations i.e. the capacity to perpetuate a given order or to transform it. (1984, p. 14)

In this sense, *all* research work is 'political' to some extent, but certain areas tend to be identified as political, whilst others can safely pass as 'neutral' or unbiased. My own research experience indicates that no such neutral or objective apolitical stance is possible. Regardless of whether I defined myself as a feminist, anti-feminist or politically neutral, I was *seen* as a feminist involved in a piece of political research, with all the various connotations that implied.

Any research which is concerned with 'sensitive' social issues, or which is seen as a potential challenge to the *status quo*, is also likely to be labelled as 'political'. On inspection, much of the research which passes as objective and value-free tends to reflect dominant ideologies and power relations. So Paul Willis' work generated few comments from the academic establishment on gender terms, but it was seen and criticized as 'controversial' and 'politically biased' in class terms, since *Learning to Labour* employed an explicitly Marxist analysis.

When we seek to construct a feminist social psychology we should be aware of the existing boundaries which aim to create a distinction between political and apolitical or non-political research. The crucial question here is not whether a specific study is defined as 'political' or not. The crux of such arguments actually concerns different notions of objectivity and value-free research.

All research workers bring their own preconceptions and assumptions to a project. Whilst positivists might strive to create a certain distance between themselves and the 'subjects' of study, I would argue that it is impossible to operate as an objective and value-free researcher. It is more important to make what has been called a 'theoretical confession', in which the aims of the research, and the values and preconceptions of the research worker(s) are made clear from the start of the study (see Willis, 1980).

If feminist social psychology is to make any significant impact on the academic 'male-stream', then the focus on female experience should eventually lead to a profound reassessment of existing gender-specific theories. This is unlikely to be a smooth or easy process, since many (male) social psychologists will cling tenaciously to the Great Theories which they hold so dear. Feminist research (and teaching) should not be confined to the margins of social psychology, or seen as relevant to only a few 'committed' or 'biased' women (Roberts, 1981). The arguments and analyses of feminist social psychology (and feminist social science in general) are relevant to *all* social psychologists, male and female, regardless of their research interests, feminist or even anti-feminist sympathies. It could be argued that the messages of feminist social psychology are most relevant to those who are most dismissive of feminist and radical social science. Similarly, feminist research need not restrict itself to analyses of women's experiences; it can also tell us a great deal about men's attitudes and behaviour.

I have no space to speculate here on the precise definition of feminist social psychology: that has been covered at greater length in other chapters of this book (see, in particular, Chapter 1). I have demonstrated some of the advantages of qualitative research and a focus on female experience for social psychology in general, and for the development of a feminist social psychology in particular. However strong our arguments, some sections of the academic establishment will no doubt prefer to see feminist social psychology in its 'rightful' (and less threatening) place: on the margins of 'male-stream' research. I have argued in this chapter that the proper place for feminist social psychology is in the centre of social psychological teaching and research.

REFERENCES

Amos, V. and Parmar, P. (1981). Resistances and responses: the experiences of black girls in Britain. In: A. McRobbie and T. McCabe (eds), *Feminism for Girls: An Adventure Story*. London, Routledge & Kegan Paul.

Armistead, N. (ed.) (1974). *Reconstructing Social Psychology*. Harmondsworth, Penguin.

Ashton, D. and Field, D. (1976). *Young Workers*. London, Hutchinson.

Bates, I., Clarke, J., Cohen, P., Finn, D., Moore, R. and Willis, P. (1984). *Schooling for the Dole? The New Vocationalism*. London, MacMillan.

Billig, M. (1978). The new social psychology and 'fascism'. *European Journal of Social Psychology* **7**(4), 393–432.

Brake, M. (1980). *The Sociology of Youth Culture and Youth Subculture*. London, Routledge & Kegan Paul.

Brannen, P. (ed.) (1975). *Entering the World of Work: Some Sociological Perspectives*. London, HMSO, Department of Employment.

Broverman, I. K., Vogel, S. R., Broverman, D. M., Clarkson, F. E. and Rosenkrantz, P. S. (1972). Sex role stereotypes: a current appraisal. *Journal of Social Issues* **28**, 59–78.

Campbell, D. (1978). Qualitative knowing in action research. In: M. Brenner *et al.* (eds), *The Social Context of Method*. London, Croom Helm.

Casburn, M. (1979). Girls will be girls: sexism and juvenile justice in a London borough. Women's Research and Resources Centre pamphlet, No. 6, London.

Connell, R. W. (1983). *Which Way is Up? Essays on Sex, Class and Culture*. London, Allen and Unwin.

Corrigan, P. (1979). *Schooling the Smash Street Kids*. London, MacMillan.

Cowie, C. and Lees, S. (1981). Slags or drags? *Feminist Review* **9**, 17–31.

Davies, L. (1979). Deadlier than the male? Girls' conformity and deviance in school. In: L. Barton and R. Meighan (eds), *Schools, Pupils and Deviance*. London, Nafferton Books.

Education Group, Centre for Contemporary Cultural Studies, Birmingham University (eds) (1981). *Unpopular Education: Schooling and Social Democracy in England since 1944*. London, Hutchinson.

Fryer, D. M. and Payne, R. L. (1983). Pro-activity as a route into understanding the psychological effects of unemployment. Memo 540, Social and Applied Psychology Unit, Sheffield University.

Giddens, A. (1976). *New Rules of Sociological Method*. London, Hutchinson.

Glaser, B. and Strauss, A. L. (1976). *The Discovery of Grounded Theory*. Chicago, Aldine.

Griffin, C. (1982a). Cultures of femininity: romance revisited. Stencilled paper, Centre for Contemporary Cultural Studies, Birmingham University.

Griffin, C. (1982b). The good, the bad and the ugly: images of young women in the labour market. Stencilled paper, Centre for Contemporary Cultural Studies, Birmingham University.

Griffin, C. (1984). Young women and work. Stencilled paper, Centre for Contemporary Cultural Studies, Birmingham University.

Griffin, C. (1985a). Qualitative methods and cultural analysis: Young women and the transition from school to un/employment. In: R. Burgess (ed.), *Field Methods in the Study of Education*. London, Falmer Press.

Griffin, C. (1985b). *Typical Girls? Young Women from School to the Job Market*. London, Routledge & Kegan Paul.

Griffin, C., Hobson, D., McIntosh, S. and McCabe, T. (1982). Women and leisure. In: J. Hargreaves (ed.) *Sport, Culture and Ideology*. London, Routledge & Kegan Paul.

Hall, S. and Jefferson, T. (eds) (1975). *Resistance through Rituals: Youth Subcultures in Post-war Britain*. London, Hutchinson.

Hall, S., Hobson, D., Lowe, A. and Willis, P. (eds) (1980). *Culture, Media, Language*. London, Hutchinson.

Hayes, J. and Nutman, P. (1981). *Understanding the Unemployed: the Psychological Effects of Unemployment*. London, Tavistock.

Halsey, A., Heath, A. F. and Ridge, J. M. (1980). *Origins and Destinations: Family, Class and Education in Modern Britain*. Oxford, Clarendon Press.

Hobson, D. (1978). A study of working class women at home: femininity, domesticity and maternity. Unpublished MA thesis, Centre for Contemporary Cultural Studies, Birmingham University.

Jenkins, R. (1983). *Lads, Citizens and Ordinary Kids: Working Class Youth Life-Styles in Belfast*. London, Routledge & Kegan Paul.

McRobbie, A. (1978). Working class girls and the culture of femininity. In: Women's Studies Group, Centre for Contemporary Cultural Studies (eds), *Women take Issue: Aspects of Women's Subordination*. London, Hutchinson.

McRobbie, A. (1980). Settling accounts with subcultures. *Screen Education* **34**, 37–49.

McRobbie, A. and Garber, J. (1975). Girls and subcultures: an exploration. In: S. Hall and T. Jefferson (eds), *Resistance through Rituals: Youth Subcultures in Post-war Britain*. London, Hutchinson.

Miles, M. B. and Oberman, M. (1984). *Qualitative Data Analysis: A Source Book of New Methods*. London, Sage.

Millman, M. (1975). She did it all for love: a feminist view of the sociology of deviance. In: M. Millman and R. Kantor (eds), *Another Voice: Feminist Perspectives on Social Life and Social Science*. New York, Anchor Press.

Norris, G. (1978). Unemployment, subemployment and personal characteristics; (A) The inadequacies of traditional approaches to unemployment; and (B) Job separation and work histories: an alternative approach. *Sociological Review* **26**, 89–106.

Prendergast, S. and Prout, A. (1980). What will I do? Teenage girls and the construction of motherhood. *Sociological Review* **28**, 517–535.

Rapoport, R. and Rapoport, R. N. (1975). *Leisure and the Family Life Cycle*. London, Routledge & Kegan Paul.

Robbins, D. and Cohen, P. (1978). *Knuckle Sandwich*. Harmondsworth, Penguin.

Roberts, H. (ed.) (1981). *Doing Feminist Research*. London, Routledge & Kegan Paul.

Roberts, K. (1984). *School Leavers and their Prospects: Youth in the Labour Market in the 1980's*. Milton Keynes, Open University Press.

Sharpe, S. (1984). *Double Identity: The Lives of Working Mothers*. Harmondsworth, Penguin.

Siltanen, J. and Stanworth, M. (eds) (1984). *Women and the Public Sphere: A Critique of Sociology and Politics*. London, Hutchinson.

Spender, D. (1980). *Man Made Language*. London, Routledge & Kegan Paul.

Stanley, L. and Wise, S. (1983). *Breaking Out: Feminist Consciousness and Feminist Research*. London, Routledge & Kegan Paul.

Thomas, C. (1980). Girls and counter-school cultures. In: D. McCallum and V. Ozolins (eds), *Melbourne Working Papers*. University of Melbourne, Australia.

Tolson, A. (1977). *The Limits of Masculinity*. London, Tavistock.

Ullah, P. and Banks, M. (1983). Does unemployment encourage withdrawal from the labour market? Paper presented at the British Psychological Society Social Psychology Section conference, Sheffield University.

Walkerdine, V. (1981). Sex, power and pedagogy. *Screen Education* **38**, 15–24.

Warr, P. (1983). Work, jobs and unemployment. *Bulletin of the British Psychological Society* **36**, 305–311.

Watts, A. (1983). *Education, Unemployment and the Future of Work*. Milton Keynes, Open University Press.

Westwood, S. (1984). *All Day, Every Day: Factory and Family in the Making of Women's Lives*. London, Pluto Press.

Willis, P. (1977). *Learning to Labour: How Working Class Kids Get Working Class Jobs*. London, Saxon House.

Willis, P. (1979). Shop floor culture, masculinity and the wage form. In: J. Clarke, C. Critcher and R. Johnson (eds), *Working Class Culture*. London, Hutchinson.

Willis, P. (1980). Notes on method. In: S. Hall *et al.* (eds), *Culture Media, Language*. London, Hutchinson.

Willis, P. (1984). Youth unemployment: thinking the unthinkable. *Youth and Policy* **2**(4), 17–36.

Wilson, A. (1978). *Finding a Voice: Asian Women in Britain*. London, Virago Press.

Wood, J. (1984). Groping towards sexism: boys' sex talk. In: A. McRobbie and M. Nava (eds), *Gender and Generation*. London, Macmillan.

Chapter 11

Exploring the Experiences of Women Managers: Towards Rigour in Qualitative Methods

Judi Marshall

INTRODUCTION

A growing literature is challenging the application of traditional scientific methods within the social sciences, and seeking to establish alternative research approaches as valid. These alternatives are variously called 'qualitative', 'experiential', 'collaborative', 'new paradigm', 'feminist', and so on. Here I mainly use the term qualitative to describe my model of research. In addition, I discuss the importance of feminism to me as a researcher.

How I describe and experience my qualitative research approach has developed over the years. Early on I would invoke Glaser and Strauss' (1967) advocacy of 'grounded theory' as a legitimating banner for what I was already doing because it made sense to me. Later, I moved on to embrace more of what phenomenological, interpretive research has to offer theoretically and practically, and to identify its challenges more clearly. This chapter gives me an opportunity to extend my exploration in this area; writing it has been a mini research project in many of the ways described below.

However, the current debate is more than a matter of methods in supposed isolation. More important are the paradigms which take life through such methods. The dominant paradigm of the social sciences is inherently positivistic, resting on assumptions of objectivity; distance; causality; abstract, generalizable knowledge which can be acquired; getting it right, and so on. I favour an alternative paradigm (sometimes called 'new paradigm', see Reason and Rowan, 1981a) which recognizes multiple perspectives, acknowledges the very personal nature of sense making, and advocates direct engagement with others involved in the research process. Researching is affirmed as 'a distinctively human process through which researchers *make* knowledge' (Morgan, 1983). Stanley and Wise

(1983) reach a similar position from a specifically feminist base. Quantitative methods are often identified with the dominant paradigm, and qualitative methods with its alternative, but the correspondence is by no means that clear cut. Many researchers use qualitative methods positivistically, trying to pin down and constrain their data into incontestable, replicable, generalizable, detached truths. This approach limits the method's potential, and burdens qualitative research with inappropriate criteria of validity.

I am, then, a qualitative, new paradigm researcher. I am also a feminist, although I am not yet sure how this will affect my future as a researcher. I became a feminist through the project described below, and in that sense feminism is a core aspect of this chapter. I am pursuing many of the concerns I have developed, with particular attention to the tradition of the muted female in society, through my current work on organizational culture, but femininism has complemented my other research identities rather than supplanting them.

In this chapter I first review the themes in qualitative research which I find most relevant and challenging. I then consider what criteria of validity can be appropriately applied to the personal approach outlined. In the third section I tell the story of a study into the experiences of women managers. I concentrate on my sense making and how it changed during the process of my research, using some of my conclusions and theorizing as illustrations. Further on, I reflect on my own validity. Finally, I explore some general issues of relevance to qualitative and feminist research theory.

In writing this chapter I am not claiming to have done my research perfectly. In agreement with Reinharz (1980), I believe that many 'methodological problems' are not resolvable, but are dilemmas which must be experienced and endured.

SECTION I: DOING QUALITATIVE RESEARCH

There are six key themes to what I am trying to achieve and how I operate as a researcher.

Research as a Personal Process

I have always chosen as research topics issues which have personal significance and which I need to explore in my own life. There was usually an initial recognition that relocation, stress, women at work, change or organizational culture carried some personal interest and, as my work continued, a deepening realization of their full relevance. This involvement provides the energy for research, heightens my potential as a sense maker and means that research has relevance to my life as a whole, not just my conceptual knowing. It also means that I bring to research my own anxieties about the area in question, and, with them, any ways in which I might hinder myself. Research can be a wonderful way of not finding out, of avoiding central issues—by erecting a façade of academic theory, for example, I can become estranged from my concerns and deal with them as if they are purely aspects of the outside world.

Embracing the personal nature of research means I live through each project, balancing my engagement with others with attention to my own processes, always with the aim of using my involvement creatively. In doing so I expect to learn about topic, method *and* person (me) (Reinharz, 1980). This also often involves change through the process of research.

Critical Subjectivity

If research is so personal, I may project my image on to the phenomena I study and discover and report about only my own reflection. 'Objectivity' is meant to guard against this by minimizing the researcher's influence; if this appears in the research in any way, it is seen as bias. I am part of any social situation I explore, and always have attitudes, values, feelings and beliefs about it. I do not therefore believe in, or aspire to, objectivity.

My perspective is what I have to offer as a researcher. But part of this is a responsibility to reflect on my perspective and develop its clarity. I aim to achieve 'a personal view from some distance' (Schwartz and Ogilvy, 1979). I seek to do this by being receptive to others' meanings; through engagement with other people and with the data; by attending to my own sense making; and through personal work with colleagues and counsellors. I also believe that any writing should include some acknowledgement and explorations of who I am, of my purposes and how I impacted the research. Readers can then judge the content in the context of the perspectives and assumptions by which it was shaped.

All this means that research can be done with passion and is usually political in the sense of expressing and exploring values. Rather than disguise this, I advise researchers to acknowledge and explore their stances and value judgements.

Concern with Meaning

One of the central purposes of my research is to access, understand and adequately portray the meanings of the phenomena with which I deal. These are meanings as they are exposed to me, the researcher, in the fullest possible familiarity; they are meanings in relationship. I maintain as open a stance as I can, bracketing my own experience—in interviews, for example, my attention is on interviewees' accounts of their own experiences, on exploring with them the ways in which they see the world and on checking back what I think I have heard. In this way I am seeking insiders' accounts, and place a high premium on being faithful to them and on using them as literal material. In making further sense of phenomena, I move backwards and forwards between this level of data and my own interpretations, so that my theorizing is grounded (Glaser and Strauss, 1967).

As meaning is paramount, sample sizes and distributions become much less significant than in traditional research. They obviously affect what aspects of the world I can claim to illuminate. I usually hope to achieve depth and that mythical quality 'richness', rather than make widely applicable but conceptually simplified statements.

Engagement with People

To learn and develop through research I need to tolerate my not knowing and to seek open encounter with the participants in my research. I seek a measure of equality and wish to be non-alienating in relationships. This involves telling participants what the project is about; discussing its aims and uncertainties; at times revealing where I stand and what I find puzzling and contradictory about the issues raised; and allowing participants to shape the research direction. Whilst, as the researcher, I have a different stake in the project from others, I expect to meet other people's needs as well as my own.

Analysis through Immersion

I have described my approach to data analysis elsewhere (Marshall, 1981), and shall go into more detail in the research report which follows. Essentially, I become immersed in the data, often using physical correlates like copying quotations on to cards, moving pieces of paper round, and creating and abandoning sense making diagrams to increase my engagement at a fairly literal level. Through this process I am looking for patterns, connections, themes, comprehension of the meanings involved which are empirically discovered rather than logically inferred. I expect these to be often complex, circular and conflicting; ecologically embedded; to do with wholes and processes. I need to take care to handle them lightly, almost playfully; to recognize that they are statements for now, but may change. It is always tempting to over-invest in theories, to make them more certain and enduring than they can sensibly be.

The open approach I adopt has links with notions of a female cognitive style (Keller, 1980) and with communion/acceptance rather than agency/control as a life strategy (Bakan, 1966; see also Chapter 5, this volume, for a fuller discussion of this distinction).

Managing Uncertainty and Anxiety

At its heart I see research as an engagement with the uncertainties and anxieties of not knowing. I meet my own issues about the chosen topic. I also experience doubts about my capabilities as a researcher: whether, after all the hard work, there *is* anything there; how I can be sure that I *know*, and so on. It is often tempting to control this anxiety by controlling and restraining the research—by reaching for established questionnaires to make the study look more orderly; by deciding not to look at certain messy areas; or by using someone else's theory rather than developing my own ideas.

To engage productively with the confusion, I need both permission (my own and that of significant people around me), and support. The latter can come from many sources. It helps if it involves both arenas in which I can explore the personal issues raised in the research and more academically oriented 'friends willing to act as enemies' (Torbert, 1976), people who will challenge me supportively. For example, there may be questions I do not ask interviewees or play down in some way so that they never get discussed. I may need someone to point this out and to ask why. Or my sense making may omit aspects of the situation which other theorists have thought important. I may need someone to question whether my theories reflect my data and how I can account for those other aspects.

SECTION II: VALIDITY

We need to re-cast the traditional concept of validity to apply it productively to new paradigm, qualitative research. We certainly need to detach ourselves from any notion that validity tells us 'how true' any piece of research is on anything like an objective scale of truth. Validity instead becomes largely a quality of the knower, in relation to her/his data and enhanced by the use of different vantage points and forms of knowing—it is, then, personal, relational and contextual. It requires continual creation and attention as research proceeds, and is always relative, sufficient to some purpose. There is a growing concern that qualitative research should become more rigorous, should pay more, but appropriate, attention to the quality of knowing. I find Rogers' definition of science appropriate to the potential of qualitative methods:

> Scientific methodology needs to be seen for what it truly is, a way of preventing me from deceiving myself in regard to my creatively formed subjective hunches which have developed out of the relationship between me and my material. (1961)

Drawing on Diesing (1972), Reason and Rowan (1981b) and discussions within my own research community as sources, I offer the following questions as a reflective checklist of my own and others' validity. Of major significance is that most of the items are directed at the researcher, whereas in more traditional approaches the focus is on method. The criteria of validity are as follows.

How the Research was Conducted

Were the researcher(s) aware of their own perspective and its influence? Were they aware of their own process?

How did they handle themselves?

Did they challenge themselves and accept challenges from others?

Were they open in their encounters?

Did they tolerate and work on the chaos and confusion? (If there is no confusion, I become suspicious that deeper levels of meanings were neglected.)

Have the researcher(s) grown personally through the research?

Relationship to the Data

Is the level of theorizing appropriate to the study and its data?

Is the theorizing of appropriate complexity to portray the phenomena studied?

Are alternative interpretations explored?

Is the process of sense making sufficiently reported?

Contextual Validity

How do the conclusions relate to other work in the area?

Are the researcher(s) aware of relevant contexts for the phenomena studied?

Is the research account recognizable — particularly by people within the area studied?

Is the material useful?

'Good' research addresses most of these issues — it does not do so 'perfectly' (whatever that means); rather, the researcher(s) develop their capabilities for knowing.

SECTION III: RESEARCH STUDY

The research project I am going to describe in detail concerned the experiences of women in management jobs, and was begun in 1978. At the outset, I realized I wanted to research women because I had so far mainly studied men's experience (of job stress), and wanted to even the balance. I was wary, however, of becoming too involved with women's studies because of the stigma this seemed to carry. As the project progressed, I realized that my own unresolved issues about being a woman in a largely male-dominated organizational world were ready for attention. The research both prompted and was facilitated by my development as a feminist.

The research progressed in two broad phases. In the first, I did some initial reading on women at work, conducted a series of interviews, analysed the data and wrote a report. The second phase opened with a contract to write a book about the material. This time I read much more extensively, revisited the research data and, painfully slowly, wrote the book (Marshall, 1984), which I shall here refer to for convenience as *Travellers*. In this project the fieldwork of interviewing other people about their experiences played a less prominent part than in any other research I have done. My own sense making and awareness of its shifts was very dominant.

I cannot tell here the full story of a process which spanned five years. I shall select certain stages for attention, mainly because they developed my thinking and personal awareness. Some were, however, important for the stagnation they marked, and the not knowing or lack of connection with the research which had to be lived through: and these will also be represented.

Phase One: The Initial Stance and How It Was Shaped

Conflicts about why I was doing the research showed through in my initial stance and the methods used. I did not particularly see women as socially disadvantaged and was certainly not prepared to voice publicly an identification with 'women's issues'. The initial study was funded by the Equal Opportunities Commission (EOC), and my contacts there had no such reservations. They, and much of the literature I read at the time, talked as if discrimination and prejudice against women were widespread. I reacted against the strength and simplicity of this position, and held firmly to my lack of commitment. The EOC wanted the study to produce a profile of the successful woman manager. At the time, I noted the caveat that career building within organizations is only one possible measure of achievement in life.

The interviewing approach I adopted partly reflected my usual preference for broad, open-ended questions encouraging interviewees to express and explore their own meanings. It also delayed, as I was doing, making any assumption that being a woman was a major disadvantage in career development and everyday working. Only after a series of questions about work history, future prospects, factors which had helped and hindered them, did I ask whether being a woman had been important in any way. I wanted to leave the managers every opportunity to mention gender in their own terms, and only then to ask about it specifically.

In many ways I later benefited from my uncommitted starting point. My perspective changed radically through doing the research, but the data remained relevant which they might not have done had I directed the questions to more clearly prescribed ends. There were, however, areas I would have later liked to know more about or to have been more confronting on, but which I had no opportunity to develop. This was a cost. Some of the interviewees who had developed their own feminism may have found me uneducated in this sense, and I may have missed out on debate I would later have valued.

Who to Speak to

Within the constraints of time and money, I could sensibly contact 30 people. I decided to interview women only, rather than a comparative sample of men and women. I wanted to see as many women managers as possible, as I knew so little about them, and had a strong impression of men managers' experiences from my recent work. Here again, a choice which made one sort of sense at the time, took on greater significance as the research progressed. I recognized increasingly that I objected to comparative studies in which men became the norm against which women's experiences were judged. Rather, my appreciation of men's work experiences served as a background; in the foreground were women in their own right.

I split the sample between two industries—book publishing and retailing—to provide a fairly coherent group, but offering one major axis of comparison. I chose those industries by eliminating ones in which other work on women was being done and identifying ones in which there were enough women in management to offer a fairly senior sample without them being singular, highly unusual, women. I had some idea that I wanted material relevant to 'ordinary women'—whoever they are!

As I look back it becomes even more apparent than it was at the time that I was tackling a major topic through contact with a small group of people. Speaking out from the research required me to achieve some depth in my resulting interpretations. My conclusions would then 'travel' because they were firmly grounded, rather than because they were deliberately 'generalizable'.

The eventual sample was split evenly between the two industries and represented the range of management jobs in which women were found. The interviewees' positions ranged from middle management to Director level; their ages ranged from approximately 26 to 50; half were married or living with long-term partners; three had young and one had teenage children; most worked in London.

Fieldwork

I enjoyed conducting the interviews, meeting a range of people and hearing about their lives. I can remember some of the detail of that activity now, but not much. It has been overtaken by the product, and the more abstract, processed level of knowing what it represents.

Whilst I was concerned to capture managers' meanings, at times I talked about my own ideas and experiences. Researchers are often shy of doing this in case they 'lead' the interviewee. Ironically, in my experience, people are made more anxious by having no feel for who the researcher is, and clutch at any clue to know what s/he 'really wants', and hence to be co-operative.

I recorded interviews to allow myself to concentrate on talking with participants, and to preserve the full content of what was said to the next stage of research. Listening to tapes later, I often find that there are things I have missed or only partly attended to at the time. This preservation of the original interview material was particularly important in this study because in the second phase I returned to the data from a new perspective. The detailed sense that I made changed very little, but I focussed on different aspects and made new connections between previously separate topics.

Movement from Phase 1 to Phase 2

Analysing the interview data to submit a report to the EOC marked the end of Phase 1. This was done in a hurry because I had taken on a new job and been involved in another research project. The report was put on one side for many months. I now have no clear idea of why I suggested to a publisher that I write a research report type of book about women managers. One motivation was that I had put much effort into the project and wanted to make some academic use of it. But it was looking backward and towards a single activity, whilst around me were other opportunities to do new things and work with others. There was certainly some unfinished business there.

The first phase had been competent but relatively flat. The final report reflected the nature of my experience. It contained much detail, but little organized sense making or structure; it was undigested. It was expressed in a monotone with few highs or lows, either in content or style. It did not involve or seem particularly relevant to me.

After some delay and debate, I signed a contract to write a book. I did not think it would take long; in fact it took a further three years. I started in a very proper academic manner, with a fresh review of the literature.

Phase 2: Literature Review—Development as a Feminist

At the time I thought I needed to read some more to 'top and tail' the research report. I did not anticipate that my engagement with the literature and the issues it presented would take over and become the major focus of my attention, learning and writing.

The first literature review I had conducted was wide ranging, but lacking in meaningful direction. I had found several general histories of women and work, and pages of statistics showing women's lowly place in the workforce. There were a few interesting studies of women managers, but these were comprehensive rather than alive. The literature review I conducted as the research entered its second phase was more thorough, went more deeply into work on women managers, and also increasingly reached out into feminist analyses of women's position in society.

I later came to realize that at this stage I was reading two separable bodies of literature. Neither is completely uniform, but they originate from two very different sets of core values and objectives. An initial computer search sent me in one direction, which I later called 'reform feminism'. Its literature seeks to prove that women are essentially the same as men in their suitability for management, and to integrate them into current organization systems. Men are used as the norm for what women should be like and do. This literature is mostly in management and personnel journals, and measures women's success (with which it is preoccupied) by their representation in senior management. The other approach has little to say explicitly about women as managers. It points to women's subordinate and disadvantaged position in society, and rejects male values as represented in patriarchy. I called this 'radical feminism'.

A critical stage came when I realized how boring and meaningless I found much of the reform feminist writing. A particular day stands out, when I had travelled to another university's library to do some concentrated study. As I plodded through apparently highly relevant articles, I felt sluggish, my eyes and brain glazed. I took detailed notes because I was not really capturing the material in any other way. I had no side-sheet of my own ideas stimulated by the reading as I usually do when involved. I returned home disappointed and puzzled, thinking I had wasted my time. But as I thought things through, and told colleagues what I had felt, I found that my dullness held its own meaning. I surfaced a source of emotional intelligence which helped me make intellectual sense. I realized that underneath my reading I was rebelling against the literature's basic assumptions. It seemed a false enterprise to argue that women are the same as men, and to plead logically for their acceptance into organizations. I resented the continual use of men as the standard to which women should conform, and noted that even writers who said they would not do so, soon slipped into this pattern. The whole approach seemed particularly senseless as my earlier research had been about stress, which is the price of some men's styles of working.

At the same time, I found in radical feminism rich pictures which resonated with my life as a woman, and respect for female experience. As I read each new book I lived its perspective and concern about the devaluing of women. This threw my life into turmoil. Some of the ideas made sense to me, but so upset my previous views of the world that I hardly knew how to behave. I became sensitive to even the most subtle forms of sexism and discrimination; my relationships with men felt difficult. Typically, I would come to live each framework for a while and then take a step back, retaining the aspects I needed to build my own personal feminism.

I was left at the end of an involving and exhausting journey seeing both reform and radical feminism from some distance, and having regained my sense of humour. Whilst I tended to identify more with radical feminism, I also felt uncomfortable with some of its views. For example, whilst rejecting patriarchy, many writers still gave the public world and employment primacy, and so, for me, followed rather than transcended male values. I am not alone in questioning whether equal numbers of women joining men in activities that (patriarchal) society currently prizes is really equality. A new wave of writers are advocating re-vision (Callaway, 1981), through which we reappraise values and renew the meaning of some traditional activities, especially those which women have done in society. It was with this intent that I identified *Travellers*. I was also dissatisfied at the sociological emphasis of many of the radical feminist theories. I needed to twin these with a more psychological approach to understanding the pattern of power relationships between women and men (Marshall, 1984).

This very important phase in my personal development and intellectual sense making was not easy to write about. I initially drafted one chapter to cover the reform viewpoint and another to cover the radical viewpoint. I spent a long time trying to lead neatly and logically from the former to the latter. It was only when I realized that the bridge was neither neat nor logical, that I could write. I had to narrate the process which had led me to dismiss one approach and embrace another, and I did not have to justify and prove my position. I noted the *discontinuity* between the chapters, and so was able to reveal and therefore develop more of my implicit theorizing.

I circulated the first draft of the book to several colleagues and outside contacts for comments. It was such a relief to have produced something which looked like a full text, that I wanted any corrections to be minimal. Happily, I had regained some energy and realized that revisions were necessary before my reviewers kindly told me so.

It is interesting that the first draft remained unclear on my values. One colleague challenged whether I really was a feminist, pointing out that in the radical chapter I had used a lot of quotations to speak for me. It was as if my intellectual knowing and ability to express myself lagged behind my emotional knowing. In the final draft I was more sure of my own voice.

Working on Personal Issues

During much of the second phase of research, but particularly as I encountered radical feminism, I needed anchor points to support the more personal aspects of the inquiry. I did some personal growth work, mainly co-counselling (Heron, 1973) and assertion training (Dickson, 1982). Coming to terms with different perspectives and eventually developing my own form of feminism (not that it was/is static) was exciting, but, at times, painful. For example, I was often hesitant about expressing my changing thinking. Intellectually, I could recognize language's exclusion of women (Spender, 1980), but I also had to break through my own silence. I also discussed my work with colleagues and in a staff/student research group. Without the support and challenge of these various arenas, I would not have achieved what I did through the research.

Returning to the Data

My first cycle of data analysis had retained much of the detail of managers' accounts, and I had the original interview transcripts to go back to. Even so, I felt strange returning after so much personal change. I might well have asked different questions had I started my fieldwork at that stage, or established a more exploratory contract with participants (maybe running some workshops). Returning to the original data was a compromise. Partly because of the separation in time and perspective from its lived collection, the final write up is a little more conceptual and less dense with description than I would have liked. It is as if I could not push it, or push into it, quite as far as usual. An academic reviewer of the first draft said that the data was 'slightly under reported'. I agree.

I was able to regain entry into the data by absorbing the detail, and patiently dwelling with the material through times when it felt difficult and fragmented. I place a high premium on working with the words used by participants rather than filtering what they have said through my second order constructs. Many of the headings and key concepts in *Travellers* are expressed through their words — experimentation, women are a risk, wanting to lead a balanced life and so on — with me playing the role of organizer, interpreter, translator.

When analysis is going well I experience myself nimbly twinning receptivity to others' meanings (communion in Bakan's terms, 1966) with categorizing them through my interpretations (agency). From this, understandings, patterns and insights emerge; for example, often apparently disparate events show the same pattern. A significant number of managers in both industries had been promoted through 'jobs which grew under them'. This was particularly evident in book publishing where the importance of selling rights (for example, to publish a book abroad or adapt it to a different medium such as film) has increased dramatically over the last 15 years. What was originally the part-time responsibility of a director's secretary grew first into a full-time job, then into a department, and now often warrants a place on the Board. Women have achieved accelerated progress with this development. Similar things have happened in other job areas such as personnel and the use of video in education. The following were elements in the common pattern: the company had not intended to promote the manager concerned, but had done so because she was their only expert in the particular area; the often official job title and other people's perceptions of her status lagged behind the manager's increase in responsibilities; and many women had become more committed to work because of their unexpected promotion.

I brought the feminism I had developed during the literature review to data analysis. My earlier impression (from Phase 1), that the managers were both accommodating to organizations' male values and living from alternative, female values was confirmed and given more substance. At this stage I tried out alternative interpretations. I was wary of making idealized statements about women's characteristics and culture, and yet I wanted to illuminate their neglected position in their own terms. I therefore explored the degenerative aspects of female ways of being alongside their strengths.

The most 'difficult', but in many ways obvious, conclusion I reached from the data, was that over half the managers I interviewed muted their awareness of being female. I took special care with this part of the analysis because it involved setting aside interviewees' replies to my so carefully timed question about whether being a women had been important to them. Most said no, or that it had been an advantage. I wanted to respect these clearly expressed views, but could not wholly believe them. There was contradictory evidence in the scarcity of women in senior management jobs. Many of the interviewees said they felt 'privileged' to have reached such positions; and this word made me uneasy. Also, when I looked more closely, many had contradicted the simplicity of their own opinion: they talked about ways they avoided or coped with discrimination, identified negative consequences of working for their personal and social lives, said explicitly that 'it is a man's world', foresaw career obstacles, and so on. Eventually, I pieced together a jigsaw puzzle of evidence to reveal a complex picture. I divided the sample into three groups according to their attitudes towards being women, and one group stood out as holding internally conflicting views.

Just over half the managers said they thought that if they did not make a point of being female, other people would treat them first as people, rather than as women. Most of this group were annoyed if attention was drawn to their gender, and did not like the resulting visibility. They distinguished themselves as particular (successful or privileged) cases from women as a general (potentially disadvantaged) group. Several were concerned that their balanced perspective on work issues would be disturbed if they identified themselves as women. Above all, they wanted to avoid becoming angry. As one put it: 'There's a danger of becoming over-aggressive if you have too strong an idea of yourself as a woman fighting against men'.

I concluded that this group allowed that there are potential disadvantages to being women, but believed that awareness of this increased the likelihood of such disadvantages becoming significant. To cope, their strategy was to disregard these issues in their surface consciousness, and so to mute their awareness of being female. Once arrived at, I found this a recognizable pattern for which there was much contextual validity. In retrospect, however, I am not surprised that it took me time to reach such a pattern, and that I did so particularly carefully.

Firstly, I felt that I risked misrepresenting interviewees' views, especially as I had not explored these areas more openly when we met. Secondly, the conclusion had undertones of an accusation of false consciousness, although being said from a different value position. I had resented, and still do, the judgemental approach of some feminist writers who criticize other women for not 'recognizing' how oppressed they are by patriarchy, and for not taking action. I did not want to join their ranks. (Condor, Chapter 6, this volume, shares these feelings.)

On reflection, I realize that muted awareness was also what I had come to recognize in myself through the literature review. It seems surprising that I was therefore slow to see or accept the same pattern in the data. But I also find this reassuring — as some indication that I was phenomenologically bracketing my own issues.

The other two groups (in terms of attitudes towards being women) were much more straightforward to identify. Three managers were acutely aware of being women in a men's world when I met them, and were finding this perspective disturbing. Each, in different ways, had had this consciousness forced upon them by confrontation with organizational practices or life choices. The final group, about a third of the sample, had already developed a clear sense of themselves as women, some because they had earlier been told that there were jobs they could not therefore do. That they were different from men and treated differently seemed to be truths they could hardly avoid. But they were not disabled by this awareness. They were concerned about women's limited opportunities; some cynically, others as active advocates of women's rights.

One reviewer of the first draft queried the moderate tone of many of my analyses, and asked where the anger was. He was identifying a difference from some other feminist writers, and challenged whether I was avoiding this aspect. Some of the managers had been wary of becoming angry—was I? Looking back, I realized that I had written little from the stage of greatest anger—that is, when I was initially exploring the more radical feminist perspectives. I had felt too 'unbalanced' at the time, and had simply allowed developments to happen until my ideas came together and felt more grounded. Anger had been a part of seeing women's position from men's values. I later came to a perspective from which I could accept and honour both female and male values. In the final write-up I tried, therefore, to do justice to the anger as an important stage and form of knowing, but was more concerned to chart the discoveries it had led to.

As I near the end of any piece of depth data analysis, there are two strong and warring voices in me. One is a deep-rooted knowing about the area of study, and this guides my writing. The other voice is a nagging fear that I have made it all up. This uncertainty never completely leaves me, but is a doubt I have learnt to manage and suspend. It is sometimes accentuated by looking back at very early research notes, and finding the germ of my conclusions there. Research is not the linear activity in time which most texts suggest. It is at least cyclic. In this study of women managers re-cycling played an especially significant part. After one phase of literature review, fieldwork, analysis and writing, I had still only scratched the surface, intellectually and personally, of the issues involved. I needed to re-visit all of these areas to do the work I had really, but unwittingly, set out to do. The productivity of the second phase would have been jeopardized if I had not had the necessary support and time (even from my publishers) to let my learning follow its own path and pace. As it was, I could have spent even longer, but there came a stage at which I felt able and willing to pause and to draw the book together, leaving further developments to other opportunities. By then I was also tired!

Expression

In writing about qualitative research, I am seeking an encounter with the reader from a densely and candidly portrayed account of the inquiry and its data. In *Travellers*, I could only do this to my satisfaction by using my own developing feminist awareness as the central theme of the book. I moved between personal material, conceptual analysis and the reported data.

When I offer my research up to be read, I always feel vulnerable. The highly personal style of *Travellers* made me even more so, and I felt reticent as the publication date neared. I also knew that that was the way it had to be written. Some people, mostly men, find my personal reflections irritating and intrusive. Others, mostly women, say they are the book's main offering. Reactions in both directions have been strong, so at least I have done my job wholeheartedly.

Since the book came out, I have toyed with the ideas in it, and found clearer ways of expressing some, but have not pushed them further. The research and writing drained me of that sort of energy, I trust temporarily. I also think the strong relevance of the material covered made me more attached than usual to the ideas expressed. I did not fully live up to my maxim of holding them lightly. Being asked to give talks and being cast into the role of 'expert on women managers' contributed to their fixity. Writing this chapter has given me some distance from the research and its products, and left me more ready to explore and move on. Significantly, I was slow to start writing and only later on did I begin to learn from and enjoy what I was doing.

SECTION IV: REFLECTIONS ON QUALITATIVE AND FEMINIST RESEARCH

It seems to me self-evident that qualitative methods are appropriate vehicles for much feminist inquiry. Even large scale studies, say a survey of women's career development patterns, need to be aware of their value positions and judgements, and to articulate these, rather than presenting their conclusions as objective data. But the case for using qualitative approaches is particularly strong in the more significant role I see for feminist research, that of illuminating the devalued, muted tradition in society which women largely represent and carry. Issues on how to express and present qualitative data require particular attention. Firstly, written accounts need to do justice to the multiple, interacting aspects — personal, social, political, archetypal — of the phenomena with which they deal. A second major challenge is that research *about* inequalities in social power is currently being reported within an academic context which mirrors this patterning of power — both socially and in what it defines as knowledge. There is a risk that feminist researchers will come to carry or express for the research community the suppressed issues which women carry for society.

This leads on to the issue of who research is for and what functions it serves in society. I find it helpful to distinguish three main audiences: research is *for them* in that it contributes to understanding within the research community; it is *for me* as I use it to explore topics of personal interest and develop my competence as a knower; and it is *for us,* as taking part in research impacts participants' lives (Reason and Marshall, in prep.). Traditional social sciences emphasize 'them' as an audience, and judge theory and data on their contribution to 'the body of knowledge'. New paradigm approaches call for an equalization of power in the conduct of research, often looking for practical usefulness, as well as awareness, as outcomes for 'us'. They also identify the researcher's perspectives and development as central (for 'me').

Feminists face a key dilemma in their relationship to the established academic world. The route to legitimacy currently lies through addressing research to 'them', and attempting to identify de-personalized truth. But amongst its purposes feminism includes the re-vision of social values. Established models of knowledge, and the attribution of knowledge development to academia as an elite social group, owe much to patriarchal values. There is no one way to address this issue. A strategy I favour, as part of a repertoire, is to strengthen the internal dialogue and validity of feminist research; to concentrate on 'me' and 'us' rather than becoming over-dependent on, or attentive towards, 'them'.

There are various traps facing any 'alternative' researchers which are relevant to both qualitative and feminist research at the moment. Inquiry, as I have portrayed it, is an uncertain, vulnerable process with immense potential for personal growth and intellectual creativity. If under attack, we can become defensive about these aspects, and seek security through control and conformity. Coping strategies we should beware of are:

> Assuming a false uniformity within feminism/qualitative research;
> Moving towards orthodoxy of method or ideology;
> Establishing new, absolute criteria of 'truth' to replace those we have seen through;
> Looking for permanent understandings of the shifting, transitory phenomena with which we deal;
> Drawing our boundaries too tightly so that we do not recognize our similarities with, and links to, other areas of inquiry;
> Splitting and de-limiting areas of study or theoretical concepts so that they become constraining rather than illuminating;
> Playing down the personal meaning in which our work is based, and seeking social or organizational power through grand theorizing;
> Focussing our attention so that we fail to appreciate contexts and ecology.

Looking back to the broad field of social science research, there are now several, if not many, challenges to the dominant, positivist approach. I see the emergence of feminist, new paradigm and qualitative methods and philosophies as linked aspects of a strengthening of female values within society as this impacts academia (in the broadest sense). They share a theme which has implicitly informed this chapter—that of balancing control, a dominant male value, with acceptance, an archetypally female value. In particular, I have highlighted accepting uncertainty; allowing the necessary time to explore change and personalized knowing fully; and handling these through self-reflection and attention to contextual reference points. At a theoretical level, we also need to accept diversity, multiple perspectives and impermanence, and develop appropriately our notions of, and competence for, valid inquiry.

REFERENCES

Bakan, D. (1966). *The Duality of Human Existence*. Boston, Beacon Press.

Callaway, H. (1981). Women's perspectives: research as revision. In: P. Reason and J. Rowan (eds), *Human Inquiry*. Chichester, Wiley.

Dickson, A. (1982). *A Woman in Your Own Right*. London, Quartet Books.

Diesing, P. (1972). *Patterns of Discovery in the Social Sciences*. London, Routledge & Kegan Paul.

Glaser, B. G. and Strauss, A. L. (1967). *The Discovery of Grounded Theory*. Chicago, Aldine.

Heron, J. (1973). *Re-evaluation Counselling: a Theoretical Review*. University of Surrey, Human Potential Research Project.

Keller, E. (1980). Feminist critique of science: a forward or backward move? *Fundamenta Scientiae* **1**, 341–349.

Marshall, J. (1981). Research as a personal process. In: P. Reason and J. Rowan (eds), *Human Inquiry*. Chichester, Wiley.

Marshall, J. (1984). *Women Managers: Travellers in a Male World*. Chichester, Wiley.

Morgan, G. (ed.) (1983). *Beyond Method: Strategies for Social Research*. Beverley Hills, Sage.

Reason, P. and Marshall, J. (in prep.). Research as a personal process. In: D. Boud and V. Griffin (eds), *Understanding Adult Learning: From the Learner's Perspective*.

Reason, P. and Rowan, J. (eds) (1981a). *Human Inquiry: A Sourcebook of New Paradigm Research*. Chichester, Wiley.

Reason, P. and Rowan, J. (1981b). Issues of validity in new paradigm research. In: P. Reason and J. Rowan (eds), *Human Inquiry*. Chichester, Wiley.

Reinharz, S. (1980). Experiential analysis: a contribution to feminist research methodology. In: G. Bowles and R. Duelli-Klein (eds), *Theories of Women's Studies*, Vol. III. California, Berkeley.

Rogers, C. R. (1961). *On Becoming a Person*. London, Constable.

Schwartz, H. and Ogilvy, J. (1979). *The Emergent Paradigm: Changing Patterns of Thought and Belief*. SRI International, Analytical Report No. 7, Values and Lifestyles Program, Menlo Park, California.

Spender, D. (1980). *Man Made Language*. London, Routledge & Kegan Paul.

Stanley, L. and Wise, S. (1983). *Breaking Out: Feminist Consciousness and Feminist Research*. London, Routledge & Kegan Paul.

Torbert, W. (1976). *Creating a Community of Inquiry: Conflict, Collaboration, Transformation*. New York, Wiley.

Author Index

A

Abel, E., 78
Abercrombie, N., 100
Abrams, D., 101
Adamec, C. S., 101
Adams, C., 125-6
Adlam, D., 78, 84
Adorno, T. W., 98
Ajzen, I., 109
Albright, D., 100, 110
Allen, C., 151
Allen, D., 98
Allport, G. W., 99
Amos, V., 181
Ardener, S., 109
Armistead, N., 178
Arnoff, 123
Arnott, C., 113
Asch, S. E., 110
Ashmore, R. D., 97-8, 106, 113
Ashton, D., 174
Auerbach, S. M., 99

B

Baetz, R., 160
Bakan, P., 10, 78, 84, 196, 204
Bales, R., 78
Banks, M., 175
Bannister, D., 18, 20, 153
Banos, J. B., 121
Bardwick, J., 79
Barker, M., 105
Barrett, M., 98
Bates, I., 174
Bean, J., 99
Beck, A. T., 26
Becker, H. S., 146
Beere, C., 98, 101, 110, 143
Bell, C., 104, 143, 145
Beloff, H., 39
Bem, S., 3, 26, 40, 80-4, 89, 99

Bennett, F., 65
Berger, P., 152
Bernard, J., 9-10, 17, 19, 100, 102-3
Bernstein, B., 65
Best, D., 106
BhaBha, H. K., 71
Bieber, I., 151
Billig, M., 178, 186
Bird, C., 99
Bland, L., 62
Blum, H. P., 137
Boulton, M. G., 137
Bowker, L., 98
Bowles, G., 8, 11-12, 15-16
Bradly, 123
Brake, M., 177
Brannen, P., 174
Breen, D., 137, 146
Breinburg, P., 167
Brittan, A., 98
Brogan, D., 101, 104, 109, 113
Broughton, J., 26
Broverman, I. K., 28, 173
Brown, G., 26
Brown, R., 101, 108
Brown, S. R., 153-4
Bumpass, L., 104
Burr-Evans, N., 87
Burris, B., 110
Burt, C., 153
Butler, R., 124

C

Callaway, H., 8, 13-14, 16, 18, 21, 202
Campbell, D., 173
Carlson, R., 10, 15, 19, 79, 84
Cartledge, S., 160
Cartwright, D., 99
Casburn, M., 177
Cattell, R. B., 153-4
Central Advisory Council for Education, 59

Subject Index

Appendix 1

Smoke
Dope!